Treating Problem Children

Treating Problem Children

Issues, Methods and Practice

Masud Hoghughi

with John Lyons, Andrew Muckley
and Michael Swainston

SAGE Publications
London • Newbury Park • Beverly Hills • New Delhi

First published 1988
Reprinted 1989, 1992

 SAGE Publications Ltd
28 Banner Street
London EC1Y 8QE

SAGE Publications Inc
2111 West Hillcrest Street
Newbury Park, California 91320

SAGE Publications India Pvt Ltd
C–236 Defence Colony
New Delhi 110 024

SAGE Publications Inc
275 South Beverly Drive
Beverly Hills, California 90212

British Library Cataloguing in Publication Data

Hoghughi, Masud
   Treating problem children: issues,
   methods and practice.
   1. Deviant children. Behaviour therapy
   I. Title
   618.9′289142

   ISBN 0–8039–8152–X
   ISBN 0–8039–8153–8 pbk

Library of Congress catalog card number 88–060144

Typeset by System 4 Associates, Farnham Common, Buckinghamshire
Printed in Great Britain by The Alden Press, Oxford

Contents

PART II   METHODS OF TREATMENT

For our partners
and others who inspired our effort

Preface

There is by now a huge and complex industry for treating children. Its hallmarks are opacity, lack of focus, huge cost, poor accountability for its sins of omission and commission and generally uncertain or frequently damaging outcomes. Despite the work of many high-calibre practitioners and claims to the contrary, we still have no coherent and valid idea of what to do with most of our problem children. The main reason for this, we believe, is the absence of a discipline of treatment which allows us to deal with children as integrated entities rather than as a collection of parts which are divided among physicians, psychologists, teachers, social workers and others.

This book is an attempt to provide an integrated and comprehensive view of children's problems and what should be done with them. We have presented the reasons for adopting a descriptive 'problem profile approach' to the assessment of children in another book (*Assessing Problem Children,* 1980). In the present one, we propose a relatively comprehensive classification of treatment methods derived from our intensive perusal of the literature and prolonged work with disordered children in a variety of settings.

We hope that the book contributes a coherent view of problem children and of what we can do to help. Having spent, between us, several decades working with disordered children, we are convinced that all children should be treated as children first and problem children second. Irrespective of the professional agency and the practitioners who deal with them, both the children and the practitioners have a great many more similarities in their problems and means of dealing with them than they have differences. It is, therefore, sensible to emphasise the similarities and provide a unifying framework for identifying problems, the aims of intervention and the methods and techniques that may be used for dealing with them. This is what we have attempted to do.

Given the range and complexity of the subject-matter and our encyclopaedic ambitions, we have no doubt of the many shortcomings of our effort, both in coverage and emphasis. Almost every topic in this book is better covered in one or more volumes by other authors. We also recognise that our contributions are variable, representing not only our own shortcomings but also inevitable clinical preferences. Equally, they reflect the patchy state of the subject. Like every working tool, however, we hope this book will be adapted and improved by the user.

The book is divided into three parts. Part I covers basic ideas of treatment and some of the current concerns of people who deal with problem children. Part II sets out our classification of treatment methods and the techniques which are encompassed within them. Part III is the specific 'cookbook' element, allowing for daily use in identifying appropriate and preferred methods of treatment for individual problems. Throughout and for the sake of brevity, we have referred to the child and the practitioner in the masculine. We trust that this will be regarded not as gender bias on our part but rather as adherence to convention.

This book has been a long time in the making. We are grateful for Farrell Burnett's forbearance and her editorial comments. In addition, a number of colleagues have helped us with various stages of preparation of the material. They include Tom Berney, J. Grimley Evans, Fran Lyons, David Moseley, Dennis O'Connor, Ruth Reay, Melvyn Rose, Stuart Whiteley and Len Wilson. We are grateful to all of them, but do not hold them responsible for the final product. We also wish to thank the Librarian of the School of Education and her staff at the University of Durham, whose help has been invaluable. The senior author is grateful to Dr James Barber, Master of Hatfield College, University of Durham, and the College officers, for providing him with the space in which much of this book was written.

Last but not least, we wish to thank Doreen Kipling, who has shared much of the agonising over unmet deadlines, botched manuscripts and a multitude of other problems that arise in the course of bringing a book into publishable shape. This book is a tribute to her sustained help, as it is to that of our partners.

PART I

ISSUES IN TREATMENT

1
Concepts and Ethics

People have 'treated' their children one way or another since the beginnings of time. When the children presented problems, something was done to sort out their difficulties. It was not, however, until the last hundred years or so that we began talking of children's difficulties as distinct from those of adults and started clarifying our ideas about whether they should also be differently treated. In this sense, treatment is a relatively modern concept, one that features prominently in all areas of the social control of children whose condition falls outside our notions of what is 'normal'. So when the term 'treatment' is used in the context of medical, penal, educational or social services dealings with a child, we assume that a specific, coherent approach is being adopted to contain or reduce the child's problems.

We distinguish this use of 'treatment' as a professional activity from its everyday meaning of the way we deal with each other in 'treating someone well or badly' or giving them a 'treat'. The words 'treat' and 'treatment' in the professional context have become synonymous with 'therapy' as a response to a diseased, disordered or unacceptable state of the child. The original Greek and Latin roots of 'treatment', meaning simply to 'attend to' and 'manage', have taken on the connotation not only of a coherent, professional response but also of something that is worthy and good.

Both 'treatment' and 'therapy' are, therefore, 'buzz' words. In most western languages the two words are used, often interchangeably, without adequate definition of what their similarities and differences are. 'Therapy' is often used in combination with another adjectival word, as in 'physiotherapy' or 'psychotherapy'. Such usages of the word denote the *process* (as in 'psychotherapy'), the *medium* ('group therapy') or the *focus* ('family therapy'). These meanings are quite different yet difficult to distinguish in the commonly loose usage of the term. Anything that can be used for the purpose of alleviating problems can be and often is called 'therapy' – as, for example, in German *Reitentherapie* (riding therapy), French *hydrothérapie* (water therapy) and English 'relationship therapy'. The word 'therapy' is now almost devoid of denotative meaning or specific reference. Its major sense is in connoting or suggesting the positive *intention* of the 'therapist' in relation to the child or his circumstances. 'Treatment' will be used as the wider term encompassing 'therapy'. The latter will be used in relation to particular methods, where the term is prevalent.

In this book, 'treatment' is defined as 'the alleviation, amelioration, reduction or remediation of a problem'. Each of these terms has its own distinguishable, fine shade of meaning, but for our purposes the critical element is the concern with a *purposive activity aimed at making an 'unacceptable condition' less so, through reduction either in the number of problems or, of their severity*. The most important implication of this definition is that treatment is not about curing, though that is always desirable and sometimes possible, particularly in the physical and educational problem areas.

This, in turn, centrally affects our conception of what is 'successful' treatment. Whenever a reduction in the number and intensity of problems has been achieved, we can legitimately claim success (or more properly, absence of failure). Clearly, however, this must be qualified by statements about the amount of success, as well as about the time and place to which the success is limited. We shall return to this topic, but for the present, whether we are prepared to accept such partial success depends on how desperately we need it and on the price we have to pay for it.

This is presumably why the terms 'therapy' and 'treatment' are so frequently used to legitimise and describe actions which are devoid of coherent concepts and allied practices. Thus, we use such terms as 'social treatment', 'intermediate treatment', 'relationship therapy' and 'milieu therapy' without much compunction about sense or meaning.

Despite the proliferation of such titles and activities and a voluminous literature on treatment and therapy, there is rarely any discussion of the *concept* of treatment and its implications for practice. This is puzzling, given the huge investment in treatment activities of one sort or another and the centrality of the concept to so many activities of the 'helping professions'. It would seem reasonable to expect an account of the main elements of the concept in at least the major textbooks, as a means of enabling students to have a coherent idea of their own activities. But we search for such a discussion in vain (for example, Howells, 1965; Keat, 1979; Rutter and Hersov, 1985; Stein and Davis, 1982; Wolman et al., 1978). Indeed, despite the extensive writings in this area and the teaching of child psychiatrists, psychologists, social workers and others, the practice of treating problem children is not a disciplined one. Much of what is done with a child is at the mercy of social processes, personal preferences and the idiosyncrasies of the treatment agent. The variability of such practice does not arise from bad faith or lack of concern for the children, but rather because little attempt has been made to create a coherent structure of ideas, methods and practices in a manner that can be learned and carried out.

That there is a need for such a discipline is rarely disputed. In the United Kingdom alone, at a rough estimate, there are at any given time about half a million children and young people subject to treatment in medical/psychiatric, educational, penal and social service settings, both 'residentially' and in the community. We do not know very much about what is done with these children and know even less how and why particular outcomes occur. The most significant results of this are that we cannot evaluate the benefits of the treatment given against its cost, in the widest sense. Nor can we learn from our mistakes systematically so as to improve what we do with the children. The picture is very much the same in other countries, despite significant pockets of exceptional practice (for example, Hobbs, 1982; Philips et al., 1972).

In this book, we hope to present the basic elements of what should eventually become a comprehensive discipline of treating problem children. In a practical book such as this it is not appropriate to devote a great deal of space to the philosophical discussion of treatment. Nevertheless, it is necessary to outline the main features of the concept as a general background against which its practice can be evaluated.

The concept of treatment

Treatment is a process with a beginning, a middle and an end, though what constitutes each of these is a matter of debate and negotiated definition. Fundamentally, the term implies an active, coherent response by a person, system or organisation to another person. The response has a purpose, aim or objectives, over a variable time span, and therefore implies planned or purposive behaviour. The purpose of the plan may be set out on a continuum from extreme vagueness to great detail, verbally or in writing, but it must be present in an articulated form before we can call the response 'treatment'.

The purpose is primarily defined by the treatment agent, rather than by the subject. This is because active intervention in the life of another person presumes power and authority to intervene. Although we tend to think of the exercise of such power usually in blatant cases of abuse – for example, the drug treatment of disruptive prisoners or the use of electric shock with sexual deviants – it is no less applicable in the case of children who are subjected to various forms of treatment, such as treatment for temper tantrums or enuresis, which they neither adequately understand nor are able to refuse. This is not to say that the use of power to enforce treatment is illegitimate, but simply that it takes place. The ethical legitimacy of treatment must be determined on other grounds, which will be discussed later. A variant of this issue of power arises in the case of those young people who refer themselves for treatment. As an example, a boy seeks help because he thinks he may be homosexual, or a girl asks for help to 'come off' solvents. In such cases, the young client 'confers' the power on the helper, which the latter then uses in the process of treatment. The differences with cases where referral has been made by other people lie in the degree of coercion and the kind of motivation created for continuing with the treatment.

Treatment is what philosophers call a 'second-order activity'. To know that someone is 'being treated' tells us nothing about *what* is being done; rather, we infer something about the intention of the activity, which is to ameliorate or heal the condition. Thus, *any* human activity can be regarded as a treatment activity if it fits in with an *articulated, purposive plan of action aimed at reducing a problem*. Whether the actions are relevant or appropriate to such a plan is a different matter and requires evaluation on different criteria, which will be set out later.

To undertake treatment presumes that the condition is sufficiently bad to demand intervention; intervention is appropriate and permissible, and the means of intervention are available. Put more systematically, as with every other form of purposive action, treatment demands (1) a basis in legitimising theory, values and laws; (2) the availability of relevant and appropriate methods; and (3) the existence of means whereby those aims and methods may be put into action. To appreciate fully the complexity of treatment and the frequent uncertainties of its better practitioners, it is necessary to set out these elements against the wider background of society's concern with problem children.

Order, values and social control

Every society's prime preoccupation is with its own survival. To this end, it must enforce *order* and achieve certain *values*. 'Order' is about sequence and predictability – when a child has changed into his night-clothes, we expect him to go to bed rather than romp around the garden; when we smile at a girl, we expect her to smile back rather than burst into tears. Without order, we cannot develop adaptive behaviour and we will therefore perish. A child who does not learn that walking in front of moving traffic is dangerous is likely to have a short life.

But order, though necessary, is not sufficient to account for the enormous complexity of purposive human action. To do that, we must also consider 'values', namely everything that matters to us in terms of standards, objectives and other mainsprings of our actions. Human values encapsulate both how things are and how they should be. Thus, we may say that 'at present religion does not seem to matter very much to most children' or that 'it is important to protect children against sexual exploitation'. Our most significant values (and sanctions against breaching them) are encapsulated in laws and other explicit codes which either require or enable us to take appropriate action with children.

To achieve order and promote social values, our actions are channelled to achieving three interdependent objectives:

1   *Enhancement* of whatever is deemed to be worthwhile, good and desirable, either for its own sake or because it reinforces other objectives. In the case of children, this would refer to such actions as promoting their health and happiness, giving them varied and enriching experiences and enabling them to achieve their potential.

2   *Conservation* of whatever is deemed to be worthy in its own right or not warranting change. We would thus not press a youngster to change his religion or politics, or (under normal circumstances) his hairstyle or colour preferences.

3   *Curbing, reducing and elimination* of whatever is considered to be damaging, bad and unacceptable, either because it is unacceptable in its own right (by virtue of our sense of order and value) or because it detracts from the achievement of other objectives. In this category we would place such matters as physical and mental ill health, non-accidental injury, solvent abuse, promiscuity and persistent delinquency.

The balance of the above objectives changes with social conditions, as do standards of what is good, neutral and bad. These standards reflect our 'latitude of tolerance', and clearly this latitude has changed over the years. We are now less tolerant of non-accidental injury but more tolerant of minor delinquency; eating disorders and solvent abuse attract more attention, and odd appearance less.

Any behaviour or condition which falls outside our latitude of tolerance is 'unacceptable' and therefore demands action. Such 'unacceptable conditions' are what we would define as *problems*. A much fuller account of 'problems' has been given elsewhere (Hoghughi et al., 1980), and it is anticipated that anyone using this book is familiar with the concept and means of assessing problem children.

Whatever the changes in social and individual standards, it is clear that many children experience conditions and behave in such a way that society finds unacceptable. Treatment is undertaken to bring the children 'back into the fold' – that is, to ameliorate their condition so that, however undesirable and imperfect, it is not so to an 'unacceptable' degree. Thus, treatment is a major form of social control of problem children (or children with problems) and can be most productively seen in this light. Social control and its 'ecology' has been presented in more detail elsewhere (Hoghughi, 1983).

Underlying our actions is the belief that intervention is likely to ameliorate, or at least contain, the unacceptable condition (the problem) which has provoked it. This is more frequently implicit than explicit. However, it can be regarded as the most fundamental 'article of faith' of the healer. The creed is usually unvoiced but, if it were, it would be something like: 'Every problem can be resolved, or at least its impact made tolerable, by the healing process; no child, however serious his problem, is untreatable; our failure to find effective treatments is indicative of the quality of our efforts so far, rather than of the child's condition, so let us try more and better; our next effort may well bear fruit; we cannot and must not give up.'

Treatment and other interventions

Treatment is only one of a range of responses in the achievement of social order which take place when the need arises. To make sense of its proper place as a purposive activity, it is necessary to set it out in the context of the totality of actions that must be taken to deal fully with the child's problems. As a guide to action, such steps are best set out in the 'critical path' or 'logical order' where the aims of one form of intervention cannot be achieved unless the requirements of those which *precede* it have been adequately met (Hoghughi et al., 1980; Hoghughi, 1983). These steps are set out in Figure 1.1.

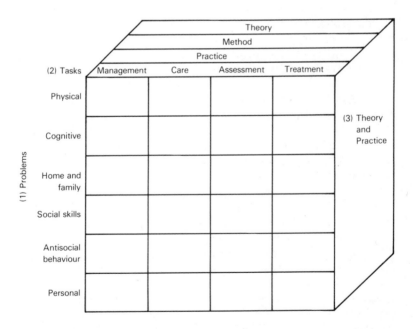

Figure 1.1 *Dimensions of work with problem children*

The 'cube' represents what philosophers call the 'total universe of discourse' – there is nothing about dealing with problem children by any profession in any context that falls outside the parameters of the cube. The power of the diagram lies particularly in enabling us to identify gaps or deficiencies in our knowledge and practice, so that we may continue to develop and improve what we do with children. In this respect it is much like Mendeliev's table of chemical elements, which has been gradually filled with the discovery of missing elements. Unlike Mendeliev's table, however, every dimension of the cube is susceptible to change, thus making it dynamic and responsive to developments in theory and practice.

Ideals and limitations

We subject a child to treatment because he experiences or presents a condition which, according to our current scale of values and sense of order, is unacceptable. The ideal of treatment is therefore the amelioration of the problem. But given that the child is a whole entity and what we do with him in one problem area will inevitably affect other areas of functioning, an ideal would be to treat him in a way that would make minimal impact on those aspects we would not want to change and maximal impact on others that we would wish to promote. Also, as part of an ideal, we should seek to maximise the length of time during which the treatment remains effective, and in such a way that the child achieves self-control or the ability to manage his own treatment.

So, for example, in treating an incontinent child, we would attempt to minimise any possible effect that our treatment may have on his schoolwork. We would not adopt a treatment approach that requires the teacher to remind him publicly that he should go to the toilet. On the other hand, we may wish to develop his swimming prowess as a way of increasing his sense of personal worth, which is desirable not only in its own right but also as an element in the treatment of his incontinence. Our child having been treated, should ideally continue to be dry and clean for ever more and become independent of others' monitoring or help in this respect.

Thus, ideals of treatment are limited by considerations of other factors such as the demand on resources, the impact on the child and the wider social context. This is the area usually referred to as 'cost-benefit analysis'. In economic enterprises, this form of analysis has become highly developed and is pursued as a disciplined activity. With changes in both economic and political climate and greater recognition of the wider social and personal implications of treatment, cost–benefit analyses are being applied in one guise or another to social interventions with children (for example, Zeckhauser, 1976; Hoghughi, 1983).

The most immediate limitation on treatment is the shortage of resources, not so much of bricks and mortar but of the number of competent people to deal effectively with problem children. A shortage of 'beds' or 'places' for children with eating disorders and poor social skills is, in reality, a shortage of people with appropriate skills to deal with these problems. This, in turn, reflects either the disbursement of resources by those who manage a service (so that, for example, not every town has an adolescent psychiatric unit) or, more probably, the fact that people with appropriate skills in this area are a relatively scarce commodity and so can be only thinly spread.

In looking at the treatment programme of a child, it is therefore necessary to consider what resources he requires, how readily available they are and how justifiably they can be devoted to meeting his requirements. This view recognises the fact that when resources are limited, not all children can receive all the treatment they require. Thus, we may give only 'minimal treatment', enough to contain immediately and possibly remedy the situation, but not enough to reduce the probability of recurrence.

A further major limitation on treatment is simply the amount of knowledge available for use with problem children. We will comment further on this in Chapter 2. In general terms, however, the usable knowledge for treating children is extremely patchy and variable in relation not only to different problem areas but also to the professionals concerned. As has already been suggested, this reflects the development both of our concerns with children and of our professions. We believe that the only way a substantive improvement will be made to this will be when treating problem children is pursued as a coherent, disciplined and co-operative activity.

In a general sense, then, feasibility, practicability or 'do-ability' in one guise or another places the major limitation on the treatment of problem children. One related and important element not dealt with so far concerns the ethical limitations of treatment, which warrants separate discussion.

Ethics of treatment

Ethics is the study of 'right and wrong', concerning the 'morality' of actions of people holding different relationships with us as professionals (such as social workers, probation officers, psychiatrists and nurses), 'paraprofessionals' (such as foster-parents), parents and friends. The major sources of ethical concern with children arise from their status as minors, from the nature of treatment as an exercise of power and from the possible consequences of treatment for the child and his wider context.

Both in law and in professional practice, children are acknowledged to be different from adults, though some of the differences (for example, in the ability to make decisions about themselves) are a matter of debate. What is generally accepted is that children, as minors, are entitled to have their health and welfare safeguarded by adults who are, or may become, responsible for them. Indeed, in most developed countries there is provision for the state to assume responsibility for the children in place of parents, if their physical and psychological health is either endangered or inadequately provided for. Whereas an adult can choose to seek treatment or not (unless he becomes subject to criminal or mental-health laws), for children treatment initiatives must be taken by adults, who must usually give consent to children's treatment until they 'come of age'. The recent ruling of the House of Lords in the Gillick case suggests that at least an adolescent owns his own body and may independently seek treatment for it (*Childright*, 1985). In general, though, the notion of parents' consent still reigns supreme.

Many of the problems of children impinge on adults, not simply because of adults' concern for children but also because the problems make adults' lives more difficult. Such problems as 'hyperactivity', 'temper tantrums' and 'staying out late' are examples of this. Adults are therefore likely to seek treatment for children because they themselves are suffering. In an important sense this is both understandable and inevitable. The distinction between 'experiencing' and 'presenting' problems is mainly one of degree and locus of impact, adopted largely for convenience. A 'depressed' child not only suffers; he also makes adults seriously uneasy about his depression and its consequences for him. Delinquent behaviour presents another and more complex example.

The distinction is nevertheless an important one, posing serious ethical questions for the treatment agent. How far should a 'hyperactive' child or one who is difficult to manage be calmed through the use of tranquillising medication, in order to make adults' lives easier? Who pays the longer-term price for the frequently unknown side-effects of the medication? How far should a girl with homosexual tendencies be subjected to the demands of sexual reorientation treatment because our culture is still intolerant of her preference? There are no easy answers to such dilemmas. The interests of children cannot be totally isolated from those of their caregivers (Houlgate, 1980; Morris et al., 1980). But the treatment agent, as the person who has to legitimise and often execute the treatment, has a special responsibility to ensure that the interests of the child and the possible impact on him by the treatment are set out and clearly understood. He should also make explicit the point at which the benefits of treatment to the child are becoming marginal and balance these with the possible damage.

This aspect is bound up with the exercise of power by adults over children. The whole process, indeed, from the definition of a problem ('unacceptable condition', but 'unacceptable' to whom?) through to the implementation of treatment, is the embodiment of a power relationship. In this respect the child is the weaker and the treatment agent the stronger of the parties. In our culture, such a relationship demands that the weaker party be protected against the possible excess or inappropriate use of power by the stronger. Whereas we have (debatably) adequate safeguards for children subjected to the legal process (such as guardians *ad litem* and legal representation), we have no parallel measures for children who are subjected to treatment by a variety of professional agencies, such as physicians, psychiatrists, psychologists and social workers (see Houlgate, 1980).

Safeguarding the interests of children in treatment becomes the more important, because not all the consequences of treatment are benign. The long-term damaging effects of medication, the build-up of resistance to further treatments that results from incompetent intervention, the unpleasant nature of some experiences and the coercive nature of much treatment at the more serious end of the scale of disordered behaviour are some of the graver consequences of treatment, however well intentioned the intervention may have been in the first place.

The consequences of treatment may be considered as part of a wider calculus of costs and benefits of treatment intervention in the lives of problem children. This calculus has been extensively set out elsewhere (Hoghughi et al., 1980) and will not be repeated here. Its elements include considerations of how well and solidly the reasons for treatment are articulated, on what basis the treatment methods are chosen and how well the detailed costs and benefits to the child, his family and the treatment agent are worked out.

Because of the complexity of the above issues, it would seem impossible to set out any universally applicable critical guidelines for treatment agents. However, there appear to be a few universal considerations which competent and ethically concerned professionals follow, and these may be set out in the form of imperatives.

- Do not coerce or use force in the interest of treatment unless you can show that all the alternatives have been explored and rejected for good reason.
- Minimise hurt and unpleasantness as much as humanly possible.
- Take account of a child's age and condition and allow him choice of treatment, if at all possible.
- Inform the child and others concerned of the reason for the treatment chosen, how it is likely to be carried out and what its effects and side-effects are likely to be.
- Even as a highly competent specialist, you are not infallible. Treat each case in the light of all its individual circumstances and *publicly* ensure that there are no better ways of treating than by your preferred method.
- Subject your procedures to rigorous monitoring and public accountability to the child, parents and other concerned people, allowing genuine opportunity for them to understand what is being done and why, how it departs from expectations and how and what further action will be taken.

- Allow participation in the treatment process by as wide a range of relevant and competent individuals as possible. Since this is a necessary corollary to treating the whole child, consensus is likely to be ethically more acceptable than a form of treatment based on a single person's judgements.
- Remember that no treatment works without fail. So, do not raise unrealistic expectations about the outcome of treatment; remember that your failure not only may damage the child but will probably make it more difficult for others to provide effective treatment.
- Remember that even a highly qualified professional is no more competent to judge what is ethically right or wrong than anyone else; his ability lies in determining the most efficacious treatment once the treatment objectives have been evaluated and determined.
- Set up appropriate records of treatment objectives, methods and outcomes to facilitate evaluation both internally and by external bodies; you should always aim to be able to identify failure of treatment, so as to learn what is least or most conducive to failure and act accordingly.
- Remember that there is hardly any form or aspect of treatment about whose beneficial outcome we can be sure; remember your fallibility and keep your treatment decisions and operations open to influence by concerned and knowledgeable others.

The gist of the above points is that undertaking any but the most trivial measures in the treatment of children's disorders raises issues of moral justification that must be explicitly accounted for. Daily experience shows that such accounting hardly ever takes place in most psychiatric, educational, penal or social services settings for the treatment of problem children. The reason for this should be sought in the poor application of moral imperatives in treating children and in the lack of demand for public accountability, as well as in the scarcity of systematic, disciplined and empirically based approaches in this area. The major safeguard proposed above is that in all treatment measures we should approximate to total public accountability. This seems to bring us into conflict with another concern, broadly within the area of ethics, which is much beloved of treatment practitioners.

Confidentiality

The process of accountability described above takes place, to our knowledge, in only a tiny minority of settings where children are subjected to treatment. Most treatment reviews, if they take place at all, do so in a haphazard way where the significance and evaluation of statements are much more related to hierarchy than to relevance or weight of evidence. Even where this is not so, significant discussions are hardly ever held in the presence of the children and their parents in such a manner as to encourage them to participate in what is being done.

The major reason for this is the tradition emanating from earlier forms of medical practice where the patient was regarded as the 'object' of treatment, who by virtue of his illness and the technicalities of treatment could not be relied upon to contribute sensibly or profitably to any discussion of the treatment. This tendency to treat children and parents as objects rather than as partners is even more blatant in those arenas where children are subject to coercive forms of treatment. The untenableness of this position on both ethical and empirical grounds is only slowly being recognised. Under the weight of persuasive professional opinion this practice is slowly changing, so that occasionally children and parents are dealt with as if they had some stake in the process of treatment.

A major impediment to the full realisation of this ideal is the reasonable concern of most professionals with how far they can discuss and disclose confidential and occasionally sensitive information, provided either by themselves or by other professional colleagues, in the presence of the child and the parents. They feel they have to carry out heavy censorship in case the material is used either in litigation or for purposes which are likely to undermine the personal and professional status and effectiveness of the treatment agents.

A central plank of the orthodoxy of all the helping professions is that the relationship between the therapist and the child (and his parents) is confidential and that the information gained through it is sacrosanct and may not be freely communicated to other professionals. The context of this book is not appropriate for a discussion of the concept of confidentiality and the complications surrounding it. It is, however, helpful to distinguish between, on the one hand, the sensitive and responsible use of information in order not to hurt a child or his parents or to damage the therapists and, on the other hand, not disclosing information at all, simply because it has been given in confidence by the child or the parents to a particular treatment agent. We take it as axiomatic that *no action* should be taken which hurts the child and the parents through insensitivity. Broadcasting damaging information is one clear instance of this and should never be practised. If a treatment agent lacks the sensitivity to communicate information in an unhurting and undamaging way, it is most unlikely that he will be a good therapeutic agent in the first place, and he should therefore be prevented from engaging in such an activity.

However, it is also a central contention of this book that the treatment of problem children is a means of achieving social order and enforcing social values, employed by a group of people who, whether they act in a statutory or a voluntary capacity, are empowered and warranted to intervene in the life of a less powerful citizen. As such, all treatment agents are of equal standing although they may vary in the organisational or (preferably) the professional/intellectual authority they carry, by virtue of their (ascribed or acquired) expertise in a particular field. The relationship between the child and one particular therapist, such as a psychiatrist, is no more confidential or sacred than that between the child and a teacher, the child and a social worker or the child and a nurse. The logical conclusion of treating information acquired from, by or through a child as confidential is that each party would refuse to communicate with the others lest the canons of confidentiality be breached. This is as counter-productive of treatment as it is unnecessary.

We believe that the notion of confidentiality in the treatment of children and their families as practised *among and between* professionals is vastly overplayed, to the detriment of children and of the interests of minimal intervention aimed at maximum benefit. One element of such maximum benefit is that all therapeutic agents should know what the others are doing so as to regulate their own actions accordingly. In any case, public accountability for all actions, which we regard as the chief ethical safeguard for the children and their care-givers, demands the sharing of information. If we do not believe in the integrity of other people involved in the treatment of the child, we should not allow them to participate in treatment in the first place.

Having conducted assessment and treatment reviews involving large teams of professionals from diverse disciplines, in the presence of parents and the child throughout, we have tested the hypothesis that there is no information which cannot be communicated openly, though sensitively, and with due regard for the understanding and coping ability of the parents and the child. In many hundreds of such meetings we have not encountered more than a handful of instances where a particular piece of information has had to be withheld because, however sensitively put, it would have been damaging to the child, the parents or the source of information. In sum, therefore, we would advocate the widest possible dissemination of information regarding the child to those people concerned with his treatment, compatible with the need for sensitivity in handling the information. Views about confidentiality are but one aspect of fundamentally different approaches to treatment, and it is to these approaches that we now turn.

Further reading

Childright (1985) 'House of Lords rule on Gillick', *Childright* 22 (Nov./Dec.).

Goldstein, J., Freud, A. and Solnit, A.J. (1980) *Beyond the Best Interests of the Child*. London: Burnett Books.

Hobbs, N. (1982) *The Troubled and Troubling Child*. San Francisco: Jossey Bass.

Hoghughi, M.S. (1983) *The Delinquent: Directions for Social Control*. London: Burnett Books/Hutchinson.

Hoghughi, M.S., Dobson, C., Lyons, J., Muckley, A. and Swainston, M. (1980) *Assessing Problem Children*. London: Burnett Books/Deutsch.

Houlgate, L. (1980) *The Child and the State*. Baltimore, MD: Johns Hopkins University Press.

Howells, J.G. (ed.) (1965) *Modern Perspectives in Child Psychiatry*. Edinburgh: Oliver & Boyd.

Keat, D.B. II (1979) *Multimodal Therapy with Children*. New York: Pergamon.

Kennedy, I. (1980) *The Unmasking of Medicine*. London: Allen & Unwin.

Morris, A., Giller, H., Szwed, E. and Geach, H. (1980) *Justice for Children*. London: Macmillan.

Philips, E.G., Philips, E.A., Fixsen, D.L. and Wolf, M.M.B. (1972) *The Teaching Family Handbook*. Lawrence, KS: University of Kansas Press.

Rutter, M. and Hersov L. (eds) (1985) *Child and Adolescent Psychiatry*. Oxford: Blackwell.

Stein, M.D. and Davis, J.K. (1982) *Therapies for Adolescents*. San Francisco: Jossey Bass.

Wolman, B., Egan, J. and Ross, A. (eds) (1978) *Handbook of Treatment of Mental Disorders in Childhood and Adolescence*. Englewood Cliffs, NJ: Prentice-Hall.

Zeckhauser, R. (1976) 'Procedures for valuing lives', in G.V. Glass (ed.), *Evaluation Studies Review Annual*, Vol. 1. Beverly Hills, CA: Sage.

2

Approaches to Treatment

Not only children but also the people who treat them are different, both individually and as groups. We should therefore not be surprised at the great diversity of treatments. The fact of the diversity, however, is easier to state than it is to analyse. Such an analysis is worthwhile because of the help it might give the practitioner to see the full range of available approaches.

Prerequisites of action

Treatment is a form of purposive action. To make proper sense of both its potential and its limitations, we must look at its basic prerequisites. These can be broadly summarised as: knowing what to do; wanting to do it; and having the ability/opportunity to do it.

Knowing what to do   This is clearly the starting-point for all action. It presumes that we have been alerted to the need for action and have a reasonable idea of what we are to do. In the context of treating problem children, whether by parents or others, this 'knowing what to do' is the result of assessment. Assessments vary in their depth and quality and will accordingly affect what is to be done.

Wanting to do it   It is perfectly possible to recognise that something must be done and to know how it is to be done, without doing anything about it. To take action requires motivation. We take such motivation for granted on the part of the professionals – after all, they are *paid* to do the job, and 'wanting' should not come into it. We cannot, however, deny that if a treatment agent is strongly motivated to sort out a child's problems he is less likely to give up than one who is less motivated. We see possible instances of this in cases of non-accidental injury or when child guidance sessions are terminated due to poor parental response.

Another important aspect of this is the need to create appropriate motivation in the child. We now recognise that, other than in tiny areas of the surgical or drug-related treatment of young children, we *cannot impose* treatment on children. Although it is often difficult we must try very hard to create some sense of commitment on the child's part. This is, of course, centrally recognised in behavioural treatments, but it is no less valid and

and necessary in the use of other methods. Underlying this is the generally accepted notion that children are not passive lumps to be subjected to treatment but rather active participants, whose co-operation will make or break the treatment. Despite the originally zealous claims of even behaviour modifiers, we now know that we cannot treat a child (that is, remedy his problems) against his will.

Because children often do not know what is in their best interests, and indeed frequently become the subject of treatment precisely because of their self-damaging behaviour, enormous difficulties result. The way out is to consider that creating motivation for and commitment to treatment is itself part of the treatment effort, directed at the child, the parents and other people significant to the child.

Having the ability and opportunity to do it   Knowing what to do and wanting to do it come to nothing if we do not have the wherewithal and the opportunity to carry out the task. 'Ability' is a blanket term which encapsulates both personal qualities (such as intelligence, warmth and sensitivity) and professional skills (such as being able to interview, to carry out microsurgery or to run a therapeutic group). 'Opportunity' refers to the availability of the setting and occasion for the appropriate interaction of the treatment agent and the child. We may believe that the only way to stop repeated suicide attempts is by sorting out the distorted relationships at home. But if the family refuse point blank to have anything to do with us, our chances of carrying out that sort of treatment are somewhat limited.

We shall return to the notions of 'ability and opportunity' in Chapter 3, but the example highlights the need not only to regard 'creating motivation' as part of treatment, but also to develop widely based approaches to treatment which may help to reduce the chances of failure.

Against this general background, we can distinguish different approaches to treatment according to orientation and context, whether the focus is on the individual child and his wider social network and the problem area involved. As regards orientation and context, it is worthwhile differentiating between informal and formal approaches to treatment. This is somewhat akin to the distinction between non-professional and professional.

Apart from the fact that such differences are more a matter of degree than of kind (everyone carries out 'physical' treatments, from a mother to a surgeon), there is also a good deal of value judgement in the distinctions as normally made. There is the implicit suggestion that 'professionals' are superior to 'non-professionals' or that 'informal' approaches may be better than 'formal' ones. Here we reject such implications, for which we have found neither evidence nor persuasive reason. We make the distinction because the contexts place different demands on practitioners.

Informal contexts

Parents and family

If we were to look closely at the process of socialisation, we would find that most children's problems are dealt with by parents in their normal setting, utilising time-honoured means of bringing about behaviour changes with the aid of family members and friends, with occasional external help from specialists. This is inevitable, because sorting out children's problems is one of the cultural functions of parents.

Parents are the chief agents of informal social control – 'informal' because they are neither legally required nor paid to look after their children in a particular way. The law may insist that they do not breach certain standards of acceptable discipline or that they fulfil certain care functions, but parents' interactions with their children remain, as yet, the most unregulated arena of children's treatment. Parents as 'carriers' and 'transmitters' of cultural values set down and enforce certain standards of behaviour (such as in toilet training and 'doing as told') using whatever methods they prefer.

In the present context, however, the word 'informal' has a wider significance. As will be seen at greater length in Chapter 3, all treatment requires resources, and to do the job those resources must be organised and paid for. Parents and 'the family' are major treatment resources whose chief feature is that they are not 'organised'.

This becomes more obvious when we look at a number of dimensions which are entailed in any treatment, such as formality–informality, 'distance'–closeness, 'office-hour'–unrestricted contact and public–private. Parents' difference from others is a matter of degree. 'Formality' concerns the training, qualification and legal and organisational basis, as well as the power relationship, in the dealings of the treatment agent with the child. Parents are not 'trained', 'qualified' or organised to deal with their children's problems, and their power, though immense, arises from kinship and the implied legal, cultural and emotional attachments to the child.

Some degree of distancing is essential in order to assess a problem and dispassionately sort out what should be done about it. On this dimension, parents are the closest people to their children. To create the necessary distance for the assessment and treatment of the child's problems would therefore be a major objective (and often difficulty) of treating the child – particularly if it is to be carried out by the parents.

Apart from the usual exigencies of family living, parents have the most extensive and intimate access to their children. Their contact is not regulated by 'office hours', demands of other patients/clients or the many other aspects of being a professional. They can also engage in the most intimate terms in the treatment of their children, not only because they are not official or paid (and therefore an object of suspicion) but also because their position is usually one of extreme trust *vis-à-vis* the child. To the extent that intensive treatment, carried out over the 24-hour period, is likely to have more impact than partial treatment taking place in an office or clinic, then parents should make the most effective treatment agents.

This is now acknowledged in the significant attempts being made to teach parents how to treat a wide array of children's behavioural problems (for example, Keat, 1977; Keat and Gurney, 1978; Patterson, 1971; Peine and Howarth, 1975). However, it is also recognised that parents play a significant part in creating and maintaining their children's problems. Indeed, their very closeness and emotional involvement frequently militate against the efficient resolution of their children's problems. Also, parents often believe they know best what to do with their children, whose problems are often tied up with other family issues and difficulties. Because of these factors, it is difficult to ensure that parents do what is expected of them. Unless problems reach such a pitch that children have to be removed from home, we have to confine ourselves to what the parents can be persuaded to do.

Foster-parents
Sometimes children's conditions are such that they cannot stay at home. These conditions range from a very young child's being neglected and ill-treated to an adolescent's being suicidal or seriously delinquent. The common thread of such conditions is that the child is not receiving adequate care or control. An increasingly popular venue for the placement of such children is 'boarding out' or 'fostering' with an alternative family. Foster-parents are paid an allowance, which may take account of a child's difficulties. They are therefore less 'informal' than parents and can be expected to carry out a suitable programme of child treatment. Although frequently not so regarded (see Shaw and Hipgrave, 1983) there are powerful reasons for believing that ideally even most short-term foster placements should be used as a medium of treatment, that is, reducing the extent and severity of a problem (Hoghughi and Hipgrave, 1985).

Foster-parents potentially come closest to natural parents in all the dimensions mentioned above, with the advantage that they should be better able to distance themselves from the child in order to assess and treat his problems. To do so, however, they require training in the relevant skills as well as help in drawing up treatment programmes, where their own role as treatment agents, *vis-à-vis* others, is made explicit. Apart from those problems which require high-level specialist attention (such as surgery) or particular settings (such as group therapy), suitably trained foster-parents should be able to use almost all the treatment methods and techniques outlined in this book.

There are many other people and agencies that can be fitted somewhere along the dimension of informal–formal, such as clergymen, friends and youth workers. It is not possible to enumerate them all and comment on their potential role. We will therefore now move further into those areas where a treatment task is explicitly recognised.

Formal intervention

Whilst recognising the grey area in the definition of 'formal', we regard any intervention in which professionals participate in an official capacity (rather than, for example, as family friends) to be 'formal'. This is because they are presumed to have certain skills for which they are employed and paid, and are often expected to do their job according to certain professional standards.

In an advanced society such as ours there are numerous professionals involved in the treatment of problem children. They are distinguishable both by the broad differences of their disciplines, such as between physicians and social workers (always allowing for great charity in the use of the word 'discipline'), and by the varying orientations within the same discipline, such as those of surgeons, psychiatrists and family therapists. Since this book is not a treatise on professional practice, it would be inappropriate to go into detail about such differences. On the other hand, given the crucial role of professionals in treating problem children, some discussion of their contributions is merited. For the sake of consistency, we shall look at the professionals in terms of the four major treatment contexts in which they *mainly* operate: penal or criminal justice; medical; educational; and social services.

Criminal justice

The treatment input in this area includes the police, probation officers and volunteers, community service supervisors and the staff of various penal establishments. Their work ranges from occasional counselling sessions in a probation office to the behaviour modification of a seriously aggressive youngster in a youth custody centre. As far as young people are concerned, they deal with a narrow band of older adolescents, who have offended against the criminal law and who are coerced into treatment. The aim of intervention in this area is primarily to contain the problem and to prevent re-offending. Because of the strong overtones of punishment and the coercive nature of involvement with the young person, there has been relatively little emphasis on treatment. In the UK at least, any pretence of treatment now seems to have been removed from the work of the penal facilities. Probation officers and those who work with young offenders in the community, on the other hand, are becoming increasingly involved in what can only be termed treatment.

There has been a tendency in the past to consider that the probation officer is concerned only with the youngster's offending and, to that extent, has no responsibility for ensuring that the youngster's care and other treatment requirements are met. This has been in part due to the partial and narrow training of probation officers. However, it is now recognised that a youngster is an integrated whole; unless his care requirements are met and his wider difficulties ameliorated (even though there may be no causal relationship between these and offending), he is likely to offend again. Other professionals may be involved with the youngster, but the probation officer is likely to be the person identified as having failed to prevent the re-offending. He is therefore required not only to do what is necessary to ameliorate the youngster's problems, but also to organise others to do so. In this respect he is both an *executor* and a *co-ordinator* of treatment measures.

Given the complexity of the task (and with small, though significant, exceptions), probation officers are at present poorly trained in assessment and treatment skills. Magistrates are in general unaware of the professional limitations of probation and appear to assign tasks to probation officers that they cannot perform. This is borne out not only by the massive breakdown rates in supervision orders but also by their relative decrease in numbers and the alarming increase in custodial sentences for young offenders. The many issues involved have been discussed at greater length elsewhere (Hoghughi, 1983).

Health services
The health services are those traditionally and most readily associated with treating children. The basis of the tradition lies in the incomparable significance of sickness (nothing else is a matter of life and death) and the corresponding sophistication of medicine. Associated with this, these services also employ the largest number and widest range of professionals – from the surgeons, general physicians and psychiatrists to nurses, occupational therapists and psychologists. The context of the services ranges from short visits to a surgery, out-patient sessions and short-term in-patient periods to long-term residential treatment in a psychiatric facility. There are so many variations in clusters and emphases of the health services that it would be misleading to generalise about what they do and how they do it. It is, however, worthwhile to distinguish the *physical* health services from those that deal with a youngster's other problems.

Physical medicine is the most advanced of human sciences. Its practitioners are the most rigorously trained and professionally regulated. They draw upon a large (though by no means equally sound or comprehensive) and well-systematised body of information directly related to treatment. Even more significantly, the whole practice of physical medicine is subject to continuous good-quality research, and the knowledge base is therefore constantly developing.

There is so much writing on various aspects of child psychiatric practice that any discussion of it is likely to be deemed either superfluous or grossly inadequate. Yet, in a book of this sort, child psychiatry cannot be left out, because of its significance in the treatment of problem children. Historically, child psychiatry is a much later arrival than its adult counterpart, and both are only latter-day, accidental offspring of a relatively grown-up physical medicine (Jones, 1977). Apart from the early application of dynamic psychological insights to children, it is only recently that, in the non-physical areas, psychiatrists have stopped seeing children as younger versions of adults. Gradually also, a body of research knowledge has developed which, in the hands of rigorous practitioners, is turning child psychiatry into a disciplined activity (see, for example, Rutter and Hersov, 1985).

The essence of child psychiatrists' contribution lies in their ability to assess and treat those conditions where the use of medication is appropriate, such as psychoses and depression. There is no other area of practice with children in which psychiatry can claim expertise *as* psychiatry, and where the knowledge base is not shared by other professions, notably psychology and social work. However, because child psychiatrists specialize in the diagnosis and treatment of children's disorders, they are likely to be of considerable assistance in evaluating the type of help a child may need and who should provide it. They are also the focus and the main organisational hub of the child psychiatric services to which children are referred for help. A good psychiatric service, utilising a wide range of expertise, should be able to provide a comprehensive assessment of children's problems and arrange for treatment. The quality of psychiatric service, however, is probably no less variable than that of any of the other services for children, particularly when we move from in-patient to out-patient treatment (Health Advisory Service, 1986).

Much treatment of children's disorders is carried out by nurses and psychologists. Nurses, though sharing a basic physical orientation, seem to be becoming more widely involved in the planning and execution of treatment for problem children (for example, Donellan, 1986; Health Advisory Service, 1986). The basically high quality of their training, with greater recent emphasis on psychological methods, combined with their greater number and approachability for parents and others, augurs well for an increasingly important role for nurses in this area.

Clinical psychologists are the most recent professional group to have become involved in the systematic treatment of children. They function in all the four treatment areas, although the majority are employed in the health services. Their widely based training, informed by both a scientific approach and its limitations, combined with concern for the total child, has placed them in a position of singular influence. Their advent seems to have coincided with and promoted increasing distaste for the use of medication as a means of ameliorating children's problems. The solid basis in experimental psychology, particularly of social learning, has enabled them to amass a considerable body of useful and systematic (though by no means comprehensive) information on treating children (see, for example, Herbert, 1978; Quay and Werry, 1979). Even setting aside our understandable bias in favour of psychology, we would still consider it as the superordinate connective tissue of all approaches to treating problem children (see Lazarus, 1976; Keat, 1979).

The health services have the greatest potential not only for treating problem children but also for helping to spearhead the spread of the relevant discipline. It cannot be doubted that considerable good work is done, particularly in the area of physical problems. The cause for anxiety is the tendency of the health services to fragment the child and attend mainly to his 'health service' aspects, at the expense of other related parts. Because of the prevalence of views in our society, mere referral to psychiatric services, plus the consequences of diagnostic labelling, is likely to have serious long-term consequences for the child. Perhaps most seriously, because of the social organisation of the health services (particularly outside physical medicine where wrong or unsuccessful treatment can be readily identified), there is little accountability for giving a poor service that is likely to result in treatment failure and in deterioration in the child's condition.

Education
Education is the only universal, mandatory service for all children, playing a major role in their socialisation. Many of the problems of children are reliably and skilfully ameliorated by teachers, particularly in the primary school. Besides mainstream education for 'normal' children, there are also extensive provisions for the assessment and treatment of children with 'special educational needs' (Warnock, 1978). These range from the provision of child guidance clinics and school psychological services to special educational facilities for children with a range of physical, cognitive and behavioural difficulties. There is now an increasing tendency to place children with special needs in ordinary schools, unless there are very good reasons to the contrary. Some special schools will, however, continue to deal with particularly handicapped or maladjusted children.

School psychological services are staffed by educational psychologists, who must have both teaching experience and specialist training. They provide primarily screening assessment and some treatment help and guidance, both directly and for use by the teaching staff. Child guidance clinics provide more formal and multi-faceted assessment and treatment.

Special schools, providing day and residential facilities, are staffed primarily by teachers who should have specialist training in the area of handicap or difficulty with which they are dealing. Much of this specialist training is concerned with assessment and treatment, though it rarely includes the necessary coaching for the inculcation of skills – as happens in nursing. Even this level of specialist training is not provided for general schoolteachers, who probably deal with more problematic youngsters than any other group.

Despite the huge expenditure on education, little is known about the efficacy of educational psychologists, child guidance clinics or special educational input beyond scholastic improvement of the child. Given primary problems of mental and physical handicap, and often serious behavioural problems, educational establishments can probably provide the most normal, productive and enhancing form of treatment for handicapped children. Lack of stigma, normality of contact with home life and quality of education usually make this a particularly attractive option for treating problem children (Howlin, 1985).

Social services

The social services cater for children whose problems do not fall readily (or by virtue of preferential definition) into any of the other three areas. They range from preventive work with children and families (such as voluntary supervision), through intermediate treatment, and fostering to placement in a variety of community homes, with and without education, with varying degrees of focused competence for ameliorating children's problems. They also run specialist facilities for particular groups of problem children, such as the physically and mentally handicapped and the delinquent.

The social services are run primarily by 'field' or 'residential' social workers, with some specialist input. 'Field' social workers are mostly qualified through the acquisition of a CQSW, whereas only a small minority of 'residential workers' have a relevant qualification.

Despite various attempts, social work training is seriously deficient in conceptual framework or an integrating, shared body of knowledge concerning children and relevant practices with them (see Beedell, 1970; Crompton, 1982; Hoghughi, 1980; Treischmann et al., 1970). Moreover, the reactive nature of social work, the fact that its clients are the most disadvantaged and damaged in our society, combined with the overwhelming pressure of work and the fear of public reaction in the cases that are bound to go wrong, lends a quality of chaotic panic to much social work with children. As a result, the 'processing' of a child in the hands of the social services is a highly unpredictable affair, and its outcome even more so. Indeed, good-quality 'monitoring' of social services intervention in children's lives remains as elusive as its occasional results are depressing. The notion of accountability for the quality of service, though not quite as conspicuously absent as in the health services, is only slowly beginning to go beyond the fulfilment of statutory review requirements.

Yet these are paradoxically the very services that are required to deal with the rejects and failures of the health and educational services whilst, unlike penal establishments, retaining a positive, optimistic stance towards the child. The problems and potentials of social workers in the community are very much like those of probation officers, outlined earlier. 'Intermediate treatment' officers are a group on whom considerable good-quality attention is being lavished (see, for example, DHSS, 1977; Thorpe et al., 1980). In time they should be able to utilise a wide range of techniques for dealing with delinquent youngsters whose problems are sufficiently light to be containable in the 'community'.

Residential facilities in the social services are likely to continue dealing with the most problematic youngsters. Despite serious cut-backs and a paucity of education and training for their workers, but perhaps because of the severity of the children's problems, these are becoming the very spearheads of the disciplined treatment of problem children (see, for example, Adler, 1981; Brown and Christie, 1981; Nethercott, 1983).

Falling between field and residential work, fostering is emerging as an important context for treatment within the social services. With increasing attention devoted to developing a discipline of fostering (for example, Shaw and Hipgrave, 1983; Hoghughi and Hipgrave, 1985), prospects for the specialised treatment of moderately disordered children in 'normal' settings are likely to expand.

We have presented the above picture of the treatment of children primarily in terms of the contexts of intervention and the major professional groups that operate within them. We shall present in Part II of this book an account of the main methods of treatment which can be used with children. It may at this stage be worthwhile to look at the state of treatment in terms of each problem area.

The state of treatment

Physical problems
Physical problems encapsulate everything that is wrong with the body and its functioning. The state of knowledge and competence in practice, though variable in relation to particular problems, is the most coherent and high level available. Medicine is secure enough to have been able to utilise a wide range of other methods in the amelioration of physical problems. Difficulties concern those physical problems such as addiction to solvents and drugs which have no straightforward physical basis or medical solution.

Cognitive problems
Although not much can be done to raise the genetically determined ceiling to intelligence, considerable information is now available on how to

improve the effective level of intellectual functioning and reduce the consequences of handicap. Remedial education is well developed, as is the teaching of vocational skills.

Home and family

This category contains a huge range of problems, most of which arise from the interaction of family members with each other and their wider social context. The susceptibility of these conditions depends upon how specifically they 'lie in the family' rather than outside it. Homelessness is relatively straightforward to sort out, but not poor emotional ties between parents and children. In general terms, despite the *theoretical* availability of many treatment methods and the proliferation of practices such as 'family therapy', the state of treatment of home and family problems is abysmal and in need of substantial development.

Social skills

Although social skills are a relatively recent area of interest, a considerable amount of systematic information is already available for the amelioration of social skills problems. The research evidence concerning outcome urges strong caution, but the basic tools are sufficiently simple and widely usable to warrant optimism about future developments in this area.

Antisocial behaviour

Antisocial behaviour is also a conglomerate of many problems with quite different characteristics. Despite a very long history of serious interest, effective treatments have remained elusive. The considerable literature, presenting systematic information on often innovative practices, is largely dismal and depressing. One major reason for this is that, as with home and family problems, offending is related to a wide range of external circumstances, not directly within the grasp of the treatment agent. Because of the social significance of this problem area, however, the search for effective treatments continues.

Personal problems

The state of treatments in this area depends on the particular condition subsumed under the label of 'personal'. Personality structure cannot be fundamentally changed; patterns of personality characteristics (such as impulsiveness) can be varied in the intensity and frequency of manifestation; neurotic behaviour can be effectively treated; the development of conscience can be accelerated; and problems of identity can reasonably be resolved. Apart from the alleviation of relatively mild personality and behaviour problems, neurotic and otherwise, however, most other treatments remain notional and theoretical. The foundations seem nevertheless to be sound enough to permit substantial progress in this area.

We are conscious that the above account does not cover, even in outline, all the important features of approaches to treatment. We could have presented many other perspectives, such as a focus on the child, the family or the social system; an emphasis on relationships as opposed to other media of treatment; or the political and sociological interpretations of treating problem children. But these issues can be pursued in some of the other texts we have recommended.

In any case, as we have pointed out throughout, many of the divisions and demarcations between problems and those who deal with them are a matter of historical tradition and current convenience rather than an eternally binding logical force. Indeed, in appraising the whole field of treatment from the viewpoint of the problems, the agencies that deal with them and the demarcations between workers in terms of qualifications, knowledge status and other factors, the most striking feature is that their common ground is substantially larger than their differences. Setting aside surgery and physical medicine, not much of the knowledge and skills involved is so esoteric and high level that the majority of people involved with problem children cannot acquire and practise them.

We believe strongly that the future of treating problem children lies in bringing as many people together, including the children and their parents, as is humanly possible. If we can then provide them with some common core orientation (but without dispensing with specialisms, where necessary) and modicum of skills, we are likely to find that we can deal effectively with many more children than we do now.

Classification of treatments

Classification of the problems and difficulties encountered by the patient/client is the necessary prerequisite of carrying out focused, purposive treatment. There are numerous classifications of problems, ranging from the general – such as the International Classification of Diseases (World Health Organisation, 1984) – to the specific, as in speech disorders (for example, Fundudis et al., 1979). The prerequisites and difficulties of classification systems are numerous and will not be discussed here (see, for example, Hoghughi et al., 1980; Rutter and Gould, 1985).

Whereas there are numerous classifications of problems, with substantial similarities, there are hardly any classifications of treatment modalities beyond those according to discipline, such as medical, psychological and educational; or within disciplines, such as chemotherapy and surgery in medicine (Morgan and Morgan, 1980); or according to particular theories or conceptions of disorders (for example, Keat, 1979). Indeed, Keat (1979), as well as Rutter and Hersov (1976; 1985), Schaefer and Millman (1977), Stein and Davis (1982) and Wolman et al. (1978), brings together a wide range of treatments in relation to particular disorders, rather than according to any coherent classification of treatment modalities themselves. This is surprising. Both to develop a science of treatment of children's problems and to improve the practice in it, it is necessary to devise a classification of treatment methods. Classification is simply and at its best a tool for organising and planning action, and its merit must be judged by its ease of use and contribution to better practice. As it is now generally accepted that problems must be multi-modally and multi-axially assessed, so it is increasingly recognised that treatment must be similarly multiplex, though focused, if it is to be effective.

For logical and empirical reasons (see, for example, Hobbs, 1975; Hoghughi et al., 1980) we believe that, in the present state of knowledge, the most fruitful classification of children's problems is likely to be a descriptive one – of which the problem profile approach (PPA) is the most comprehensive example. Extended use of this approach with wide-ranging groups of children has shown us that even problems within the same area – for example, physical or personal – are responsive to and warrant the application of diverse treatment methods. This book is the result of bringing together those treatments in so far as they relate to particular problems.

Our classification of treatment methods is, like all others, arbitrary in the last analysis. Our guiding principle has been pragmatically to group treatments according to the *medium* or *modality* they use in order to alleviate problems. Accordingly, we have distinguished seven broad categories of treatment method. These are:

- provision of goods and services;
- physical treatments;
- behaviour modification;
- cognitive treatments;
- talking therapies;
- group therapies;
- environmental treatments.

These methods are further described and elaborated in Part II. For the moment, it suffices to note that the seven categories encompass the most common and important treatments, though some treatments fit less comfortably than others into the category to which they have been allocated.

The medium of treatment, according to which we have devised our classification of methods, is but one parameter by which treatments can be classified. Others include whether treatment is individual and/or group orientated; whether it involves only one discipline/profession or is multi-disciplinary in approach; whether it relies on elements of a system to carry out treatment or on specific individuals; whether it is carried out in the natural environment or requires specialised settings; whether it requires the active co-operation of the child or can be passively administered; and whether the treatment medium is readily practicable or requires highly specialised skill and other resources. It is important to recognise that these elements are but extremes of dimensions and therefore matters of degree rather than of an either/or kind. Because determining the boundaries of a particular treatment programme in time, place, context, content and medium is ultimately an arbitrary matter, it is unwise to insist that a particular treatment is 'residential', 'systemic' or based on the actions of a single professional group, rather than to assert its complements or opposites.

Further reading

Adler, J. (1981) *Fundamentals of Group Child Care: A Textbook and Instructional Guide for Child Care Workers*. Cambridge, MA: Ballinger.

Beedell, C. (1970) *Residential Life with Children*. London: Routledge & Kegan Paul.

Brown, B. J. and Christie, M. (1981) *Social Learning Practice in Residential Care*. Oxford: Pergamon.

Crompton, M. (1982) *Adolescents and Social Workers*. London: Heinemann.

DHSS (1977) *Intermediate Treatment – Planning for Action*. London: Department of Health and Social Security.

Donellan, M. (1986) 'The nursing of adolescents', in D. Steinberg (ed.) *The Adolescent Unit*. Chichester: Wiley.

Fundudis, T., Kolvin, I. and Garside R. (1979) *Speech – Retarded and Deaf Children*. London: Academic Press.

Health Advisory Service (1986) *Bridges over Troubled Waters*. London: Health Advisory Service.

Herbert, M. (1978) *Conduct Disorders of Childhood and Adolescence*. Chichester: Wiley.

Hobbs, N. (ed.) (1975) *Issues in the Classification of Children*. San Francisco: Jossey Bass.

Hoghughi, M.S. (1980) 'Social work in a bind', *Community Care*, 3 April.

Hoghughi, M.S. (1983) *The Delinquent: Directions for Social Control*. London: Burnett Books/Hutchinson.

Hoghughi, M.S. and Hipgrave, T. (1985) *Towards a Discipline of Fostering*. London: National Foster Care Association.

Hoghughi, M.S., Dobson, C.J., Lyons, J., Muckley, A. and Swainston, M. (1980) *Assessing Problem Children*. London: Burnett Books/Deutsch.

Howlin, P. (1985) 'Special educational treatment', in Rutter and Hersov (1985).

Jones, K. (1977) 'Society looks at the psychiatrist', fifty-first Maudsley Lecture, delivered to the Royal College of Psychiatrists, York.

Keat, D.B. II (1977) 'How to discipline children' (tape). Harrisburg, PA: Professional Associates.

Keat, D.B. II (1979) *Multimodal Therapy with Children*. New York: Pergamon.

Keat, D.B. and Gurney, L.G. (1978) *What Every Parent Needs to Know about Raising Children*. University Park, PA: Cope Press.

Lazarus, A. (1976) *Multimodal Behaviour Therapy*. New York: Springer.

Morgan, A.J. and Morgan, M.D. (1980) *Manual of Primary Mental Health Care*. Philadelphia, PA: Lippincott.

Nethercott, R.E. (1983) 'The special unit: five years on'. Aycliffe, Durham: Aycliffe Studies of Problem Children.

Patterson, G.R. (1971) *Families: Applications of Social Learning to Family Life*. Champaign, IL: Research Press.

Peine, A.H. and Howarth, R. (1975) *Children and Parents*. Harmondsworth: Penguin.

Quay, H.C. and Werry, J.S. (1979) *Psychopathòlogical Disorders of Childhood*. New York: Wiley.

Rutter, M. and Gould, M. (1985) 'Classification', in Rutter and Hersov (1985).

Rutter, M. and Hersov, L. (eds) (1976) *Child Psychiatry*. Oxford: Blackwell.

Rutter, M. and Hersov, L. (eds) (1985) *Child and Adolescent Psychiatry*. Oxford: Blackwell.

Schaefer, C.E. and Millman, H.A. (1977) *Therapies for Children*. San Francisco: Jossey Bass.

Shaw, M. and Hipgrave, T. (1983) *Specialist Fostering*. London: Batsford.

Stein, M.D. and Davis, J.K. (1982) *Therapies for Adolescents*. San Francisco: Jossey Bass.

Thorpe, D., Smith, D., Green, C.J. and Paley, J.H. (1980) *Out of Care: The Community Support of Juvenile Offenders*. London: Allen & Unwin.

Treischmann, A., Whittaker, J. and Brendtro, A. (1970) *The Other 23 Hours*. New York: Aldine.

Warnock, H.M. (1978) *Children with Special Educational Needs* (the Warnock Report). London: HMSO.

Wolman, B., Egan, J. and Ross, A. (eds) (1978) *Handbook of Treatment of Mental Disorders in Childhood and Adolescence*. Englewood Cliffs, NJ: Prentice-Hall.

World Health Organisation (1984) *International Classification of Diseases*. Geneva: WHO.

3

The Organisation of Resources

The concept of treatment as a focused, *purposive* activity demands the organisation of resources and activities. The people who have the competency to carry out treatment must be brought together with those who are to be treated at an appropriate time and in a suitable place. Taking the steps in the logical sequence, a place must be designated for treatment, human resources recruited and equipment acquired, human resources inducted, trained, guided, supervised and appraised. The delivery of treatment service must then be monitored and the results fed back to the service in order optimally to adapt and develop it.

Organisation and venues

As already indicated in Chapter 2, treatment servies are organised in four broad categories of criminal justice, health, education and social services venues. Each of these covers a wide range of different agencies, frequently within different organisations, management and funding arrangements. These have evolved over a considerable time, presumably in response to changing social conditions and demands on services.

They each have separate national and local organisations with relevant funding. They range in time scale of intervention from early or preventive to heavily reactive; they employ distinct though sometimes overlapping personnel with varying training requirements and regulatory codes of practice. Their time and places of practice range from short-term intervention in the natural setting to long-term involvement under highly structured, secure settings.

There are numerous permutations both within and between the services and not a few areas of overlap. Some antisocial youngsters are dealt with by courts on 'mental health' grounds and placed in mental hospitals; schools for the mentally handicapped and the maladjusted take children from hospitals and, indeed, many operate within them; community homes and other social services resources are devoted to dealing with youngsters who have sometimes been through penal, psychiatric and educational processes and, in return, call on many of the above services to help them cope with children in their care.

The development of these four distinct organisations with appropriate enabling and mandatory legislation is indicative of society's perception of distinguishable clusters of children's problems, responsive to particular forms of professional, specialist intervention. Much of this claimed responsiveness is based on special pleading and on sectional interest, rather than on evidence of effective intervention.

There are, at any given time, serious reservations about the quality of service delivery of each of the above categories and of particular agencies within them. This is reflected by frequent commissions of inquiry, working parties and other forms of review. Nevertheless, the fact that treatment agencies continue to operate would indicate either broad approval or, at least, an absence of serious disapproval of the quality of treatment. The purpose of this book is not to provide an organisational critique. Furthermore, it is unlikely that such complex organisations as those cited would be responsive to recommendations to change based on narrow considerations of treating problem children. The rest of this chapter is therefore concerned with outlining some of the issues in the organisation of treatment for children which may be of wider interest.

There is some writing on aspects of the organisation of treatment of problem children (see, for example, Barker, 1974; Howells, 1965; Steinberg, 1986). Some of the studies are based on research (for example, Street et al., 1966) which attempts to compare different types of organisation for treatment. However, although the research findings are valuable in giving some clues to therapeutic relevance and efficacy, the sources of error and variation in the treatments have not been made adequately explicit to enable any substantial conclusions to be drawn (see Rutter, 1985).

The main issue in the organisation of treatment is how best to match the service to the child's treatment requirements. In reality, however, because the child is relatively powerless and his problems are identified in different settings by people with particular treatment orientations and access to finite resources, it is the child who is fitted to the treatment service and not vice versa. This would be reasonable if the child could be properly and 'economically' fitted, but this is often not done because we do not have many independent agencies with personnel who have the necessary wide-ranging knowledge to attempt to match the child and the service. Instead, we have a situation in which most children most of the time seem to find the kind of service which they are *thought* to need on the basis of narrow, partial judgements rather than comprehensive assessment.

As we have already suggested, however, whatever the 'presenting' problem – be it physical, educational or antisocial – it is manifested by a child who is an integrated whole and therefore likely to suffer from other problems. Thus, at best, a child should be referred to that service or agency which seems most suited to his most urgent or most serious problem. This works best where the problem is both easily recognisable (because the assessment expertise is highly developed and widely available) and considered important enough to warrant action. Physical problems are at present the only ones to fulfil these criteria. They are therefore most easily and most frequently given the necessary treatment – which is why, irrespective of other problems, children with *serious* physical problems are unlikely to be dealt with by any other than the medical services.

Resources: material and human

Treatment is not achieved through a miraculous process of self-fulfilment. Rather, as a purposive activity, it requires people to undertake it, and they require an environment and appropriate materials with which to achieve treatment. The chief function of resources is to create the *capability* or the competency which is necessary for undertaking treatment. Resources are of two types – material and human – and each can be evaluated in terms of such questions as 'how much?' and 'what kind and/or quality?'

Material resources

Environment and space

We cannot separate human activity from the environment in which it takes place. The environment or place of treatment is, apart from in this logical sense, also an important positive element in the treatment process. We speak of 'therapeutic' or unhealthy environments, because we consider the interaction of the features and events of a person's perceptual world, or 'life space', to be the critical element which, in interaction with biological and organismic features of the person, leads him to behave in a particular way. In Part II we devote a chapter to environmental methods of treatment. The features of what may be regarded as a 'therapeutic environment' are therefore not repeated here. But because the context is a major determinant of this quality of treatment, it warrants brief mention.

At its most basic, the task of an environment as a 'treatment resource' is twofold: (1) to reduce stress and pressure towards creating and maintaining dysfunction, maladaptive behaviour or whatever else is regarded as the basis of the problem; (2) to activate, foster or enhance potential for the amelioration of problems and growth towards healthy, adaptive behaviour.

We are most conscious of 'unhealthy environments' in the case of physical ailments. Asthma and skin rashes, for example, are more resistant to treatment in a dirty and polluted setting. But equally, treatment of other problem conditions is likely to be undermined or negated if there are contrary pressures; remedial work with a child is difficult if the room is very cold, hot or otherwise distracting; reducing aggression among family members is almost impossible if the home is so overcrowded that they cannot help but trip over each other; teaching co-operative behaviour is not easy when the only opportunities for interaction are competitive; a child with poor internal controls cannot be expected to resist the temptation of stealing easily accessible, desirable goods; and anxiety states cannot be eradicated if major features of the physical environment are threatening.

Whilst it is not always difficult to point to the stressful and unhealthy elements in an environment, it is less easy to identify what constitutes a healthy one that encourages treatment and enhances therapeutic potential. Part of the reason for this is the huge potential of human beings to survive and grow even in the most therapeutically arid conditions. Another reason is that, apart from knowing very little about conditions which enhance treatment, we are also almost wholly ignorant of the contribution of the spatial and physical environment to the total treatment outcome. The whole topic is, indeed, conspicuous by its absence from all the major writings on the treatment of children's problems (see, for example, Rutter and Hersov, 1985; Wolman et al., 1978). The major exception is in the treatment of delinquents, where substantial though inconclusive material has been provided concerning the contribution of environmental factors to treatment (for example, Hoghughi, 1978; Cornish and Clarke, 1975; Street et al., 1966). Even so, we can state with reasonable confidence that every environment must make provision for meeting the basic requirements of management and care (as defined earlier) demanded by the problem condition and the basic requirements of every human being in terms of food, shelter, sleep, social contact and emotional support.

The range of spaces, buildings and rooms within which treatment takes place is vast, from one extreme of tents and open spaces (such as in 'camping therapy') to highly specialised settings, such as operating theatres and simulated real-life environments for purposes of social skills training. The choice of the physical environment is usually predetermined by its availability, designation for a particular purpose and limitations on access to alternatives. This, in turn, reflects the allocation of resources and society's response to its priorities. There is no evidence to suggest that, other than with small but significant exceptions, particular physical environments are necessary for carrying out treatment. To a large extent, *what* happens seems to be more important than where it is happening. Behaviour modification can be carried out as effectively in the home as in the clinic, provided that the environment can be regulated to the same degree. The exceptions concern such obvious cases as a 'germ-free' operating theatre for surgery and a 'secure' environment for those whose movement must be curtailed before treatment can take place.

Appropriateness of the environment is a matter of degree, reflecting the demands of particular treatments. Such 'appropriateness' can and should be looked at from the viewpoint of both the treatment agent and the child; what may be appropriate for one may be intensely disliked by another. A restrictive environment for a severely disordered youngster may be a necessary prerequisite for behaviour change but likely to be found frustrating and provocative to a youngster. Children are rarely taken seriously enough to be asked about the type of environment they prefer, so we know little about how to create settings which achieve the best match of children's and their treatment agents' requirements. In this respect, as in so many others, we continue to treat children as passive recipients of our beneficence.

The demands of management, care and treatment vary according to the definition of problems with which the agency deals. One way of looking at this is along the dimension which extends from one extreme of 'natural home' and environment to the other extreme of a highly specialised setting. To some extent, which point of this spectrum is considered suitable for the child reflects judgement of the seriousness of his problems. Many mentally handicapped children are well managed, cared for and treated in their own homes; some require additional help from perhaps a day centre, and others need provision for respite care; yet others spend much time in a residential school for the mentally handicapped; some are so seriously handicapped that they become long-term hospital residents.

Another viewpoint concerns the major defining task of the treatment agency, according to whether it is in the criminal justice system or in the health, education or social services. The coercive nature of criminal justice 'treatments', for example, combined with the quality of their clientele, in the context of our prevalent attitudes to offenders, results in stark, cheerless and largely forbidding environments. The social services, on the other hand, utilise a wide range of treatment settings, from the natural home and small day centres to the other extreme of secure facilities for disordered and delinquent adolescents. The quality of social services environments is as variable as the aesthetic standards of the local authorities that provide them, but they are on the whole moderately 'soft' and in tune with what we regard as suitable for children.

In the course of their growth, children need to recognise and observe behavioural boundaries in relation both to themselves and to others. The idea of 'defensible space' (Newman, 1972) therefore becomes an important prerequisite for the development of what must, in time, become wholly internalised controls. In view of this, it seems reasonable to suggest that the size and freedom of a treatment environment should expand with the child's increasing ability to relate to and control it, as the seriousness of his problems diminishes. This sequencing of spatial form in relation to treatment has been tried in a variety of settings (see, for example, Blumenthal, 1985) and has been found to contribute significantly to effective treatment (Nethercott, 1983).

One aspect of spatial variation is concerned with the degree to which a child can relate it to his personal experiences and needs. There is a widely accepted view that the more 'domestic' a child's environment the more he is likely to be happy in it. This view, however, is more an instance of folk wisdom than the result of any hard evidence. Children's domestic environments are widely variable. In any case, treatment settings in which professionals operate, other than in the child's own home, are usually 'business' premises which, though preferably 'domestic' in scale, have quite different functions from those of a home.

'Domesticity', then, does not appear to be a particularly important or relevant concept in this context. What is more important is to create an environment of a scale and aspect which the child finds positive and calming, and where stimulating activities can take place. In doing so, the settings must also conform to requirements of health and safety, security and vandal-proofness, as well as aesthetic and developmental standards of providing a suitably stimulating environment.

Equipment

As will be evident in Part III, there are many forms of treatment which cannot be carried out unless the appropriate material equipment is available. These range from medicines and biofeedback machine to paper and pencil for remedial teaching and tools and props for 'play therapy'. Clearly the range of equipment needed is extremely wide and cannot be enumerated. However, apart from many physical problems, to which medicine has responded by providing drugs and surgical measures, there are fortunately not many other forms of treatment which require material resources over and above what is commonly available. Indeed, most behaviour modification, cognitive, talking, group and environmental treatments do not demand much equipment of a kind not commonly available in most ordinary environments.

Human resources

Earlier in this book, treatment was defined as purposive action aimed at ameliorating problems. A purpose must exist in somebody (the treatment agent), and the 'somebodies' make up the most critical resource, human beings. People are likely to remain the crucial treatment agents until we have self-activating robots or long-acting drugs which increasingly take the place of personal face-to-face intervention by the treatment agent. In this respect, treatment is no different from other tasks of management, care and assessment which also demand substantial human resources.

The starting-point of treatment as the alleviation of a problem depends on a judgement of unacceptability which must be made by a human being, although a machine (such as a heart-function monitor) can be programmed to sound the alarm if a danger zone is approached. But the importance of the human agent in treatment goes beyond the simple practical necessity. As will be seen in the later parts of this book, most treatments, as currently conceived, can take place only through human agency. Indeed, most of them *depend* on the establishment of a positive therapeutic relationship between the treatment agent and the 'client' child.

'Therapeutic relationships' have been generally regarded by everyone as being crucial prerequisites of all treatment, particularly in relation to adults (for example, Truax and Carkhuff, 1967). In the phrase 'therapeutic relationship' the word 'therapeutic' is intended to connote the intention of the treatment agent in relating to the client as well as the outcome (optimistically) of the interaction. The word 'relationship' is, however, more complex. Apart from denoting straightforwardly that a treatment agent and his client are related through their respective positions as seeker and giver of help, the word connotes a cluster of positive feelings, views and expectations by one towards the other and preferably shared. In this sense, the word 'relationship' has come to take on substantial extra meanings which impose their weight by implication rather than explicit statement. Indeed, because of its positive connotation, it has been elevated to the position of a therapeutic method or technique (the writings are too ambiguous to allow the distinction to be made) without in any way either identifying the theoretical basis or producing the evidence for such elevation.

More importantly, the word 'relationship' has come to act as an excusatory umbrella in many forms of intervention with problem children, where, instead of being one element of treatment, it has become an end in itself, based on the dubious and unsubstantiated premise that most children are disturbed or delinquent due to 'difficulties in relationships'. This is not to deny that positive relationships are desirable in *all* treatments, but they are not indispensable. It would be nice for the child with a hole in the heart to think well of the surgeon, but so far as is known, such a positive view is not a necessary precursor for a successful surgical operation. Nor has the same sort of relationship been shown to be essential in many forms of behaviour modification, remedial teaching, psychotherapy, group therapy or environmental treatments (Mitchell et al., 1977; Kolvin et al., 1981).

To establish a therapeutic relationship, *both* the treatment agent and the child must have the basic personal qualities and interpersonal skills which enable such a relationship to be established. These qualities and skills include mutual liking, interest, caring, trust, consistency, resilience and the ability to withstand set-back and disappointment. Such a relationship, if established, is likely to act as an important bridge and lifeline during those lean times when treatment seems to be proceeding slowly and both the therapist and the child and his family have hit a low mark and are beginning to question the validity and the efficacy of the treatment. The relationship will allow the motivation to be maintained at a high enough level to ensure an upturn.

Therapeutic relationships are established in a variety of settings, such as a foster home, a hospital, a secure unit or a child guidance clinic, though both the form of the relationship and its content are largely determined by the form of treatment that is likely to be undertaken in these settings. An important corollary of such forms of treatment is the length of time the therapist and the child are engaged in them. A visit to the surgery or out-patient clinic demands hardly any relationship, whereas long-term stay in an ESN school or in a psychiatric adolescent unit makes the development of relationships of some kind inevitable. Other elements relate to the gender of the therapist and his position, whether the treatment is taking place individually or in groups and whether the therapist is acting alone or in partnership with other treatment agents.

Whilst we strive after positive relationships with children who are subjected to treatment, we ought to be aware that often only negative relationships are engendered, particularly where a coercive element is allowed to prevail. The major exception to this occurs in such settings as a foster home. In such cases, positive, supportive and dependent relationships are not only the norm but the prerequisite without which neither the contact nor the treatment could be sustained (see also Herbert, 1981a).

In general terms, the less urgent the child's problems (truancy compared with physical violence) and the more voluntary the child's participation in treatment (a foster home as against an adolescent unit), the more such a negotiated, 'therapeutic relationship' *seems* to be necessary for the maintenance of the treatment programme. The professional writing on relationships is too diffuse and full of special pleading for us to be any less tentative in our conclusion. Treatment agents vary not only in relation to the above factors but also in ways that reflect their personal qualities and skills. Their personal characteristics and professional competencies affect what they do and how they do it – not only by themselves but, more crucially, in conjunction with other people. It is to these qualities and skills that we now briefly turn.

The requirements of human resources

What are the requirements of human resources? We need resources to deal with anything that demands effort. In this sense, resources are best seen as 'capability to respond'. This capability is made up of the interaction of individual characteristics of treatment agents, their skills and their numbers.

Numbers
The number of people available to do a job determines whether and how well the job will be done, depending on its complexity. There is some

general, though vague, consensus about the complexity of tasks and their resource requirements. The consensus has its roots in the 'power' of the professional groups involved. So, for example, teachers in special schools operate on 1:7 maximum ratios by virtue of a government circular, whereas there are no general guidelines for regulating social workers' case-loads of difficult children.

The numbers needed to do a job cannot be sensibly separated from the demands of the job, as well as the quality and skills of the persons involved. There are no satisfactory formulae for working out this equation, though attempts are made within each venue of treatment to set down the bases of resource provision. Since this matter is intimately tied up with particular circumstances prevailing in each setting, no further space will be devoted to it here. It should, however, be remembered that treating problem children, whatever the problems and numbers involved, is labour intensive. Under-provision of resources not only is uneconomic when treatment fails and has to be repeated at an even higher level, but also has larger and longer-term costs for society.

Personal qualities

Personal qualities are the characteristics with which people are born, which determine their development and ultimately the way they operate as treatment agents. We may broadly distinguish the 'census' characteristics such as gender from the less immediately apparent aspects of personality.

Although there is the occasional suggestion in the literature that problem children need 'mothering' (and therefore presumably female treatment agents) or enforceable boundaries (with the need for occasional use of force), no systematic evidence is available concerning the need for specific deployment of male and female people. This issue is bound up with our complex, historical and contemporary views of capabilities and legitimate roles for men and women. The chief indisputable difference between the genders is the greater physical strength of men, which may or may not be required as either a primary or a back-up resource for dealing with problem children. It is not difficult to imagine children in any of the problem categories who may require physical restraint at some time. Once we set aside this aspect (or can cope with it by other means than force, as in the use of medicines), there is no presumptive need for having more or less of a particular gender in a treatment facility.

The more important point, however, is that children ascribe to and expect particular roles from their care-givers. These seem to follow the broad cultural patterns where females carry out most of the nurturance tasks and males most of discipline and direction. This distinction, however, is rapidly being eroded even in traditional institutions; and it is in any case not applicable to any setting such as a foster home or a psychiatric unit where, of necessity, treatment tasks have to be shared among a group of adults.

Such other matters as age and appearance also potentially affect the quality of treatment, but they are not features of which anything sensible can be said *in general*.

Despite universal agreement about their crucial importance, much less is known systematically about the personal characteristics and style necessary for effective treatment. Part of the reason for this is that selection for professional training – for example, of a doctor or a social worker – presumes that the professional has the necessary qualities for effectively operating in that role. Another reason is that the whole area is so complex and bound up with sensitive personal and professional issues that researchers have tended to leave it alone (see Hoghughi, 1978; Robertson, 1981). There has also been a tendency to confuse personal qualities with professional skills, of which they are a necessary but not a sufficient condition.

This whole area is the subject-matter of study of personality, personal style and the social psychology of interpersonal behaviour, of which treatment interactions are but one instance. We do not know, in a systematic way, how treatment differs from other human interactions to be able to claim distinctive requirements for it. All aspects of dealing with other human beings demand intelligence and problem-solving ability, sensitivity, stability, resilience, compassion, maturity, humility and optimism. These qualities are given essential force in dealings with children, because children are more vulnerable and less powerful than adults; they can be more readily subjected to fashionable or idiosyncratic treatment and they cannot so easily express what they find wrong or unacceptable about treatment. These potential difficulties are accentuated as the number and severity of children's problems increase and they therefore require apparently 'heavier' intervention.

Each of the above characteristics is a variable on a dimension of personality. The most sensitive people are not necessarily the most resilient, nor are the most intelligent necessarily the most humble in the manner they approach their task. Personal qualities are easier to find singly than in plentiful combination. They are also elemental and inherent in people, whether genetic or as a result of upbringing. They cannot be taught. If people have the qualities, training both in attitudes and in skills can help to enhance them.

However, treatment agents, like human beings, are 'packages'. Choice must therefore be made on the basis of a balance of weaknesses and strengths in relation to the job. This balance changes even within the same individual over a period of time, not least as a result of doing the job. The best that any person responsible for staff resources can do is to choose the best-balanced individual from among those who have offered themselves for employment and then set about maximising their strengths and minimising the impact of their weaknesses.

It is not only the treatment agent who is a resource for the amelioration of problems and growth. The child himself, his family and other significant people in his environment must also be counted amongst the treatment resources available. Although a child is not referred for treatment unless he has problems, he also has strengths which can be utilised in his treatment. He is a source of motivation for therapeutic change and can act as an extension of the treatment agent in implementing a treatment programme, such as taking his cough medicine at the right time, doing homework for his bad spelling and keeping a star chart for his bed-wetting. Additionally, all but the most problematic children can also contribute to ideas about how best their problems may be ameliorated. As an example, although the parents may be able to speak reasonably authoritatively about what a child likes and dislikes, the child himself is a much better judge of his preferences, on the basis of which a 'reinforcement schedule' may be prepared.

Families, other professionals, volunteers and other agencies share the same diverse characteristics as the focal treatment agent and the child. Given their various levels of interest and involvement, as well as life experience and ingenuity, they can contribute significantly to a child's treatment. Indeed, increasingly the major task of treatment agents is the identification and co-ordination of services and 'external' competencies that exist for ameliorating a child's problems. The community and ordinary people are as much a part of this competency as are those more specifically designated as having treatment skills. A core concern of this book is to emphasise the 'ecological' approach to treating a problem child, taking account of his whole 'life space' or extended context and the networks that may be utilised to provide treatment.

Treatment skills
If possessing the 'right' human qualities was all we needed in treatment agents, then roughly two-thirds of the population (those in the middle lump) could satisfy the requirements of most treatments and start practising them. But, in reality, we expect those to whom we entrust our children to have specialist ability or expertise which is usually the result of training and relevant experience, rather than of their inborn aptitudes.

Bearing in mind the complexity of events and interactions that we summarise under the term 'treatment', it is awesomely difficult to classify the skills involved, even if one took for granted that no list of skills could be exhaustive. This may be the reason why no classification of treatment skills has so far been devised. It may nevertheless be worthwhile to attempt a tentative classification of such skills as a basis for analysing the variables in the treatment process. We may still end up by saying that some people are indefinably better than others at treatment – that they have the equivalent of 'green fingers'. But, in evolving a discipline of treatment, we must attempt some analysis of generic skills.

Skills of treatment include the following: information processing; managerial; technical; and interactional. *Information processing skills* are concerned with the ability to analyse and synthesise the relevant information about what is wrong; with what possible 'causes'; in what order of urgency; what should be done about each individual or cluster of problems and how the process is likely to continue with or without particular forms of intervention. The development of such skills clearly requires a *knowledge base* about the problem conditions; *ability to differentiate* the conditions and relate them to hypothetical underlying conditions; knowing *what treatments* are available and in what order of preference; and being able to extrapolate the interaction of the above elements to arrive at a statement of *probable outcome*. This set of skills, perhaps more than others in the treatment process, requires high levels of fluency and openness in thinking and the ability to classify and reclassify the information concerning the child and his conditions in the light of ever-shifting circumstances – not least those brought about by the treatment agent.

Knowing what the problem is and what should be done about it may be the essential starting-point, but the treatment agent is likely to remain rooted to that point unless he can acquire, organise and monitor the interaction of the problem (child and family) with the interventions, and keep the two aligned. Whilst underlying such *managerial skills* is again a body of knowledge of relevant *treatment resources*, the bigger part of the treatment agent's task is *gaining access* to them and *utilising* them as necessary.

The task includes such elements as the treatment agent's problem-solving ability, unwillingness to take 'no' for an answer, sympathy and sensitivity as a basis of negotiating and ability to motivate others to want to help. We may not be able wholly to inculcate such skills in our treatment agents, but we can go a long way towards highlighting them and improving the way they are practised. The outcome of these managerial skills is the creation of a 'right package' of treatment measures, including a wide basis of contributors to ensure that the child's total treatment programme is not at the mercy of idiosyncratic actions.

Technical skills relate to the particular requirements of a treatment task. For example, a surgeon must know how to wield a scalpel; a remedial teacher must know how to conduct a graded reading programme; a social worker must know how to set up a contract between a child and parents; a foster-parent should know how to improve a youngster's self-presentation; a probation officer should know how to conduct a group counselling session with young offenders; and a psychologist should know how to carry out a desensitisation programme with a phobic child.

Each of these examples presumes knowledge, training and experience in carrying out multiple tasks assigned to treatment agents, whether professional or not. Given the variable personal qualities which underlie the acquisition of professional skills, as well as variations in the length and quality of training and experience, it is not surprising that technical skills are so unevenly distributed. In general, the more rigorous the discipline or the profession, the higher the level of technical skills that we may presume in its practitioners. We expect substantially more of a surgeon than we demand of a social worker and, in turn, of a foster-parent. But skills are teachable, and there is in principle little reason why the same high level of technical skills should not widely prevail among a wide variety of treatment agents. This book is, indeed, about such a development.

What we have called *interactional skills* are those personal qualities which are identified, distilled and gradually developed in the service of helping people with problems. Taking a sequential view, these skills include being able to create the appropriate feeling in the child and the family (whether of relaxation, anxiety or a complex of both); generating trust in the treatment agent's benevolence and competence; ability to gain commitment to treatment proposals; maintaining hope and appropriate level of motivation in the course of treatment; being able to listen and talk sympathetically without colluding or being phoney or blandly neutral; self-distancing or becoming involved as appropriate.

Many of the above skills entail a complex process of role-taking on the part of the therapist. These can and sometimes do come into conflict with each other and demand an ever greater exertion of professional skill in disentangling them and setting them out in the appropriate order of priorities. The whole notion of being a therapist or treatment agent presumes placing a value high enough on the child to warrant expenditure of personal resources. The American designation 'behavior change agent' or BCA neatly encapsulates this idea. It demands a non-judgemental acceptance of the child (and his family). Much has been written in the therapeutic and social work literature on this topic (Hill, 1985; Marzillier, 1976: Rogers, 1951; Truax and Mitchell, 1971). Yet the whole business of treatment is about changing, and if the condition were not unacceptable (and hence implicitly undesirable) we would not seek to change it. What we seek is therefore a balance between honest appraisal that a child's condition is unacceptable and acceptance of the child as a person of dignity and worth who warrants our respect.

A treatment agent has frequently to act as the child's advocate while at the same time recognising, in the manner of an ombudsman, that the child may have failed to respond to a reasonable amount and quality of help. With seriously delinquent or uncontrollable children, some form of 'moral' judgement of the child is particularly tempting. In recognising this temptation, the whole weight of a treatment agent's efforts must be towards continuing to do what is best for the child. Another conflict is between directive teaching, training and shaping, on the one hand, and non-directively enabling the child to choose from alternative courses of action, on the other. The difficulty arises from our knowledge that children, particularly those with serious problems, have a limited understanding of treatment alternatives and their consequences. Additionally, if children are to be self-determining, this may bring them into conflict with the organisation and threaten its stability.

Many treatment agents, such as foster-parents and nurses, are also in the position of care-givers, however temporarily, and must satisfy the requirements of good care as perceived by them. This often demands that the child be directed to a particular course of action. But this may clash with their wish to allow the child to make his own choice, even at the expense of making mistakes. The example of a 16-year-old girl suffering from VD who wishes to continue a loose, 'communal' life-style illustrates this. The many clamourings for the 'rights' of children further complicate the issue.

There are no easy answers to any of these conflicts. However, a good professional's competency lies precisely in being able to reconcile them and arriving at an acceptable conclusion. Remembering the requirements of management and boundary setting, it is not difficult to see that the balance between directiveness and self-determination must move slowly but surely more from the former to the latter if the child is to become able to function with the appropriate degree of autonomy in a society in which he cannot be eternally protected from taking the consequences of his actions.

Supervision, support and appraisal

Treatment resources, having been acquired and organised, must then be supervised, supported, appraised and developed not only to create a flexible response to changing requirements of problem children, but also to bring out the professional and human potential of those who work with them.

The first prerequisite is that the treatment agent and others in his network should know what he is supposed to be doing. This is not simply about terms and conditions of service (as in the case of a teacher or a social worker) or of the broad requirements of the job (a doctor doctors, and a probation officer deals with offenders). Rather, each worker should have particular objectives in terms of both what is to be done (content) and how it is to be done (standards). There are different approaches to 'management by objective' (Drucker, 1977) although the prevalent one emphasises the negotiated nature of all objectives.

Once the objectives have been set, they and the total performance of the worker become the subject of regular review and updating (see, for example, Payne and Scott, 1982; Westheimer, 1977). Supervision is formally built into the structure of the social services, probation, probationer clinical psychology and the training of medical registrars. Encompassing what has been done, with whom, how and with what outcomes, supervision is a most important form of monitoring treatment agents towards the provision of better service.

A critical element in setting up an effective treatment service (whether by psychologists or foster-parents) is the creation of a support network for the treatment agents. Treatment of all sorts is difficult and stressful. It is therefore essential to ensure that those who are entrusted with it are not isolated or under undue pressure, as a result of which they may either be damaged or develop questionable, defensive means of coping. This reinforces the need for a close support network for sharing information, experience and feelings with others who have similar problems. In the best organisations for treatment such a support network is provided at a variety of levels, ranging from the very formal meetings of teams to informal chats among co-workers (see also the chapters by Wilkinson, Foskett and Lampen in Steinberg, 1986).

Formal appraisal is simply the continuation and culmination of the regular supervision sessions. Its important distinguishing element is the overall evaluation of the worker's weaknesses and strengths and the provision of a strategic plan for his training and development, ideally stating what each party is to do to achieve the objectives. Appraisal is even more infrequently carried out than supervision. It is at present non-existent in medicine and allied professions, most criminal justice areas, all education and most social services. Although professional references and promotions are some form of commentary on performance, they have the enormous disadvantages of secrecy, possible idiosyncrasy and an absence of guidelines for the development of individuals and so of *whole* services.

Monitoring

We commented in Chapter 1 on the concept of monitoring. In the present context, monitoring is concerned with noting, recording, analysing and evaluating the performance of the treatment service. Such monitoring can be carried out at quite different levels of detail and specificity. The appraisal process mentioned above is clearly one particularly relevant form of monitoring. By evaluating who has done what and how, we can give a coherent picture of how well the heart of the system is ticking. But there are other aspects of monitoring, ranging from the number of referrals and cost per unit of work to 'process analysis' and long-term outcome evaluation.

As with every other aspect of treatment, monitoring requires tools, recording instruments and people to use them. Many forms of monitoring are carried out, their subjects ranging from the total cost of the health service to the recidivism rate of community homes for delinquent youngsters. Much monitoring, however, is based neither on universally agreed criteria nor on shared practices. Though complex, monitoring is an essential prerequisite of good practice and development of a discipline. We shall return to the topic in Chapter 4 in relation to individual treatment programmes. At present its practice is both patchy and of variable quality, in general reflecting the quality of the parent discipline – for example, medicine, as opposed to social work.

Development
If a service is to continue to fulfil the primary task of alleviating children's problems, it must be kept in touch with the relevant developments in the ideas, methods and practices of treatment. But there is a difference between improving an individual's knowledge and possible competence, on the one hand, and generally achieving better service delivery, on the other. Most treatment agents operate in organisations, and their operations are restricted by organisational constraints. To our knowledge, there are not many services which allow, enable or carry out a regular audit of their practices with a view to providing better services. Yet such an audit would be of benefit not only in tuning the service to demand but also in setting strategic aims and enabling the human resources to develop accordingly.

We believe that most people in the children's services have an enormous concern for children and desire to give them better service, frequently frustrated by the apparent indifference of the people who are responsible for managing the services. We believe that in this most important of areas the coherent, though sketchy, view we have given of aspects of resource management and development can go some way towards harnessing the available potential of the people involved. The new 'monetarist' spirit in evaluating service delivery may be a boost to this process, if positively perceived and implemented.

Training for treatment

Training is the means by which professionals acquire competence and skills for providing specialist services. Training for treatment is relevant and necessary in every aspect of theory, method and practice. This is under-taken to a satisfactory standard in the health services and some aspects of education, but far less in social services or criminal justice. Even in the health services, the levels of competence outside physical treatments are very variable. Also, sophisticated training in some areas such as medicine has tended to emphasise skills in one area at the expense of a wide understanding of the child and his family and the mainspring of their behaviour.

A first priority seems to be to bring up the level of competency of workers in the justice and social services systems to those of their colleagues in health and education. Training is the only means of achieving this, emphasised by too many bodies and committees of inquiry to warrant enumerating here. However, before training can be undertaken, we require a *comprehensive and integrated ground plan* of treatment (of the type attempted in this book) and competent trainers. The former may now be available, but the latter are conspicuous by their scarcity. There are signs that this is being gradually recognised – as, for example, in the new plans for the training of social workers.

We have also emphasised throughout that parents and the children themselves have considerable potential for being trained in the skills of management, care, assessment and treatment. Unless we are concerned with perpetuating a kind of professional hegemony which requires an ever-increasing investment of public resources in an ever-expanding army of professionals to deal with problems of children and their families, it seems sensible that we should attempt to teach parents and children how to use the many methods and techniques set out in this book. Whilst we are unlikely to reach the ideal of getting each parent to become an effective treatment agent, some attempt in this direction may result in a reduction of pressure on the current treatment agencies so that we may all do a better job with those who are entrusted to us. There is an extensive literature on parenting and teaching parents treatment techniques that may be of help in this area (for example, Patterson and Gullion, 1971; Peine and Howarth, 1975).

Research into treatment

Although the whole process of development of such professions as medicine, clinical psychology and remedial education is towards achieving a disciplined approach to treatment, we are yet a long way from attaining this goal. Our knowledge of treatment of particular problem areas varies from the primitive extreme of treatment of antisocial behaviour to the advanced treatment of physical disorders. Taking the child as a whole, treatments are overall more primitive than advanced (see Rutter 1985).

This book is not about the development of a methodology of treatment research, but we cannot pass by the opportunity of making a plea that ideally every practitioner should become a researcher who can contribute to the development of a discipline of treating problem children in a manner which recognises that they are integrated entities. There are, broadly, three sets of variables which must be researched, each independently and then in conjunction with each other, towards the development of a discipline of child therapeutics:

1   *Input variables* relate to all the characteristics of the child, from his demographic background and socioeconomic status to a comprehensive problem profile and other relevant aspects of his context or functioning and the statement of treatment objectives.
2   *Treatment process variables* – everything that is done to, with and about the child, with such detailed specification as who, did what, under what circumstances, in what order and context. This is a huge and complex

area because, ideally and finally, it includes *everything* that happens to the child either externally or internally, both independently and as a result of the interaction of one set of treatment variables with another, both intended and otherwise. The more complex the treatment process, environment and resources which are brought to bear on it, the more elaborate the specification of the treatment variables becomes.

3   *Outcome variables* are concerned with the state of the child and his wider context after treatment, from the short to the medium and the long term.

The above sets of variables encompass between them *everything* that happens to the child in the course of treatment. To develop a discipline of treatment, it is necessary to specify each of the three sets of variables and determine their relationship to each other retrospectively at varying levels of detail, from the grossest statement (such as, 'fat girls placed on lean diets have lost weight') to elaborate ones relating clusters of input variables to particular treatment processes and outcomes.

All retrospective research is subject to statistical and other forms of error. At best it would form the basis of predictive hypotheses about whether the relationship between the above treatment variables in fact exists. If in further prospective trials the previous hypothesis is not disproved, then it becomes increasingly probable that the treatment may not be irrelevant or inappropriate. For complex logical and methodological reasons, it is not possible to be certain that a particular treatment has been successful or that the treatment undertaken is the reason for the beneficial outcome. It is, on the other hand, easy to ascertain the failure of a treatment, and all attempts at the testing of a hypothesis are therefore aimed at disproving that a particular treatment works (see, for example, Kuhn, 1962; Popper, 1972).

An important consideration in evaluating all treatment is that the effects of treatment are invariably limited to a time and place, however wide ranging these may be. So it is important to specify the criteria that are used for evaluating 'success' or other measures that are thought to be related to the improvement of a child's condition. This implies that we can never talk of the failure or the uselessness of a treatment without qualifying it in terms of the population and conditions to which it was applied.

At this stage of development of systematic treatment, our concern must be to establish broad-based connections between children's characteristics, certain treatment processes and the eventual outcome (see also Rutter, 1985). Once we have done this over a wide area, we may then begin to refine our knowledge base so that we may be able to 'precision-tune' our treatments. One serious problem remains – most workers are not trained in or required to undertake research, and those who are so trained and required pursue their own interests, irrespective of the urgency of filling the void in knowledge over the whole spectrum. This is what accounts for some very good detailed sectional maps in an otherwise ill-charted terrain.

Further reading

Barker, P. (ed.) (1974) *The Residential Psychiatric Treatment of Children*. London: Crosby Lockwood Staples.

Blumenthal, G.J. (1985) *Development of Secure Units in Child Care*. Aldershot: Gower.

Cornish, D.B. and Clarke, R.V.G. (1975) *Residential Treatment and its Effects on Delinquency*. London: HMSO.

Drucker, P.F. (1977) *Management*. London: Pan Books.

Foskett, J. (1986) 'The staff group', in Steinberg (1986).

Herbert, M. (1981a) *Behavioural Treatment of Problem Children: A Practice Manual*. London: Academic Press.

Hill, P. (1985) 'The diagnostic interview with the individual child', in Rutter and Hersov (1985).

Hoghughi, M. (1978) *Troubled and Troublesome*. London: Burnett Books/Deutsch.

Howells, J.G. (ed.) (1965) *Modern Perspectives in Child Psychiatry*. Edinburgh: Oliver & Boyd.

Kolvin, E., Garside, R.F., Nicol, A.R., Macmillan, A., Wolstenholme, F. and Leitch, I. (1981) *Help Starts Here: The Maladjusted Child in the Ordinary School*. London: Tavistock.

Kuhn, T.S. (1962) *The Structure of Scientific Revolutions*. Chicago: University of Chicago Press.

Lampen, J. (1986) 'Aspects of leadership', in Steinberg (1986).

Marzillier, J.S. (1976) 'Interviewing', in H.J. Eysenck and G.D. Wilson (eds), *A Textbook of Human Psychology*. Lancaster: MTP Press.

Mitchell, K.M., Bozarth, J.D. and Krouft, C.C. (1977) 'A reappraisal of the therapeutic effectiveness of accurate sympathy, non-possessive warmth and genuineness', in A.S. Gurman and A. Razin (eds), *Effective Psychotherapy: A Handbook of Research*. Oxford: Pergamon.

Nethercott, R. (1983) 'The special unit: five years on'. Aycliffe, Durham: Aycliffe Studies of Problem Children.

Newman, O. (1972) *Defensible Space: Crime Prevention through Urban Design*. New York: Macmillan.

Patterson, G.R. and Gullion, M.E. (1971) *Living with Children*. Champaign, IL: Research Press.

Payne, C. and Scott, T. (1982) 'Developing supervision of teams in field and residential social work', NISW Papers No. 12. London: National Institute of Social Work.

Peine, A.H. and Howarth, R. (1975) *Children and Parents*. Harmondsworth: Penguin.

Popper, K. (1972) *The Logic of Scientific Discovery*. London: Hutchinson.

Robertson, J. (1981) *Effective Classroom Control*. London: Hodder & Stoughton.

Rogers, C. (1951) *Client Centred Therapy*. Boston, MA: Houghton Mifflin.

Rutter, M. (1985) 'Psychological therapies in child psychiatry: issues and prospects', in Rutter and Hersov (1985).

Rutter, M. and Hersov, L. (eds) (1985) *Child and Adolescent Psychiatry*. Oxford: Blackwell.

Steinberg, D. (ed.) (1986) *The Adolescent Unit: Work and Teamwork in Adolescent Psychiatry*. Chichester: Wiley.

Street, D., Vinter, R.D. and Perrow, C. (1966) *Organization for Treatment*. New York: Free Press.

Truax, C.B. and Carkhuff, R.R. (1967) *Towards Effective Counselling: Training and Practice.* Chicago: Aldine.

Truax, C.B. and Mitchell, K. (1971) 'Research on certain therapist interpersonal skills in relation to process and outcome', in A.E. Bergin and S.L. Garfield (eds), *Psychotherapy and Behaviour Change*. Chichester: Wiley.

Westheimer, I. (1977) *The Practice of Supervision in Social Work*. London: Ward Lock.

Wilkinson, T. (1986) 'Education for nurses: support, supervision and training', in Steinberg (1986).

Wolman, B., Egan, J. and Ross, A.E. (eds) (1978) *Handbook of Treatment of Mental Disorders in Childhood and Adolescence*. Englewood Cliffs, NJ: Prentice-Hall.

4

The Practice of Treatment

Treatment is a continuous process whose roots lie in society's concern with problem children, whose branches are the work of the many agencies and whose final fruit should be a less problematic child. Awareness of (and preferably consensus on) the foregoing issues provides the bedrock of ideas and values from which the practice of treatment should proceed.

In our ground plan, treatment follows management, care and assessment of the child. The last is the foundation on which treatment is based. Wrong or inadequate identification of the problems can lead only to wrong and inadequate treatment. Poor treatment is still possible with good assessment, but poor assessment will inevitably lead to poor treatment. Good assessment will have identified the problems at the necessary level of detail and indicated what might be done to ameliorate them. Treatment is concerned with (1) translating those indications into a treatment plan of appropriate detail and (2) implementing that plan and evaluating its outcome, with a view to determining whether and what other treatment steps should be taken.

Planning

Assessment (and the *treatment plan* on which it is based) forms the fulcrum for the whole process of treatment. Unless treatment actions are planned, they may not be carried out at all coherently, efficiently and with due regard to expectations and implications. 'Unplanned treatment', because it is not purposive, is no treatment at all.

Plans, like maps, can range from general outlines to extremely detailed accounts. The level of detail is determined by both the resources of the agency and the requirements of treatment, arising from the number and complexity of the child's problems. Every treatment action taken, if effective, changes the nature of the problem, and every plan must therefore be updated and revised. If treatment is ineffective, then equally it requires revision to ensure that time and resources are not wasted. How fundamentally treatment plans are changed depends on the comprehensiveness and time scale of the initial treatment plan and how much it took account of probable outcomes and the response to those outcomes. Similarly, the level of detail of treatment plan will reflect the ability of the agency to draw up complex plans and carry them out. There is little sense in detailed planning if the resources are not such as to allow those plans to be implemented. However, unless an attempt is made to increase the detail of treatment plans, the child's condition is unlikely to improve, nor will the competency of the agency.

Detailed treatment plans are the most important source of public account-ability concerning why a child is being subjected to a treatment process, and are the means of monitoring whether treatment intentions have been carried out. The greater the level of (appropriate) detail, the easier such monitoring will be.

Several attempts have been made to set out the steps in the process of treatment planning, from the one micro-extreme (for example, Herbert, 1981a) to another of creating a macro-system (for example, Hobbs, 1982). Herbert provides a comprehensive and most helpful list of twenty steps, set out in the form of imperatives, linking assessment and treatment process, in the context of behaviour modification. Whilst his approach would be welcomed by well-trained clinicians, we feel that the numerous steps, combined with the behavioural emphasis, may not be appreciated by a wider range of people with different qualifications and backgrounds involved in treatments. Furthermore, he specifically aims his recommen-dations at behaviour disorders, whereas throughout we have emphasised the essential integratedness of a wide range of children's problems and their treatment. We therefore propose below an alternative and more parsi-monious list of the necessary and sufficient steps in treatment planning before we go on to the issues which arise from implementing the plan.

Individual treatment plans (ITPs)
Throughout we use the phrase 'individual treatment plan' (ITP) to denote the actual programme document concerning a named child. We distinguish between (ITP1) and ITP2). The former is the long-range, *'master' strategic* plan of treatment; the latter is more akin to an 'action programme', con-cerning the 'nuts and bolts' practicalities of who is to do what, how, and so on. The two can be combined, but considerable experience has shown that if more than one person is to be involved in treatment there is much advantage in separating the two to allow for the different time scales and concerns of such treatment agents as the psychologist, social worker, the child and the parent. In this way, ITP1 remains the same, but different ITP2s are devised for particular workers.

Steps in treatment planning (ITP1)
The sequence of steps is as follows:

1 Set out the *problems*.
2 Set out the *aim*.
3 Set out the preferred *method(s)* of treatment.

4 Set out the *technique(s)* to be used.
5 Set out treatment *priorities*.

The ITP is a document which can be designed in a variety of ways. The example shown in Table 1.1 is one which we have found very useful in practice.

Table 1.1 *Individual treatment plan (ITP1)*

Name: . . . . . . HB . . . . . .
Date: . . . . . . 1.3.87 . . . . .

Code	Problem	Aim	Preferred method	Technique	Priority
01.11.04	Eczema	Eliminate	Physical	Chemotherapy	1
01.13.03	Abuse of alcohol	Eliminate	Talking	Counselling	2
01.13.04	Excessive smoking	Eliminate	Cognitive	Educational programme	3
02.67.02	Spelling	Develop skills	Cognitive	Remedial	2
02.09.02	Maths retarded	As above	As above	As above	2
02.10.03	Poor achievement motivation	Increase motivation	Behaviour modification	Contracting	1
03.06.05	Father works in Abu Dhabi	Reduce impact	Talking therapy	Counselling	3
03.13.02	Inadequate parental guidance	As above	As above	As above	3
03.13.03	Inconsistent parental guidance	As above	As above	As above	3
03.14.01 03.14.02	Inadequate and inconsistent parental control	As above	As above	As above	3
03.11.02	Parent/child rejection (mother)	As above	As above	As above	1
03.16.01	Brother has *grand mal* seizures	As above	As above	As above	1
04.02.04	Stands too close	Teach appropriate distancing	Behaviour modification	Prompting	2

1 Set out the problems   This should be the comprehensive list of problems obtained through assessment. The problems are set out *in order* according to some classificatory system, such as the PPA (Hoghughi et al., 1980), DSM III (American Psychiatric Association, 1980) or Basic Id (Lazarus, 1976; Nay, 1979). We have already presented the case supporting the preferred use of the PPA (see page 28); but whatever classification is used, the structure of treatment planning remains the same. The problem 'names' are set down, in a comprehensible manner and with their appropriate identifying code, if so desired. The codes enable the storage and retrieval of information concerning 'input variables', which allow computerised evaluation of the treatment and would facilitate development of a discipline of treatment.

2 Set out the aim   This is the critical step in identifying what the treatment is hoping to achieve and therefore enabling treatment evaluation. Aims are *long-term goals*. We distinguish them from 'objectives' or 'actions' which are the intermediate or short-range steps taken towards achieving the long-term goals. As an example, the aim for treating an 'anorexic' child is 'normalise eating' and for one who is suicidal to 'eliminate' suicidal behaviour. The aim is the 'ideal' of treatment and says nothing about whether it is achievable or not, nor about how it may be achieved.

This is perhaps the most important and yet the most difficult step in the whole process. It is the most important because it provides the constant reminder of what the treatment agent is trying to achieve, thus allowing him to regulate his actions. It is the most difficult because we do not generally, often even in the most developed professions, think in terms of long-term goals.

Experience and intensive deliberation have persuaded us that, for every problem, *no more than one aim* is valid. In the consideration of any problem, many possible aims frequently present themselves. However, close scrutiny will show that only one of those aims is pertinent to that problem. Generally, if there is more than one aim, either the problem has been wrongly formulated or there are perhaps other related but unstated problems which are bunched with the one cited. In Part III we set out, for every problem cited, the appropriate aim, so that it can be readily transferred from the book to the ITP.

3 Set out the preferred method(s) of treatment   As will be evident from Part III, every problem can usually be treated by a variety of methods. Which method is chosen depends not only on the professional preferences and orientation of the treatment agent (for example, a physician would use primarily physical methods) but also on the availability of other resources. A careful and *comprehensive* look at alternatives is valuable to enable the treatment agent to decide whether the child's requirements may not be better served by the use of another method which may be available in another agency.

In any case, to achieve maximum treatment effect in minimum time, wherever possible more than one method of treatment of the same problem should be used. This will complicate the determination of which method has had the more significant impact and, to that extent, retard the development of an analytical discipline. But this consideration is ethically less urgent than achieving effective treatment. In any event, there are enough real-life variations in the components of any treatment package still to allow the emergence of a discipline.

It is possible that the use of some methods for treating a particular disorder (such as the use of 'time out' in treating temper tantrums) may be incompatible with the use of another (such as focal counselling, which requires both a trusting 'relationship' and enough opportunities for a discussion). For this reason, when the whole ITP has been prepared, it should be scanned to iron out such conflicts. This suggests that the person drawing together the ITP should know enough different treatment methods to be able to detect practice problems.

4 Set out the technique(s) to be used   As will be seen later in this book, techniques are detailed variants of methods. Theoretically, any number of methods and techniques are suitable for the amelioration of problems, but in practice their number is severely limited. The choice of technique is determined (by a knowledgeable person) according to empirical evidence of effectiveness and suitability to the problem (and the child) and its practicability. Counselling, for example, is not a suitable technique for treating bed-wetting, and not everyone has access to 'bell and pad' and the specialist advice on its use. But in general we know very little about what is an appropriate treatment for a problem (in a cluster of conditions), and unless we try a treatment we cannot discover what practical difficulties it raises (see also Rutter, 1985). The choice of technique must therefore be based on a compromise of evidence of suitability (where available) and consideration of probable difficulties of implementation.

An important element in the compromise is that, other things being equal, the least 'costly' treatment in terms of effort and possible hurt to the child and his wider context should be used. This demands an explicit consideration of resources that either are available or can be made available. In turn, this is based on an appraisal of the costs and benefits of alternative techniques of treatment, something on which our current information is less than perfect.

5 Set out treatment priorities   Not all problems can be tackled at the same time. The problems must therefore be set out in an order of priority. The bases of such rank ordering are primarily twofold: *ease* and *urgency*.

Reinforcement of hope and confidence in the treatment agent's competence is crucially important in all but the simplest physical treatments. The treatment agent may therefore tackle the easiest problem on his list to get rid of the simple problems *and* build up confidence and hope in the treatment.

Urgency, however, is the more critical factor in determining priorities, because of the 'risks' involved. Although bed-wetting is easier to treat than wrist-cutting, the latter carries a much higher risk 'price tag' than does the former and so must be given higher priority. The judgement of urgency emerges through negotiation between the child, parents, referral agent and the therapist. In the event of a conflict between views of what is most urgent, it seems sensible that those of the referral agent, as modified by those of the therapist, should prevail.

If a number of people are to be involved in the treatment, it may be possible for each to have both common and individual priorities. So, for example, the first priority in 'physical' problems may be the youngster's VD; that in 'educational' his illiteracy; that in 'home and family' parental hostility; and so on. The first can be treated by a special clinic, the second by the teacher and the third by the social worker. Thus, priorities may be assigned either to problem areas or to the treatment agent or to both as appropriate.

If single treatment agents, such as probation officers or foster-parents, are to be involved, then they can have only one list of priorities, selected from the problem profile according to appropriate criteria, identifying the order in which they should proceed. In general terms, it does not appear possible or sensible to state more than three priorities in any one problem area at any given time, or in the case of one treatment agent, for the whole child. Bearing in mind that the treatment of one child is but one element in a complex series of tasks carried out by any potential treatment agent, whether a parent or a psychologist, it would seem unlikely that they can cope with a longer list at any one time. The lists should, in any case, be revised at frequent and regular intervals.

Another source of confusion in deciding the order of priorities is the causal inferences which are likely to be drawn about the child's condition by the various therapists who deal with him. For example, a particular child's suicidal gestures may be thought to be related to his social incompetence or his conflicts with his family or, alternatively, to his sense of frustration and inadequacy arising from his hearing disorder. However, as has been previously argued, it is not possible even to be moderately confident about the causal origins of particular difficulties. In view of this, it is inappropriate to give the most urgent priority for treatment to what are thought to be the 'causes' of a particular problem condition unless there are exceptionally good reasons for doing so. In planning treatment, those 'causes' themselves should be specified as problems and the methods and techniques of alleviation highlighted. We should not identify one problem and then proceed to treat another which we believe may be its cause. This is the kind of confusion, at present massively prevalent in psychiatry, social work and probation, which simply compounds the probable failure of intervention.

Preparing the action plan (ITP2)

The action plan or ITP2 is concerned with setting out in detail who is to do what, how, when, for how long, where and any other matters which must be sorted out and monitored in the course of that phase of treatment. Thus, there may be many more ITP2s than ITP1s. Of a potentially long list of details, we shall consider only the who, the how and the how long because of their importance and potential complexity. The other questions can and should be considered in the specific context of the treatment agency.

Who carries out the treatment?

The answer to the question of who carries out the treatment emerges from a consideration of the setting (such as hospital, foster home or special school), the problem (such as physical or psychological) and the resources available for treatment. We have already set out in outline the different venues of treatment which, to a large extent, determine the kind of treatment that may be given to a child. So, although teaching may be arranged for a child in a long-stay hospital, the treatment is predominantly medical. The reverse is broadly true in a special school. In less specialised settings, such as a children's home, a foster home or in an IT group, the choice of 'who' is already determined because of the small number of people who may be realistically drawn upon to carry out the treatment.

The nature of the problem and the choice of treatment method and technique are probably the most important determinants of who undertakes the treatment. We have already extensively commented upon this as far as general treatment responses are concerned. In a nutshell, we are often left with whoever may be available. A related and important question concerns the effects of changing the treatment agent. This is an extension of the general view that parent figures should be constant and is more prominent in the 'relationship-related' therapies than in the others. Change of the treatment agent may be sought or forced for a whole range of reasons, from the child's dislike of a particular person to the treatment agent's departure. In considering the costs and benefits of such a change, it may help to remember that competence in and consistency of treatment are more important than the specific person.

With all this in mind, it still seems sensible to designate one person as the 'key worker' or 'tutor' for the child, responsible for initiating and co-ordinating treatment. Clearly this does not arise in settings where only one person (such as a probation officer) or two people (such as foster-parents) take responsibility for the whole treatment process. The designation, however, ensures that the child's treatment programme is given high priority by at least one person, who can, in addition, act as a confidant, repository of detailed knowledge of the child and advocate at review meetings. To guard against inevitable gaps and changes, the sharing of treatment by 'co-workers' or 'co-tutors' seems sensible.

What treatment?

The answer to the question of what treatment to carry out is provided by the detailed evaluation of the technique(s). So, for example, in considering the behaviour modification responses to bed-wetting, we can elaborate in substantial detail the different treatments, such as bell and pad or differential reinforcement. In some cases it is necessary to break down the problem and therefore the 'what' into smaller, manageable bits. We shortly discuss this matter under 'time targeting', to which it is related.

How should treatment be carried out?

The 'how' is simply a more detailed specification of the 'what' but refers mainly to the *manner* in which the treatment is to be carried out. 'Prompting' a child may be done sharply or gently, by single words or whole sentences. How much detail should be provided in 'how' depends on both the complexity of the treatment proposed and the 'expertness' of the treatment agent. Giving medicines three times a day, for example, does not require much skill, but giving a particular form of physiotherapy to a child with cystic fibrosis does. A psychologist may have no difficulty in drawing up reinforcement schedules, but a generic social worker or a foster-parent is likely to find such a task more difficult.

Although ideally we should have robust treatment techniques which can stand up to some variations in how they are carried out, in reality we have not reached that position. If possible, therefore, the 'how' should be stated in great detail, in the light of the ability and motivation of the treatment agent and the wider setting to sustain that level of rigour. To do so, of course, demands that the person drawing up the ITP2 should know of the technicalities of the 'how' or be able to get another person who does to contribute to the ITP.

Time targeting – how long should treatment last?

As already indicated in Chapter 1, treatment is a process with a beginning, a movable middle and an end. Given that the only justification for treatment is the existence of a problem condition, the intervention should cease when we are prepared no longer to judge the condition as 'unacceptable'. Putting a time limit on treatment assumes particular significance in cases where a youngster is coerced into doing something he does not like – for example, receiving treatment under conditions of security, or taking an unpleasant medicine.

Thus, 'time targeting' is bound up with the criteria for judging improvements in the problem condition. Whilst the ideal remains the total removal of the child's problem, we have already indicated that in the non-physical problem areas this ideal is not often likely to be reached. In any case, even if the ideal were to be reached, this must be done in *stages*, which increasingly approximate to the desired end. In behaviour modification this process is given a special name, 'shaping', but the term and the process apply across the board, in all treatments. This demands that the problem be broken down into achievable elements. Given the severity of the condition and the concentration of resources that can be devoted to it, a target date can then be set up for achieving that particular objective. So, for example, the return of an abused child to the family might be broken down in (1) getting parents to recognise their abusive behaviour; (2) enabling them to learn, theoretically, better methods of managing the child; (3) short-term contact with parents with a view to practising the management skills; (4) weekend-long management; (5) week-long demonstration of competence in problem solving; and so on. Each of these would be given a time target to be achieved by a named person.

Depending on the nature of the problem, the named person may be the child, the parent, the nurse or anyone else. Further aspects of this will emerge when we consider 'treatment reviews' later in this chapter.

There is, of necessity, a variably large element of 'guesstimating' involved in this process. But setting targets is essential because (1) it gives a necessary time limit for evaluating effective treatment; (2) it limits intervention in a child's life; (3) it allows the treatment agent rigorously to implement the treatment programme or account for why it has not been implemented; and (4) it prevents drift. As is already the case with youngsters treated under conditions of security, it is likely that time limits will eventually be placed on all non-voluntary treatments of children's problem conditions.

Implementation

All we have said so far is preliminary to the actual practice of treatment – someone doing something purposive to, with, for or about a child with problems. We have already discussed the elements that must be present for treatment to take place: knowledge, motivation, skills and opportunity. Of these the most serious difficulty is the maintenance of an appropriately high level of motivation on the part of both the child and the treatment agent. The latter is clearly concerned with doing a job, whether as voluntary or statutory worker. But as long as the task of treatment is seen just as a job and is devoid of the strong element of professional involvement (wanting to succeed, not taking 'no' for an answer, not giving up in the face of difficulty and not finding other 'reasons' for being deflected from the treatment), then it is unlikely to get very far other than with the simplest problems with compliant children. It is the absence of these strong motivational factors, rather than the absence of adequate treatment knowledge, that is responsible for the deterioration and failure of so many children (see, for example, Hoghughi, 1981). These factors take us back to the earlier discussions about human resources and the need for support and guidance. Failure of treatment often reflects a poor quality of effort from the treatment agent, though this itself may reflect poor training, support and resources.

A further complicating factor is that treatment often takes place in groups, where each child has a different profile of problems and corresponding treatment needs. There are usually numerically more children than there are treatment agents. Whereas each child knows his own problems and what is to be done with them, the treatment agent has to remember each child's specific problems and what should be done with them at every stage of treatment. It is therefore likely that opportunities for the treatment of individual children will be missed if for no other reason than because the treatment agents are just not numerous and omniscient enough to be able to do everything necessary. This is particularly true in group treatment settings. Concentrating group treatment times on shared elements and augmenting them by individual treatment sessions will go some way towards meeting this difficulty.

Almost exactly the same problems arise in generating and maintaining the motivation of the child and his family and others who are significant to him towards treatment. Here above all the need for involving the child and the family in open and honest communication and decision-making becomes self-evident. Unless the child and the family actively want the treatment to succeed, it will not do so. Many of the problems of implementing treatment arise from the ups and downs in children's views of their treatment, how much good it is doing them and what pleasure or whim they have to forgo to acquire it. The more socially and behaviourally disordered the children are, the more likely they are to engage in periodic contests of oppositional will with their care-givers.

There is no short answer to this difficulty. All that can be said is that, whereas a child is not paid to maintain the momentum of his programme, the treatment agent usually is. The child should be told that ups and downs in treatment are usual and not always undesirable; that the treatment agent has encountered the difficulty before and no doubt will do so again, but that he is not proposing to give up, so nor should the child. The more a child has experienced previous failure of treatment, the more resistance he is likely to show to new interventions, even setting aside normal difficulties of treating particular conditions. He is likely to engage in avoidance and confrontational or hostile testing out to try to discover whether and how soon the treatment agent will give up. This matter has been extensively treated elsewhere (Hoghughi, 1978; Hobbs, 1982). Suffice it to say that, in our experience, even the vast majority of extreme children are likely to be won over if they learn to trust the dogged persistence (even if not the therapeutic brilliance) of their care-givers.

Over and above this fundamental problem of maintaining motivation in the face of difficulties, there are others arising from changes in the circumstances of the child and/or treatment agent and the setting in which they operate. Children's problems change, sometimes for the worse, thus demanding a reassessment and redrawing of priorities. Apart from understandable frustration, this should be accepted as a fact of life and the new treatment plan drawn up implemented. It is worth remembering that, even if a youngster deliberately sets about sabotaging his treatment programme, such behaviour is itself a problem to be tackled.

The changes in the child are often a reflection of the changes in the child's wider 'life space', of which the treatment agent and setting are (optimistically speaking) a significant part. We have already commented on the inevitable changes in personnel for both personal and professional reasons. This is sometimes complicated by ebb and flow in levels of performance from the treatment agent. As with children, there are no major cures, only treatment agents are *paid* to do a good job and should not be allowed to inflict mediocre treatment on the children with costly long-term consequences. This is where effective developmental supervision of the treatment agents becomes imperative.

The structure and the prevailing atmosphere of the treatment environment are critical elements in shaping the treatment agents' attitude to their task. If treating the children is seen as the focal task, and the rest of the organisation is set up accordingly, brilliant work may not be done, but at least treatment will not be impeded. If, on the other hand, those who direct the treatment environment – from the consultant psychiatrist directing the registrar and nurses, the fostering officer advising the foster-parents and the senior social workers supervising their juniors, to heads or directors of complex facilities – are more concerned with bureaucracy and administrative expediency, then clearly there will be ample opportunities for frustrating the treatment effort and justifying why it has not taken place. Administration should always be a servant of treatment, not the other way round; in any case, the requirements of efficiency and accountability are not incompatible with effective, focused treatment.

Monitoring

As an essential element of treatment, monitoring can and should be conducted at a variety of levels, from the 'macro'-extreme of the operation of the whole system to the other, 'micro'-extreme of the detailed changes in the condition of the child. In a large and diverse society such as ours, with huge investment in academic and professional research, most of the 'macro'-systems research is usually conducted by people other than the treatment agents themselves. So we have research bodies concerned with the operation of criminal justice and the health, education and social services.

Over and above these, there are at any given time numerous researchers looking at one or another aspect of the input/process/output of parts of each of the above systems. They are likely to have a range of empirical and methodological concerns which cannot be covered in this book. Here we are primarily concerned with the systematic monitoring of individual children's treatment, *primarily* for purposes of evaluating what has been achieved and what remains to be done to ameliorate the unacceptable conditions. We will look at this process in the context of 'treatment reviews'. We have chosen this term not only because of its equal applicability across all treatment settings, but also because it is task centred and does not have the woolly and ambiguous connotations of the term 'case conference'.

Treatment reviews

Treatment reviews are meetings for the purpose of determining what has been done (as against what should have been done), with what consequences, and what further measures should be undertaken. The vehicle for this meeting is the detailed presentation of the ITPs and the outcome of their implementation. The end product of the review is either another set of ITPs or the termination of the treatment programme. As such the review is a focused activity, aimed at receiving, analysing and evaluating information relevant to the child's treatment. Although the meeting should, where possible, infuse new hope and enthusiasm for the whole treatment process, this is not its primary purpose. Nor is the meeting itself meant to be therapeutic. If the meeting is to be used for therapeutic purposes, then it should be set up as such, where group dynamics can be maximally utilised. This aim is not compatible with the relatively dispassionate, analytical, evaluative and planning meeting that we believe a good review meeting should be.

The structure of the meeting is therefore centred around the tasks of review, evaluation and decision-making. To do this, it requires a person who acts as a focus for the initiation and termination of discussions on particular aspects of a child's treatment. Such a meeting can be conducted privately between a child and a probation officer; between a child, foster-parent and social worker; as a small review in a special school or children's home; or as a large, formal review in a hospital or specialised facility for disordered children.

The necessary participants in the review comprise the child, the parents, the treatment agent, the referral agency and any other such people whose presence may be required (such as guardians *ad litem*) or desirable (such as the head-teacher of the child's school). The person who acts as this focus (the chairman/woman) need not be in a hierarchically superior position to the rest, although this may help where there is a conflict of views and the agency may be pushed into undertaking treatments that may not be possible or appropriate.

The frequency of the meetings would depend on the severity of the case and the complexity of treatment intervention. Certain problems, such as high temperature or refusal to eat, require much more frequent and continuous evaluation than do other areas, such as social skills deficits.

The following steps provide a reasonable structure, supported by extensive experience in a variety of settings, for reviewing the treatment of a child:

1 Introduce the participants and describe the purpose of the meeting and how it is to be conducted.
2 Present (or have presented) the treatment information on each of the six functional areas in as fine a detail as you consider desirable or appropriate.
3 In each area state the problem, the aim of intervention and what actions were recommended.
4 Collect evidence, accounts and views on what has been done towards achieving the particular aim.
5 Consider the reliability and validity of the information received and how far the actions approximate to what was supposed to have been done.
6 At every stage, collect evidence and views from the maximum number of people who are concerned with that particular area or are likely to be able to make informed comment on it. The parents and the child could make sensible comments about every area.
7 In relation to each area and based on the evidence of effectiveness and efficiency, determine whether the problem should be deleted from the list because the condition is no longer unacceptable), whether it should remain with the same aim, methods and techniques or whether it should remain but with changes in the latter.
8 Having covered the functional areas, cover any other such general matters as are deemed important in that particular setting – for example, general response to treatment, relationships with peers and adults and significant events in each area since the last meeting, as well as the child's wishes and expectations. Thus, every review is in effect a reassessment of the child's condition and will form the basis of a new ITP.

9   In relation to each area, as well as the totality of the treatment programme, ask specifically (a) has anything been done that should not have been done? and (b) has something not been done that should have been, in relation to the child's condition?

10 Collect the subjective views of all the participants (including the child and the parents) about what is happening to the child in as wide-ranging and supportive a manner as is appropriate to the circumstances.

Having analysed and evaluated the treatment information in each of the problem areas, the meeting is now in a position to consider the wider question of whether there should be any 'macro'-changes to the venue and content of the child's treatment. This should be the forum for the determination of whether, for example, a child should come out of fostering and go back home, or live independently; whether the probation or the care order should be discharged; whether the child should now leave the hospital or the special school. The discussion should centre on the question of why the child's treatment should not be terminated or at least carried out in a less structured, restrictive or demanding manner. The onus of 'proof' will therefore always be on those who demand the 'heavier' forms of intervention. Because the child, the parents and others who advocate their interest are participants in the meeting, any decisions taken in this light will be at least with their knowledge, even if not always with their concurrence.

Presenting information

A treatment programme or review record is a document intended to convey information. It should aim at maximum clarity, unambiguity and standardisation of both structure and phraseology to permit easy retrieval and evaluation of change. Given these aims, a treatment document is preferably written in phrases rather than in long sentences, setting out, in columns and in the order of the PPA, problem, aim, what has been done, what remains to be done and subsequent action programme. To achieve this end, it may be better to strive for standardised forms rather than longhand reports. Clearly a decision must be made according to the needs of the organisation as to how much detail should be presented in relation to each treatment programme. In general terms, such a decision would be based on the minimum specificity of each of the steps as is compatible with both evaluating the treatment undertaken and the steps that must be subsequently pursued.

Criteria for evaluation

The criteria for evaluating treatment are akin to those which are employed in the case of assessment or similar evidence-based activities.

Reliability is a measure of the stability or dependability of the treatment from one setting or occasion to another.

Validity relates the degree to which we can be sure that the treatment given is an answer to the problem with which we are concerned, that it is dealing with that problem rather than another which may accidentally alleviate the target problem. An example would be the treatment of distractability through the use of anti-anxiety drugs which, by achieving a reduction in the level of arousal, may also reduce distractability.

Efficiency is concerned with the judgement of costs and benefits of treatment. Some treatments, such as extended psychotherapy, are inefficient because the heavy investment of skilled manpower is not usually reflected in the gains made in the child's condition. One important element in the consideration of costs and benefits of treatment is its side-effects, sometimes referred to as 'iatrogenic'. These are most obvious in the case of medication, where side-effects may demand special attention or even treatment. But almost all treatments may have harmful side-effects which may have to be countered. Counselling, to give the child a more realistic self-concept, may make him more hopeless, or secure treatment of a drug taker may damage his family relationships. It is, however, unlikely that any rational person will undertake treatment unless the overall benefits significantly outweigh the costs. In treating children, as in all other rational acts, a positive balance sheet of costs and benefits must be obtained.

Relevance is a more ambiguous notion and concerns the degree to which our present theoretical understanding of a condition, its origins and correlates, would indicate particular treatments. Thus, our theoretical understanding and experience may suggest that remedial education is a reasonable response to educational retardation but not to poverty or severe aggressiveness.

Rigour is concerned with the degree of detail, conceptual economy and operational 'tightness' with which the treatment ideas are articulated and carried out. In this context we would consider, for example, a token economy or remedial education programme to be more rigorous than group counselling, because every stage of those operations is more tightly worked out and practised than the latter.

Integrity is a relatively new concept, relating both to the ethical, commitment dimension of treatment and to the interdependence of theory and practice.

Complexity is related to rigour but different from it in being concerned with how elaborate and interdependent the elements of the treatment and its operational correlates are. As an example, the administration of painkillers or the treatment of short-sightedness is simpler in both theory and practice than family therapy or cognitive behaviour modification. The concern here is that the more complex the theory and practice in an area of treatment, the fewer people would be able to practise it at a satisfactory level, and so it may turn out to be ineffective.

Effectiveness is the ultimate and guiding light of all treatments. It is concerned with the degree to which the intensity and impact of a problem are alleviated or reduced by purposive intervention. The concept is as important as it is elusive. Effectiveness, like all the other earlier criteria, takes its force from the appropriate matching of the problem condition and its relevant treatment; the readiness of the child and his condition to respond to treatment; the competence of the treatment agent to carry out and reinforce effective treatment; the degree to which conditions following treatment reinforce or counteract it; and the time scale over which effectiveness lasts. At every one of the junctures above we can claim or disclaim effectiveness of treatment, depending on our particular interest.

Terminating treatment

The ideal of every treatment agent is to achieve the amelioration of the child's problem. His nightmare is blatant failure. Probably even the most hardened professionals are not immune to the feelings of dismay and frustration that result when treatment is not working or, even worse, when the child's condition is deteriorating.

A reasonable starting-point is to remember that the treatment agent is not the proverbial omnipotent God and therefore cannot take success for granted. Indeed, as a good empiricist, he may start with a presumption of failure but bend all his efforts to averting or minimising that failure. This position becomes the more sensible as we begin to deal with increasingly damaged and disordered children who have suffered other failures of treatment. In the behavioural arena we should remember that, for good (learning theory) reasons, we can never undo hurt and damage, though we may be able to overlay it and reduce the probability of its manifestation. This is because, in the interests of adaptation, we need to maintain residues of our past experiences, just in case we need to use them.

Inevitably, then, the treatment agent is faced sooner or later with the prospect of failure of a particular treatment. In the physical arena this is relatively straightforward. Other than in the gravest of cases, medicine can usually offer more than one technique of treatment; if one does not succeed over the expected time scale, another will be tried.

In education, the process of inculcating skills is tied up with the child's developing cognitive capacity. The teacher pursues a programme of remediation whose time scale will be related to the child's condition. He may be slow, and the teacher may have to take a long time, but the question of failure will rarely arise if a reasonably thought-out programme is being pursued.

A similar situation seems to occur with the clinical treatment of specific neurotic or behavioural disorders by psychologists and psychiatrists. If the treatment has been well chosen in relation to the *cluster* of the child's problems, there should be few surprises which result in failure and therefore demand a change of treatment programme.

This issue arises unfortunately too often in the case of children with multiple behavioural, family and social problems, such as those who become the responsibility of criminal justice and social services agencies. Such problems as disordered family relationships, poor social skills, delinquency, promiscuity and drug abuse are bound up with a whole ecology of parents, peers, schools, community and social agencies. It is often not possible to bring them under control as a prelude to treatment. Management and treatment merge, using similar techniques, which often do not work.

The treatment agent/reviewer must then decide whether and how to modify the treatment programme. But in evaluating the apparent failure, he should consider (1) how long the treatment has been going on (has enough time been given to the treatment, knowing its intensity?); (2) whether there have been associated beneficial changes in other aspects or conditions of the child; and (3) what the alternative ploys are and what the reasons are for considering them to be better bets. Having reached this point, then all the other questions about resources raised earlier must be considered.

Whereas changing the treatment package is wholly sensible, it is quite different from giving up treatment and considering the child as untreatable. For powerful logical reasons we can never say a child is 'untreatable', only that we have so far failed to treat him. We can and should continue our treatment efforts in bringing in other resources and approaches as appropriate. We strongly believe that treatment agents, particularly those in the statutory sector, should not give up treating a child unless evidence has been provided publicly that *all* reasonable measures have been taken but have failed to produce the desired outcome.

In our terms, therefore, the treatment agent never gives up, he simply goes on trying harder and more diversely than before. Almost above everything else, children must have time and benevolent attention, and they will not have these if people keep giving up on them.

Further reading

American Psychiatric Association (1980) *Diagnostic and Statistical Manual of Mental Disorders*, 3rd edn. Washington, DC: American Psychiatric Association.

Herbert, M. (1981a) *Behavioural Treatment of Problem Children: A Practice Manual*. London: Academic Press.

Hobbs, N. (1982) *The Troubled and Troubling Child*. San Francisco: Jossey Bass.

Hoghughi, M.S. (1978) *Troubled and Troublesome*. London: Burnett Books/Deutsch.

Hoghughi, M.S. (1981) 'Is minimal intervention best?', *Community Care*, 5 November.

PART II

METHODS OF TREATMENT

5

Classification of Methods

In Part I we discussed some of the issues which arise whenever any treatment of children is undertaken. In this second part we present an outline overview of methods and techniques of treating problem children.

The idea of a 'method' has a long history. From its Greek root meaning 'a way through', the word has come to be very widely and loosely used to refer to almost anything that anyone claims to do in a particular way. This is not the place for engaging in a critical examination of such claims. It nevertheless seems to us that it is not very profitable to have a wholly open-ended, infinite list of methods which show little coherence. Because we are interested in a disciplined practice of treating problem children, it seems to us necessary to develop a classification of treatment methods. For this reason, we have developed a classification of methods of treatment, where the distinguishing mark is the *medium* of intervention, to which some notion of the underlying 'system' or target problems to be changed has been added.

Thus, in our view, methods of treatment can be categorised in terms of (1) delivery of goods and services; (2) physical treatments; (3) behaviour modification; (4) cognitive remediation; (5) talking therapies; (6) group therapies; and (7) environmental treatments. Our classification is pragmatic rather than based on theoretical or statistical analysis. It has been used and refined over many years in a number of agencies concerned with the treatment of seriously disordered children and adolescents. It has withstood the test of time and been found useful in creating coherence in treatment. It is intended to be no more than an aid to focusing on the content and target of the treatment. All classifications are, in the last resort, arbitrary (for a wider discussion, see Davison and Neale, 1982; Grinker, 1977; Hobbs, 1975) and can be sensibly evaluated only in terms of their comprehensiveness, rigour and usefulness.

We do not claim that the classification offered is unambiguously comprehensive. There are many statements of methods in the treatment literature, often supported by organisations and specialist practitioners. Examples include dance therapy, play therapy, transcendental meditation, yoga, faith healing, hypnosis and many others. These practices have their ardent supporters, because they are deemed to be beneficial. No doubt in the hands of practitioners with appropriate personal qualities almost any method of treatment may be perceived as producing beneficial results.

These approaches to treatment have not been included in our list, however, because of the relative infrequency of their usage with problem children and the poor literature on them, and because their practitioners often claim an exclusive uniqueness for their work which would disallow banding together with others which are similar.

Nor can the methods and techniques offered be neatly and exclusively compartmentalised. Giving a pair of spectacles (service delivery) is accompanied by instructions for use (cognitive); surgery (physical) is usually preceded and followed by reassurance (talking therapy); and behaviour modification is invariably concerned also with environmental contingencies. Hardly any treatment is practised in pure form, and classifications therefore need not be pure either. There is, however, equally little sense in not having a reasonably parsimonious classification, because it would then not be possible to develop any of them to a high degree of rigour in the interests of the disciplined treatment of children. In any case, many of the less widely practised treatments can be usefully construed as falling within one or another of the categories we have identified.

Distinction has been made between methods and techniques. This is not very common in the literature on treatment, where even in medicine the terms are frequently treated as interchangeable. However, we believe the distinction to be worthwhile, because it permits the drawing out of theories and elements of practice which are common to the variants of a method – here called 'techniques'. The method is therefore regarded as a super-ordinate or wider category, of which the technique is a variant and example. The number of techniques can be enlarged, as has happened in behaviour modification, without losing the common theoretical or practice threads that bind them together.

The lists of techniques and the descriptions given are not exhaustive. They simply encompass the main techniques claimed to be in use and their chief features. We have described briefly what each technique is; what its basic assumptions are; how it is practised; when and to whom it is thought best to apply; and what its current clinical status is.

We have refrained from giving references for every detailed statement made, in the interests both of brevity and of usability by people who will probably not be expert practitioners in each of the areas. They may nevertheless require some familiarity with the basic concepts in order to consider whether the particular technique is practicable in their setting. We have provided a list of further reading at the end of each chapter which, taken together, should enable the readers to advance their knowledge to an appropriate level.

The following chapters set out the methods in detail. The varying length of the chapters is not only indicative of the amount of writing and practice associated with particular areas, but also reflects to some extent our own evaluation of its relevance to problem children. Clearly in a general 'cookbook' of this sort it is not possible to set out the amount of detail that is necessary for inaugurating a particular form of treatment in a particular environment. We have therefore confined ourselves to a description which is broad enough to acquaint those who are not familiar with a particular treatment technique but detailed enough to distinguish the methods from one another and one technique within a method from others which are apparently similar. Clinical practice, however, also requires coaching and training. We cannot pretend that our descriptions remove the need for such training, but they do provide a core exposition of each technique which can be used as a basis of 'shop-floor' practice.

Given the dramatic variations in the state of knowledge and practice of different methods, our chapters and their coverage are bound to be uneven. We have also exercised judgement on what level of detail to devote to each topic. So, for example, surgery (a highly specialised field) receives the briefest general mention, while psychoanalytic therapy (also highly specialised) receives a longer exposition. This variation reflects the relevance and appeal of a subject to most of the probable readers of a book such as this. The same variation is reflected in the overall length and detail of the chapters.

How to use Part II

For general information   (1) Find the name of the method or technique from the Contents list at the front of the book. (2) Look it up under each of the headings.

For treatment planning and practice   (1) Look up the appropriate problem in Part III. (2) Find the method(s) and technique(s) you are interested in. (3) Find the page number from the Contents list at the front of the book. (4) Look it up in Part II.

Further reading

Davison, G.C. and Neale, J.M. (1982) *Abnormal Psychology*. New York: Wiley.
Grinker, R. (1977) 'The inadequacies of contemporary psychiatric diagnosis', in V.M. Rakoff, H.C. Skinner and H.B. Kedward (eds), *Psychiatric Diagnosis*. New York: Brunner/Mazel.
Hobbs, N. (ed.) (1975) *Issues in the Classification of Children*. San Francisco: Jossey Bass.

6

Delivery of Goods and Services

The whole development of advanced, welfare-orientated societies is geared to the provision of an increasing range of goods and services for people who are deemed to be 'in need'. As a major client group, children presenting or experiencing a range of problems can be provided with goods and services to fulfil a particular need.

Basic premises

The definition of a condition as unacceptable presumes some account, however implicit, of what *sort* of action must be taken to contain it and put it right. This process is made explicit during assessment. Such assessment frequently identifies gaps or deficits, which in our culture have readily identifiable answers. Thus, a child with poor eyesight is deemed to require glasses, and one without parents must have some sort of long-term parent substitute.

In such cases, the problem is seen as relatively simple and compartmentalised, requiring a similarly simple, unitary response which is likely to ameliorate it. Although the treatment is given in the hope of long-term benefit, there is no presumption that the condition will not further deteriorate and thus require further and perhaps different treatment. Whilst it may be difficult and tortuous to find the 'right' answer (for example, substitute parents) there is usually little ambiguity about what must be done. The difficulties therefore revolve around ease of access and the availability of appropriate resources for getting the right response. It is because of the immense variety of goods and services in relation to particular problems that we have given the generic recommendation to 'seek specialist advice'.

Practice Goods and services are available in all the four sectors of treatment: criminal justice; health; education; and social services, whether statutory or voluntary.

Criminal justice services include a variety of personnel such as the police and probation officers, whose help may be sought in sorting out a child's difficulties through an informal 'word' or 'caution' for a refractory child or informal 'intermediate treatment' by a probation officer. There are a number of national and local organisations (such as NACRO) concerned with the welfare of offenders, young and old, which may be able to help with a youngster through their schemes.

The formal provision of the criminal justice services includes not only the police and probation but also the judiciary in the full exercise of their powers. These range from formal caution by the police through sentences of the court in issuing attendance, supervision, care, detention and youth custody orders, fines or other sanctions.

The *health* services are organised on an out-patient or in-patient basis for both physical and psychological problems, with varying degrees of specialism. Although school health and child guidance services are organisationally part of the education service, we include them under this heading because they are primarily concerned with a child's health.

Out-patient services range from the dentist and optician, hearing and speech specialists, the GP, the school and the child guidance clinic to all the hospital-based services, from one extreme of first aid to the other of long-term hospital care. In-patient services are invariably in hospitals and accessible after prior assessment by a specialist.

The *education* services are available in a variety of settings and usually concern themselves with a child's problem if it is impinging on his educational performance. These services are primarily school based, even though they may operate outside the school. They range from school social workers or educational welfare officers, school psychological services and various specialists (such as reading and language units) to residential special schools and other facilities concerned with more serious forms of physical, intellectual or 'emotional' handicaps.

The *social services* provide the most diverse range of services for children and families, since they are the only agency legally charged with the *total* care of their clients. Their services are also classifiable along dimensions of 'community'–'residential', generic–specialist, voluntary–statutory and children alone–whole families.

There are many and diverse issues of practice in the provision of the above services and goods to which they give access. Those issues and the guidelines for practice that arise from them are considered in the course of professional training and inculcated in the practitioners. They are therefore not discussed here. However, each of the above services' practice of treatment falls in one or more of the methods of treatment which are described in the following chapters. The access route to each of these services is well defined and known, not only to the general public but more specifically to practitioners within each field, such as magistrates, nurses and doctors, teachers and social workers. If in this chapter we do not set out the 'techniques' in greater detail, it is because such detail is either unnecessary or so extensive as to demand several books because it encompasses the totality of the provisions of a complex welfare state.

Application   The extent of the provision of goods and services for the needy is probably the most universally shared criterion of how developed a society is. As such its status among methods of treatment is supreme. Indeed, we have included this as a method of treatment precisely because so much 'treatment' is simply confined to providing the child and his parents with particular goods and services. It is estimated, for example, that over 80 per cent of social workers' time is taken up with this, rather than with the exercise of treatment skills required in the use of the methods that follow.

The disadvantages of this method lie in the unequal accessibility of services to different client groups and social classes, and the more detailed consequences of what and how a particular good or service is delivered. These will be tackled in the subsequent chapters, when we discuss specific modes of treatment. The advantages lie in its ready availability to a wide range of client groups, its 'normality', the familiarity of both consumers and providers with its legitimacy and its ethical propriety, as judged by legislative sanction.

Further reading

Halliburton, P. and Quelch, K. (1981) *Get Help*. London: Tavistock.
Hughes, J. (ed.) (1986) *School Leavers' Handbook*. London: Adamson Books.
Wilmott, P. (1973) *Consumer's Guide to British Social Services*. Harmondsworth: Penguin.

7

Physical Methods

The physical treatment of children's disorders covers an enormous area, substantially the same as for adults, though with some major differences. The similarities and differences in the use of this method with children arise from their physiological and developmental differences from adults, as well as from the differing patterns of disorder. For example, more children than adults suffer from bed-wetting; more adults than children suffer from heart disease.

Our coverage of this method will include brief outlines of medication, physiotherapy, biofeedback and physical exercise. This is in no way a true reflection of the complexity and extensive range of physical treatments. On the other hand, a unique feature of this method is that some of its techniques, such as medication and surgery, may be prescribed and practised only by legally accredited professionals. It is therefore unnecessary to present detailed descriptions of these techniques in a book such as this. The specialists already have their texts, and the non-specialists are unlikely to require anything other than a general introduction and familiarisation to acquaint them both with the theoretical basis and with some of the implications of the use of physical methods for other treatment modalities.

The need for a basic knowledge of medical practice becomes the more important, since the tendency has grown to couple physical with other treatments. Examples are anticonvulsant medication combined with biofeedback in the treatment of epilepsy and dieting with behaviour modification in the treatment of overweight children.

Basic premises

Physical treatments attempt to alter abnormal functioning by intervening directly in bodily processes. This implies that assessment/diagnosis has identified the 'cause' of the disorder to lie in the physiological state, whether or not the abnormality is in fact a physical one. Enuresis is a case in point. Many children, particularly boys, continue to wet their beds well into puberty. Children who are taken to a GP or a psychiatrist for this condition are often prescribed a mild antidepressant. It is not particularly relevant in the present context to consider the efficacy of the medication. But it is worthwhile to note that the prescription implies either that the cause of enuresis is a physiological one for which the particular medicine is the remedy or that, even if it has other causes, it is treatable by altering the child's physiology.

It is fundamentally for this reason that physical techniques of treatment, particularly medication and surgery, demand *diagnosis*, which has specific treatment implications. Medical diagnoses and physical treatments associated with them have the oldest and most distinguished history of all the treatment methods. Scientific research has not only refined old techniques and developed new ones; it has also cast doubt on certain long-held views of human functioning. The field is therefore constantly changing.

There has been a notable shift of emphasis in the drug treatment of children's behaviour disorders, although paediatric medicine has continued to develop apace, and medication continues to be used as much as before for appropriate physical disorders. In the case of behavioural and psychological disorders, however, physicians are now much more cautious about using drugs than before. This is related to diagnostic uncertainty, serious anxiety about the unknown long-term consequences of medicines on a developing organism and the occasionally uncertain outcomes of medication.

The use of physical exercise, biofeedback and physiotherapy is based on the rationale of re-establishing body balance. The growing organism must be suitably fed and exercised if it is to function properly. The general theme of physical treatments is that of returning to or producing the normal state or equilibrium.

Practice The use of medication and surgery is limited to trained and accredited medical practitioners. The health services are exceptionally well developed and access routes to them well established. Although it is beneficial to know about what medical specialists do and why, this is primarily useful as knowledge for its own sake and possibly as a safeguard against inappropriate treatment; obviously it does not allow a non-medical person to engage in medical practice.

Biofeedback, physiotherapy and physical exercise are all fairly straightforward and uncomplicated, although inappropriate use may cause considerable additional difficulty. There are no special practice issues which have not already been covered in previous chapters.

Application Physical treatment is undergoing continuous change as a result of research. Surgery has always been very carefully used with children and continues in this vein. Drug treatments are now subjected to closer scrutiny from both ethical and professional standpoints than before. Physical exercise is being much promoted as an essential component of well-being, including psychological health. Physiotherapy has always been highly regarded as a corrective to the inadequate or improper use of limbs and muscles. Biofeedback, though gaining in popularity, is still too new as a technique to be accurately evaluated, although it is positively regarded.

The disadvantages lie in the tendency to see behavioural and psychological problems in medical terms and to resort readily to physical treatments. Although this should be expected from the legitimate bias in the training of physicians and surgeons, once we move beyond strictly physical problems, both diagnosis and the treatment on which it is based become very dubious. Associated with this is the tendency to see the child as a passive object or simply a manifestation of his physiology, which, suitably altered, will produce an unproblematic child. This not only denies the ever-changing, problem-solving nature of the child's interaction with his environment, but also deprives him of the opportunity to develop alternative coping strategies.

The supreme advantage of the physical method lies in the relatively high quality of its practitioners and the well-developed health services. The ideas, concepts and practice of medicine, for example, are advanced and supported by high-level and widely available resources. With this background, medical practitioners are frequently (though by no means always) capable of identifying the difficulty and dealing with it in a rapid and efficient manner. The rigour, immediacy and availability of medicine are its chief strengths.

In general terms, physical treatments enjoy the highest reputation of all treatment modalities, supported by a complex health service and powerful professional groups. The fact that physicians are seen to deal with matters of life and death, and have been instrumental in the dramatic improvement in our standards of health, has created this pre-eminence and is likely to continue supporting it. The possibility that such a position is occasionally associated with inappropriate treatments, that it may subvert the development of other treatment modalities or, indeed, that it may result in long-term damage to the organism, is not sufficiently powerful to alter this state of affairs.

Medication (chemotherapy)

Drugs have a limited usefulness in treating children's problems. Paediatric pharmacology and psychopharmacology are relatively undeveloped clinical fields. Many chemotherapeutic approaches to treating children have been based on experience rather than systematic research, but findings have nevertheless continued to establish the bases for measuring the efficacy of treatment. Many problems exist that complicate the development of well-designed research concerning children, which lags behind that for adults. Only recently have we begun to discover how various forms of medication are absorbed, used and broken down. There is also understandably greater hesitation about experimenting or using drugs with children, with the result that clinical and experimental findings about the usefulness of drugs with children are even less solid than in the case of adults, particularly in terms of after-effects.

Chemotherapy is just one of many modes of therapy for treating problems in children and should be used only as part of a broader, more comprehensive approach. This demands that the child's problem be seen within the context of social and family dynamics; and to achieve this, open communication with parents is as important as maintaining contact with the child or adolescent. This is particularly crucial in emotional and behavioural disorders. Nevertheless, there will be times when medication can and will be prescribed without a full assessment. These should be limited to those disorders that are persistent and seen to have a predominantly physical basis.

Some adolescents tend to be distrustful of adults and so may accept medication less readily than younger children. Others may abuse their medication in attempts to assert their independence or to manipulate authority figures. Some, indeed, may refuse outright to take medication. An important priority should therefore be the development of trust, whereby the possible uses of medication are discussed openly to alleviate the adolescent's anxieties.

In prescribing medication for children and adolescents, choices of drug and level of dosage are crucial factors and are often contentious issues. On the one hand there are the conservative, psychotherapeutic 'doves' who totally oppose the use of drugs, on the other the 'hawks' who advocate wider use of new, unproven drugs in high doses. Moderation, then, guided by therapeutic principles, clinical common sense and caution, should dictate the use of medication with children. Relevant factors include indication for use, individualised dosage within the recommended range, limited (rather than open-ended) duration of courses of treatment, the use of well-tried drugs and the frequent monitoring of effects. Other characteristics, such as age, intelligence, maturational level, body mass and severity of disorder, also need to be taken into account. Because the rates of the true course of absorption, distribution, metabolism and excretion of drugs vary, standardisation of dosage can be a problem. Dosage can be based on either body weight or surface area, the latter being regarded as the most satisfactory guideline.

As is evident from the breadth of medical practice, a vast range of drugs is available to deal with physical problems. Here we shall confine ourselves to a brief description of those drugs that are used to deal with children who present or experience emotional, behavioural and learning disorders. They can be dealt with under the following headings:

- antipsychotic medication;
- antidepressant medication;

- anti-anxiety ('anxiolytic') medication;
- anticonvulsant medication;
- drug treatment for sleep disorders (hypnotics);
- drug treatment for enuresis;
- drug treatment for minimal brain dysfunction, hyperkinesis and learning disorders.

Antipsychotic medication
Antipsychotic drugs are variously referred to as the 'major tranquillisers', 'neuroleptics' and 'antipsychotic agents'. In these drugs there are two main components: an antipsychotic agent and a tranquillising or sedative one. Of these the antipsychotic element has the primary role. The antipsychotic effect is specifically to reduce thought disorder, the hallmark of schizophrenia. The more marked the psychotic symptoms, the more likely the child is to respond. These drugs have a more marked effect on hallucinations, delusions, tension, restlessness and social withdrawal than on insight and judgement. The tranquillising effect is that of slowing down movement, emotional quietening and a reduction of emotional responses. Both antipsychotic and neuroleptic properties are important in the clearing of schizophrenic episodes. Many of the antipsychotic drugs cause sedation, and this property may contribute to their effect on some patients. The two major classes of antipsychotic drugs are phenothiazines and butyrophenones. The general principles of usage of the antipsychotic agents are based on the more extensive experience with the phenothiazenes, such as chloropromazine (Largactil), trifluopazine (Stelazine) and thioridazine (Melleril); the butyrophenones include haloperidol (Serenace) and their derivatives, such as pimozide (Orap).

How do they work?   Antipsychotic drugs are considered to act by interfering with dopaminergic transmission in the brain by blocking dopamine receptors. Dopamine is a neurotransmitter, a substance that acts as a vehicle of communication between nerve cells.

Practice   Oral medication is generally appropriate, the dosage dependent on age, body weight and severity of symptoms. The provision of a reasonable explanation will tend to produce a better acceptance of medication by children. A child will occasionally require drug by injection, to ensure compliance, evenness of dosage and consistency of effect on the brain.

Application   These drugs are beneficial in the treatment of childhood psychosis; severe, uncontrolled behaviour disorders (which cannot be contained in any other way); and very severe anxiety arising from other disorders. 'Functional psychosis' in children may be divided into early-onset, latency-onset and adolescent-onset. Early-onset psychosis, which usually develops in children under four years of age, includes infantile autism and infantile symbiotic psychosis. Infantile autism may respond to antipsychotic medication to help with aggressive, self-destructive or hyperactive behaviour.

The use of antipsychotic drugs may also be helpful in the following situations: absence of appropriate controls of sexual or aggressive impulses; manic-depressive psychosis; severely aggressive behaviour towards self, others or property, not able to be managed by other methods (this may be encountered in children with minimal brain dysfunction, severe behaviour disorders, organic brain disease or mental retardation); severe anxiety, depression or withdrawal not responding to other drugs or other treatment methods; heightened anxiety, such as seen in some school-phobic children.

Side-effects The most common side-effects include nasal congestion, drowsiness and dry mouth, postural hypertension, overeating, sensitivity to light (perhaps requiring sun-screen preparations), occasionally impaired learning, disruption of menstrual periods and urinary symptoms (including enuresis). Some children will develop neurological withdrawal symptoms when a neuroleptic is discontinued. This is more likely in those who have been given an adult dose and/or a dose over a long period. The withdrawal symptoms include involuntary movements of the extremities, trunk and head, impaired fine co-ordination and tremor. Some clinicians advise drug-free periods because the long-term effects of these drugs are unknown.

Antidepressant medication
The tricyclic antidepressants are a group of compounds characterised by three interlinked carbon rings. In clinical practice, chemical manipulation of the middle ring yields different classes of antidepressants. The tricyclics are a similar group which vary in strength but are similar in clinical effect and in metabolic transformation and excretion. This group of compounds is most effective in primary unipolar, severe, autonomous depressions. Another group of antidepressants used less frequently than the tricyclics and related antidepressants are the monoamine-oxidase inhibitors (MAOIs).

There are dangers of dietary and drug interactions in the use of MAOIs. For example, Bovril, Oxo, other meat or yeast extracts, broad bean pods, cheese, wines, beers, other alcohol, pickled herrings and flavoured textured vegetable proteins should not be taken in combination with MAOIs. Also MAOIs may potentiate the actions of many other drugs. A young person's behavioural signs and symptoms must be closely evaluated to ascertain whether or not they represent depression. Difficulty in diagnosis has been one factor contributing to the small number of clinical drug trials with antidepressants in children. When depression is diagnosed, environmental changes, psychotherapy and behavioural techniques should always be tried out prior to medication. If the symptoms persist, tricyclic antidepressants may be considered, taking into account also that side-effects may be encountered. When a significant depressive syndrome in an adolescent does not respond to other measures, medication may then be indicated.

How do they work?   The 'biogenic amine hypothesis' postulates that there is a depletion of catecholamines at central CNS sites and that some tricyclics increase catecholamine availability. A newer body of data suggests that a second major subtype of depression results from a serotonin deficit, and some tricyclics seem to be preferentially effective with this subgroup by blocking the uptake of serotonin. The data from research divide the tricyclics into groups that treat different types of depression. Thus, if one tricyclic does not work, one from another group with a different biochemical effect is appropriate for a second choice.

Practice   Oral medication as tablets or in syrup is generally appropriate, the dose dependent on age and body weight. Tricyclics should be started on low doses and increased every few days if necessary. Tricyclics are also available by injection if required.

Application   Tricyclics are not recommended for children below the age of 12. Children above 12 may require adult doses.

Side-effects   The most common side-effects may include insomnia or sleepiness, blurred vision, tremulousness, restlessness, postural hypotension and stomach upset, water retention, headaches, appetite and weight loss, irritability, dry mouth and skin rash. Most of the effects abate within the first weeks of treatment. If this does not occur, the dose should be lowered or the drug discontinued.

Anti-anxiety ('anxiolytic') medication
Anxiety is a normal part of life. In the case of children it is often a reaction to some disturbance in their 'life space' and does not warrant any special measures apart from gentle care. When a child's anxiety is so disabling as to interfere with normal functioning, a range of intensified measures such as reassurance, support and relaxation should be tried. If these fail, the use of minor tranquillisers might be considered. The child should be carefully assessed to rule out depression or psychosis. Only when other methods have failed should tranquillisers be considered, and when used they should be used only intermittently and as an adjunct to other treatment measures.

The minor tranquillisers (benzodiazepines) are a group of sedative-hypnotic agents which have a spectrum of central depressant effects ranging from mild sedation to sleep. Variation of dose determines each agent's action. Hypnotic agents induce sleep. In general, the sedative dose is one-third to one-quarter the hypnotic dose. The sedative-hypnotics are addictive and anticonvulsant and can produce muscle relaxation, anaesthesia and respiratory depression. They also have the effect of removing inhibitions and internal controls. The best known benzodiazepines are Valium and Librium.

How do they work? Minor tranquillisers work by depressing the central nervous system. The sedative action calms by alleviating anxiety with a minimum of interference with motor co-ordination or mental alertness. The muscle-relaxant properties also contribute to anti-anxiety effects.

Practice Oral medication is usually appropriate, the dosage being related to age, body weight and symptom severity. Injection preparations are also available and may, on rare occasions, be necessary for the child disabled by severe anxiety.

Application Oral anxiolytic medication may be used with children over 6. Injections of the minor tranquillisers should not normally be given to children below 12 years of age.

Side-effects Side-effects include drowsiness, blurred vision, muscle weakness and skin rashes. Some benzodiazepines may produce loss of self-control by releasing aggressive behaviour. This has been noted on rare occasions with Valium and Librium. On such occasions other benzo-diazepines may be substituted.

Anticonvulsant medication

Anticonvulsant medicines are given to most children who take fits. Although the prescription of anticonvulsant medication is a matter for the doctor only, the family, social, intellectual and educational factors in psychosomatic seizures require a wide-based approach if the medication is to be appropriately utilised. When the diagnosis remains in doubt or the child has had only one epileptic attack (especially where fever, unusual excitement, a flickering light or some other recognised factor was operating), it may be best to withhold medication until corroborative evidence has been obtained.

Anticonvulsant drugs comprise a range with varying properties, aimed at controlling a wide variety of epileptiform phenomena, which vary widely in type, frequency and intensity from one individual to another and may also vary in the same individual at different times and under different circumstances. From the transient and minor 'absences' or *petit mal* to the psychomotor seizures and on to the marked convulsions and loss of consciousness in *grand mal* seizures, there exist a wide range of epileptiform manifestations, requiring different types of medication. Commonly used anticonvulsant drugs include phenytoin (Epanutin), carbamezapine (Tegretol), sodium valproate (Epilin) and phenobarbitone. Minor tranquillisers may also be used (see anti-anxiety medication, above) for this purpose.

How do they work?   There is generally some sedating effect in anticonvulsant medication. The purpose of medication is to redress the chemical balance so that, as far as possible, the orderly flow of electrochemical impulses in the brain is not interrupted. However, the control of seizures is often a complex problem. The administration of the appropriate drug in adequate dosage may frequently be impossible because of the increase in general rate of activity and antisocial behaviour which is often manifested in this type of disorder. Many children with temporal lobe epilepsy are eventually given two drugs simultaneously to control the disorder.

Practice   The aim of therapy is to provide the most suitable and efficacious drug by the most appropriate route. The doctor may decide in some cases to give intravenous or intramuscular injections urgently to treat convulsive episodes. However, most treatment is through taking tablets orally or by the use of rectal anticonvulsants. When more than one attack has occurred, the doctor will make a decision whether to start continuous, regular medication over a long period (perhaps two or three years). Dosage depends upon age, body weight, severity and type of seizure.

Application   Epileptic and epileptiform seizures may occur at any age and thus require seizure control for which anticonvulsants may be used.

Side-effects   Common side-effects include drowsiness, nausea, poor eating or excessive appetite (though often temporary), general irritability and temper outbursts.

Hypnotics
Drugs producing sleep are called hypnotics. Some of the minor tranquillisers have proved efficacious for this purpose (see anti-anxiety medication, above). Sleep disorders can be manifested as insomnia, nightmares, night terrors or sleep-walking.

In insomnia, if the condition has lasted three or four nights, *with serious consequences for the child or others*, a hypnotic may be prescribed briefly and intermittently. Children generally outgrow nightmares. Use of drugs is inappropriate other than in cases of extreme disturbance.

Night terrors occur usually during the first third of the night. They are generally transient, and parents can be reassured that the child will outgrow them, and advised on how to cope with them. If they are frequent and persistent and continue over a period of weeks or months, the child may have an underlying disturbance, and medication should be considered as an option.

Sleep-walking is rarely associated with psychological disorder and does not by itself warrant the use of medication. Alterations to food intake and pre-sleep activities may be more appropriate.

How do they work? The minor tranquillisers work by central depression of the central nervous system, and the higher doses produce sleep.

Practice Oral medication is usually appropriate, the dosage being related to age and body weight. Injection preparations are also available.

Application Hypnotics are generally used with children over 12.

Side-effects Side-effects include blurred vision, muscle weakness and skin rashes. Benzodiazepines may produce disinhibition characterised by assertive and aggressive behaviour.

Drug treatment for enuresis
Nocturnal or primary enuresis is the most common form of bed-wetting and is usually present from infancy. Its origin and development are not completely known, although a hereditary component may be implicated. It is estimated that in about 10 per cent of children with enuresis an emotional disorder or family stress is the underlying cause or major contributing factor. In the majority of cases, enuresis can be traced to inadequate or deviant habit learning. As with other forms of drug treatment, therapy must be carried out in conjunction with other methods. In enuresis this is particularly important, and medication (not least because of its side-effects) should be used as a last resort. The commonest drug treatment is some form of antidepressant medication. The tricyclic antidepressants, amitriptyline and imipramine, have some impact on the short-term control of bed-wetting (see also antidepressant medication, above).

How do they work? It is not known with certainty how treatments for enuresis work. One theory postulates that enuretics have immature bladders characterised by decreased capacity and increased irritability, which leads to poor bladder contractions and thence to enuresis. Imipramine has parasympathetic and atropine-like actions, which may relax the relevant muscle, decrease muscle irritability and decrease involuntary contractions. The other theory is related to imipramine's effect on the normal sleep pattern.

Practice   Oral medication in tablets or syrup, the dose being calculated according to age and body weight. The drug should be administered until the child is dry every night for three months. Although tricyclics may be effective whilst being given, there is a high relapse rate following gradual or sudden withdrawal. If relapse does occur, the same drug may be reinstituted for another three months. This often results in longer-term bladder control.

Application   For children above the age of 6.

Side-effects   These include irritability, headache, dizziness, insomnia and constipation.

Drug treatment for minimal brain dysfunction (MBD), overactivity and learning disorders

The phrase 'minimal brain dysfunction' (MBD) is one of a number of terms applied to behavioural, affective, perceptual and cognitive disorders of childhood. The term is typically reserved for cases in which the patterns of thought and action are such that some organic abnormality is suspected but none is apparent. The term is often used as though there were some identifiable MBD syndrome, but the evidence to support a single MBD syndrome is largely unconvincing. Generally included as indicative of MBD are attention deficit disorder, hyperactivity, impulsivity, various neurological soft signs and often a variety of learning and language disabilities.

The drugs used are central nervous system stimulants. They include methylphenidate, d-amphetamine, l-amphetamine, caffeine and pemoline.

How do they work?   These drugs, in producing CNS stimulus, produce a decrease in hyperactivity, impulsivity and aggression and, in consequence, increase concentration and goal-directed behaviour.

Practice   Oral administration in gradually increasing doses. If improvement is not noticed in one month, the drug should be discontinued. Drug 'holidays', when the drug is discontinued at weekends and holidays, are a useful form of monitoring.

Application   For children over 6 years of age.

Side-effects   Side-effects include poor eating, which may be decreased by taking the drug at mealtimes or reducing the dose. Other side-effects include mild insomnia, palpitations, abdominal pain, increased motor activity, withdrawn behaviour and tearfulness.

Surgical treatment

Consideration of surgical treatment for children and young people is initially a matter for the GP, paediatrician or psychiatrist, and ultimately for the surgeon. Minor surgical procedures may be carried out by qualified nursing staff. However, it is important that those responsible for and involved in the care of children should be aware of the conditions for which referral to the appropriate medical personnel should be made. In this book, specific problems are listed for which surgical treatment is indicated. These particular problems will provide a basis for action in other similar cases. The child should always be referred to a physician if there is any doubt.

Surgery is an advanced form of medical practice, and dramatic relief may follow its use in some cases, in terms not only of the physical result but also of psychological improvement. An example may be the correction of a squint which not only remedies the sight defect but is cosmetic and leads to increased self-esteem and confidence. Surgery may be minor (perhaps under local anaesthetic), as in the case of the removal of warts, or major, as with remedy of a congenital deformity, carried out under a general anaesthetic.

How does it work? The correction of problems by surgical methods is increasingly successful due to advancements in anaesthetic and surgical techniques. Plastic surgery is also now an advanced and refined procedure. These refinements in anaesthesia and surgery provide minimal trauma and pain, as well as a reduced risk of subsequent infection. It is well recognised that basic physical changes in surgical treatment are accompanied by improved emotional and social functioning.

Practice The wide range of surgical treatment methods and techniques is a matter for trained medical and nursing staff.

Application Children of all ages.

Physiotherapy

Physiotherapy is the treatment of problems, usually physical ones, by physical means such as massage, heat and electricity. Massage is a very old and traditional practice but it has only relatively recently received appropriate recognition in orthodox medical circles. Its traditional role of palliative treatment for rheumatic aches and stiff limbs is now only a part of the wide range of treatments. These include restoration of function after injury, attention to the breaching of bed patients and the training of muscles and joints to maximise function after nerve injuries, strokes and such other physically damaging events. Even those with severe physical disability can be helped to gain a degree of independent functioning. Stress and tension can cause illness and pain, and techniques such as massage can help to break the cycle of stress by relaxing taut muscles and stimulating the systems of the body to work efficiently (see also relaxation training in Chapter 8). Among the physiotherapy techniques the following are perhaps the most commonly employed: massage; exercise; application of heat; electrical stimulation.

How does it work?   Physiotherapy works in a variety of ways. Massage stimulates the tissues and circulation, increases muscular tone and speeds up sluggish metabolism. Exercise in physiotherapy is designed to return to normal functioning parts of the body following operation or injury, by a programme of graded activity. An example would be the strengthening of the leg muscles after a cartilage operation on the knee. Heat treatment has three main effects: (1) it relaxes muscle spasm by relieving pain and easing stiffness; (2) it encourages blood flow to a specific area, bringing blood and oxygen and taking away damaged cells; (3) heat has a direct effect on painful nerve endings, soothing them by direct action and occasionally providing a counter-stimulus to the pain previously felt. Electrical apparatus is specially designed to provide such actions as vibration in massage and infra-red and short-wave treatment for surface and deep heat respectively.

Practice   Massage can be administered in four main actions: 'effleurage', 'pétrissage', 'kneading' and 'friction'. *Effleurage* involves stroking lengthways up the back, chest and limbs with a light to moderate pressure, exerted by the whole of the hand. The effect is to warm the tissues and tone up the circulation. *Pétrissage* is a firmer stroke with a moderate to deep pressure, most of the contact being made with the heel of the hand, one hand reinforcing the other. *Kneading* is deep manipulation, directed especially at stiff, contracted areas. It can be done with thumbs only or between thumb and fingers. *Friction* is a series of deep, often circular motions, using thumbs, knuckles or fingertips. Pressure is concentrated on one small area through repeated strokes as deep as necessary. Relaxation of tense muscles indicates when to move on to a new area. Electrical apparatus is frequently used to provide vibratory action.

Heat treatment can be used to alleviate aches, muscular spasms and stiff joints, and can be provided in the form of hot baths, hot water soaks, hot water bottles, embrocations and liniments, and infra-red and shortwave electrical apparatus. Heat treatment is often used in conjunction with massage and exercise. Exercise will be designed by the physiotherapist to prevent the deterioration of muscles and to improve the strength and power of muscles following operations or injuries to joints.

Application   All age groups.

Biofeedback

Biofeedback is the process or technique for learning voluntary control over automatic and reflexively regulated bodily functions. The term 'biofeedback' was conceived as an abbreviated expression to describe the process of biological or physiological 'feeding back' information to the individual client or patient. This information can be about a 'simple' physiological phenomenon such as the electric conductivity of the skin or about something as complex as the probable onset of an epileptic fit. The feedback can equally range from the extreme simplicity of a light or buzzer to complex tracing of the brain's electrical impulses. A simple example is of a 'relaxometer': electrodes are attached with a velcro pad to the fingertips; when the child becomes tense, a red light or a buzzer goes on, and when he is in a peaceful state again, the light goes off. The child *learns* to see how long he can keep the light off.

Biofeedback is a relatively recent development and has evolved out of advances in biophysical science. The results of these advances have provided new insights into the mind–body control systems, and this new perspective is contained in the word 'biofeedback'. It is also an unprecedented therapy. It is both psychological and physical. It encompasses a wide range of human emotional and physical disorders, and its uniqueness lies in the fact that the therapeutic process takes place in the mind (or mind-brain) of the client. The therapist and the machine provide information and guide and assist the client, but the process itself is a reversal of the traditional client–therapist roles. The client is no longer the object of treatment. He is the treatment. More important than the varied uses of biofeedback, perhaps more important than its apparent universality, is its potential for restructuring therapies in which the individual client assumes, or at least participates in, the responsibility for his own health or illness. The suggestion from some recent research is that biofeedback may be more effective with younger (less completely matured) individuals than with adults.

How does it work? The process of achieving voluntary control over automatic, reflexively regulated body functions is still not clearly understood. The information about biological activities (including those of the brain) is made available to the brain. When this has been received, cognitive faculties (that is, perceptual, linguistic and problem-solving abilities) are set in motion to restore a state of well-being or equilibrium. Biofeedback therapy is a learning process. The client must 'learn' how to control his internal biology just as he has learned how to control his muscles to perform everyday functions. Essentially, it is operant conditioning of autonomic, electrophysiological and neuromuscular responses. The nature of biofeedback learning demands a new attitude towards learning, because the entire learning process is internal and self-actuated. When the particular physiological activity involved is externalised in the form of the biofeedback signal, only the relevant information and mental activity are needed to accomplish learning how to change that physiological activity. Since the client has little knowledge either of his internal biological processes or of how to control them, he must rely upon the therapist to provide the appropriate information. The task of the therapist is to have a clear understanding of the types of information the client needs and of the situations in which the information can most effectively be used.

Biofeedback training has the following requirements:

1 Biological information; that is, the biofeedback signal.
2 Cognitively useful information, which facilitates the use of the bio-logical information; that is, what the physiological activity does, how it behaves, how it is measured, what the instrument does and other relevant information.
3 Strategy information; that is, clues or directions for changing physiological activity by internal psychological means.
4 Psychologically supporting information; that is, encouragement and reinforcement of performance that acts to consolidate the learning experience.
5 Experiential information; that is, the information derived from memories and biofeedback information associated with internally perceived changes in mind and body states.

Winking is an example of biofeedback learning. It is the intervention of voluntary action over a reflex. Blinking is the reflex activity that ensures the even distribution of moisture over the eyeball, a reflex performed automatically many times per hour. Yet we can also learn to control this reflex. Most people learn how to wink as youngsters, either using a mirror or with another person, such as the mother, giving feedback. They get biofeedback information about what the eyelid is doing and whether it is moving correctly, either as visual information from the mirror or as auditory information from the other person. The result is learning to wink.

Practice   The technique is essentially one in which a selected biological activity is monitored by an instrument which detects, by such means as electrodes or transducers, signals of physiological activity such as heart rate, blood pressure, muscle tension and brainwaves. This detected activity is amplified, then used in the instrument to produce a display (visually, by ear or otherwise) which then reflects any change in the particular biological activity. This process is analogous to feeling the pulse, taking blood pressure or taking the temperature, where the information is detected and is translated into numbers, as beats per minute, millimetres of pressure or degrees of temperature. Although special instruments are not always used, the instruments developed especially for biofeedback are preferred because of their convenience and accuracy. Most instruments have been designed so that the client can see or hear (or both) the monitor of his selected biological activity more or less continuously and is able to observe, for example, light changes or hear changes of tone from the monitor.

Application   All age groups, provided the client can supply subjective information on his experiences. Although very young children may not be capable of participating in this way, older children and adolescents provide very good subjects. Two specific areas of application for bio-feedback with children have been the subject of research with promising results: seizure disorders (including epilepsy) and hyperactivity. Relaxation training is a common form of treatment for children experiencing these problems.

Further areas where biofeedback has also been found to be effective include: *cardiovascular biofeedback* (heart rate, blood pressure, vaso-constriction and vasodilation, skin temperature); *gastrointestinal biofeedback* (functional diarrhoea, faecal incontinence, oesophageal spasm, gastric acid secretion); and *brainwave biofeedback* (alpha biofeedback, neuroses, behaviour problems, pain, psychoses, hyperkinesis, epilepsy).

Physical exercise

Good health is not just an absence of disease but a state of vitality in which the various parts of the body are efficient, well co-ordinated and able to respond easily to needs during work and recreation. Our social condition no longer provides us with enough physical activity. School, travel and work are increasingly sedentary, and leisure is often a matter of just sitting watching (or spectating). The object of regular exercise is to create and maintain a degree of physical fitness that will provide a wide margin of safety for daily activities and also allow us to derive pleasure from their performance. Although children are generally more active than adults, it is increasingly observed that problem children tend to engage in fewer and less demanding physical activities than their ordinary peers.

How does it work?   The immediate effect of exercise is to increase muscle tone. Even when the muscles are at rest, a certain amount of tension still remains. The tension ensures that the body is always ready to respond if demands are placed upon it. Regular exercise will strengthen the muscles and increase the ability of the heart and lungs to supply oxygen to the tissues.

Practice   The main forms of exercise are: isotonic, isometric, callisthenic, circulo-respiratory and yoga. Isotonic exercises consist of weight-lifting, rowing, push-ups and similar activities. This develops muscle strength and stimulates heart, lungs and circulation. Isometric exercises are motionless. They are the force of one body muscle against another or against a fixed point such as a wall. Towels or ropes can be used or more complex machinery (bullworkers, flexorciser). Holding the muscle tension for six seconds or more produces the best gains, but ten to twelve seconds are generally recommended. Intensity of effort is more recommended than frequency. Callisthenic (muscular endurance) exercises are the training needed for fitness for all competitive sports from athletics to football where endurance is needed. Exercises can be with or without equipment, such as push-ups, sit-ups, pull-ups, on a bar. Equipment is increasingly being used and can help to increase the motivation and satisfaction with exercise. Circulo-respiratory exercises include brisk walking, jogging, running, cycling, swimming, rope skipping and running on the spot, as well as using cycling and rowing machines. These exercises place demands on the circulation and respiration to supply oxygen to the muscles involved and are 'aerobic'. Yoga consists of posture and breathing exercises. These increase flexibility in the joints of the spine, arms and legs. This tones up muscles and improves circulation. Physical and mental relaxation are features of yoga.

General advice

A general fitness programme should include:

(a) circulo-respiratory exercises;
(b) endurance exercises for shoulders, arms, abdomen, back and legs;
(c) flexibility and stretching exercises for neck, shoulders, back, hips and hamstrings.

A programme of therapeutic exercises for children should take the following into account:

1 Daily exercise if possible; some callisthenic exercises give good results, however, on two to three work-outs a week.
2 Regular exercise; days should not be missed.
3 A particular time should be set aside for exercise, whether this is morning, afternoon or evening.
4 Realistic targets should be set; the intensity of exercise should be gradually increased; a child's strength should be under-, rather than overestimated.
5 The body should be given a general warm-up and started with less difficult exercises.
6 Measures should be taken to counter the period when a child is not making any progress; he should be taken back to a lower level of effort and allowed to progress upwards again.

7 It is important to ensure that other associated factors are also taken into account; the child should get sufficient sleep, eat sensibly, stop smoking and receive help to reduce stress.

8 Although gentle exercise is likely to hasten recovery after illness or operation, great care should be taken not to exercise the child who is still ill and to exercise him only gently during the recovery period.

Application   For children and adolescents of all ages.

Further reading

Brown, B. (1978) *Stress and the Art of Biofeedback*. London: Bantam.

Carroll, D. (1984) *Biofeedback in Practice*. London: Longman.

Duquesne, T. and Reeves, J. (1982) *A Handbook of Psychoactive Medicines*. London: Quartet.

Gatchel, R.J. and Price, K.P. (1979) *Clinical Applications of Biofeedback: Appraisal and Status*. Oxford: Pergamon.

Hare, M. (1986) *Physiotherapy in Psychiatry*. London: Heinemann.

Harris, D.V. (1972) *Involvement in Sport: A Somatopsychic Rationale for Physical Activity*. Philadelphia, PA: Lee & Febiger.

Kan, J.E. (ed.) (1972) *Psychological Aspects of Physical Education*. London: Routledge & Kegan Paul.

Kaplan, C.A. and Kolvin, I. (1985) 'Drugs in child psychiatry', in K. Granville-Grossman (ed.), *Advances in Clinical Psychiatry, No. 5*. London: Churchill Livingstone.

Parish, P. (1982) *Medicine: A Guide for Everybody*. Harmondsworth: Penguin.

Taylor, E. (1975) 'Drug treatment', in M. Rutter and L. Hersov (eds), *Child and Adolescent Psychiatry*. Oxford: Blackwell.

Werry, J.S. (1978) *Paediatric Psychopharmacology: The Use of Behavior-Modifying Drugs in Children*. New York: Brunner/Mazel.

8

Behaviour Therapy

Behaviour therapy consists of a set of procedures derived from experimental research on the psychology of learned behaviour. Its basic premise is that, if disordered behaviour is learned, it can also be unlearned, using psychological methods. It is an approach to dealing with and seeking to alleviate maladaptive behaviour. It is a collection of techniques rooted in scientific evidence based on relatively objective and measurable evidence. It aims to modify current behaviour and focuses attention on how that behaviour is manifested in terms of observable responses. Although behaviour therapy has tended to emphasise *current behaviour*, paying little attention to its antecedents and 'causes' and more importantly to its longer-term outcome, there is growing evidence that both these areas are now receiving systematic attention.

In this chapter we will set out a brief description of behaviour therapy and its foundations, a short account of its use with disordered children and a look at its main advantages and disadvantages, prior to presenting a selection of the more widely applicable behaviour therapy techniques for use with disordered children.

Theoretical basis

There are two major underlying assumptions of behaviour therapy: current observable behaviour and the shared basis of both normal and abnormal behaviour in the same principles of learning.

Every behaviour has antecedents ('causes') as well as consequences. Behaviour therapists do not deny this any more than any other sensible person would. However, they emphasise current behaviour, not only because this is what has been deemed 'unacceptable' but also because this is the only segment of the past-present-future of the child's behaviour that is *available* to us for treatment. We cannot undo the death of the child's mother or the episode of being bitten by a dog, but we may be able to do something about his present depressed state or his debilitating fear of dogs. His future welfare would also depend on how far we can alleviate his present problems.

In the past, this led some behaviour therapists to emphasise current behaviour so heavily that they seemed to ignore the shaping of that behaviour by past events. This left them open to the charge by more traditional therapists, particularly psychiatrists and psychoanalysts, that they were concerned with symptoms which, if successfully removed, would only be replaced by other symptoms. That early emphasis has now been corrected by a more balanced approach which looks at the background factors in the comprehensive assessment of the child's problems, though with a behavioural emphasis. Furthermore, there is now ample evidence that the removal of problematic behaviour (such as bed-wetting or temper tantrums) does not result in the emergence of another, substitute problem behaviour.

The second assumption of behaviour therapy is that both normal and abnormal behaviour are governed by the same laws. This assumption is both an article of faith and a hypothesis. It is an article of faith which arises from the scientific training of psychologists and their conviction that the universe (which includes human beings and their behaviour) is governed by laws which determine all fundamental processes – whether normal or abnormal. It is a hypothesis in that psychologists use an ever more sophisticated (but not always more productive) array of concepts and methods derived from experimental research on *normal* processes such as learning, perception, group behaviour, memory and personality development to make sense of and ameliorate abnormal behaviour. It is scientifically wasteful to look for new principles and explanations until those already acquired in this way have been shown to be inadequate or inappropriate. But, of its nature, the conviction cannot be logically disproved and must therefore always remain hypothetical.

Behaviour therapy recognises two major groupings of disorders: *deficient behaviour*, when a person has failed to learn acceptable and/or adaptive responses and therapy seeks to make up for and teach him these responses; and *maladaptive behaviour*, when a person has learned inappropriate responses to a variety of conditions, so that he cannot cope with the demands of the environment in a manner acceptable to significant persons in that environment, including himself. Behaviour, deficient or maladaptive, is deemed to be 'abnormal' not exclusively because of its nature (such as wrist-cutting) but also because of the frequency, duration and intensity with which it occurs or does not occur. For example, crying, running around or fighting may be judged abnormal when they occur with excessive frequency. On the other hand, not being able to speak properly, look after basic personal needs or play with other children may be regarded as abnormal because their rate of occurrence is too low. Other behaviours are considered abnormal because they occur in inappropriate situations, such as bed-wetting or exposing oneself.

The value judgement that a behaviour is considered abnormal depends in part on the characteristics of the child (such as age or sex), in part on wider cultural standards of acceptable behaviour and in part on our psychological theories of 'normality' in development and social behaviour.

Whether the problem behaviour is deficient or maladaptive, treatment involves learning, unlearning and/or relearning. This corrective action is known as behaviour therapy. It assumes that behaviour can be modified (hence the synonym 'behaviour modification') by studying in detail the current conditions under which behaviour occurs and planning remedial action on the basis of the information thus obtained. Many behaviour therapists use the experimental methods of psychology to monitor the appropriateness of their treatment by looking at treated and untreated groups; evaluating the child's response before and after treatment; varying the intensity of treatment; and a wide range of other methods. These are essential for the long-term development of a discipline of treatment as well as for the evaluation of individual treatment. Although it is recognised that many treatment agents do not have the resources to carry out such strict scientific evaluation, this should not detract from the immediate usefulness of behaviour therapy techniques.

All behaviour results from the interaction of the psychological organism with the environment. A new-born infant has a certain innate potential for becoming a normal child but he has to *learn* all the behaviours which will achieve that normality. Thus, learning is the central process of behaviour change and is itself the end product. The three major forms of learning are achieved through association ('classical'), by outcome ('operant') and through observation ('social').

At its simplest, classical conditioning (and the learning which results from it) is achieved by *associating* or pairing an ordinary or neutral stimulus with another until the latter elicits the same response as the former. An important feature of this form of treatment is that the client or patient has little control over his responses (which are involuntary and controlled by the autonomic nervous system) and can therefore be treated *passively*. If the taking out of a handkerchief (which is a neutral act) is sufficiently often followed by a shout (which is frightening), then eventually the handkerchief by itself will arouse fear.

This form of conditioning, which is associated with the name of Pavlov (1927) is the basis of many forms of psychological treatment where emotional responses such as fear, anger, relaxation and happiness are concerned. Perhaps the most successful and universal application of this form of behaviour therapy in the area of children's problems is the bell-and-pad technique of treating bed-wetting.

In *operant conditioning*, by contrast, the child is an *active* operator of his environment, and his behaviour is instrumental in bringing about a desired result. Indeed, this result or consequence is the chief reason for the learning that occurs. If the consequence ('reinforcement') is positive (other things being equal), the behaviour will probably be repeated; if negative, then probably not. A positive reinforcement can take the form of either a *reward* (smile, money, late-night TV) or the cessation of something unpleasant (going to bed later, parents stopping fighting). Conversely, negative reinforcements can take the form of either positive punishment (being put in own room, loss of pocket-money, having to do more chores) or the withdrawal of something positive ('loss of privileges', being ignored).

What complicates operant conditioning of problem behaviour in children is that, dependent on their history and personality, positive and negative reinforcers vary quite markedly for different children. Although there are certain common physiological (for example, pain of physical punishment) and cultural patterns (for example, loss of privileges), there are so many differences among children in their responses that we cannot be at all sure that what is intended as a reinforcer (positive or negative) will be perceived as such by the child.

When the behaviours we wish to reduce or strengthen through conditioning are not parts of the child's normal behavioural repertoire (such as bed-wetting) or are likely not to occur in the presence of the therapist (such as setting fire), then one of two procedures is used: (a) chaining and shaping, where increasing approximations to the target behaviour are reinforced; or (b) prompting, where the appropriate behaviour is produced through instruction or modelling and appropriately reinforced.

This form of treatment is associated with the name of Skinner (1938; 1953) and has now been developed into a variety of sophisticated techniques for reshaping many forms of maladaptive behaviour.

Observational or social learning occurs in the natural environment where children witness both adults and peers engaging in a variety of activities. Depending on the conditions associated with or the outcome of the activity and the child's perception of it, he is likely to learn either to imitate or to avoid that behaviour. Because of the element of reinforcement, there is some controversy as to whether or not this is a variant of operant conditioning. It is sometimes used in behaviour therapy in coaching or tutoring a child to acquire a new response.

Status

The theory and method of behaviour therapy are based on scientific and experimental evidence and clearly related to observable behaviour. Thus, subjective inference and intuition, though still present, are minimised. Changes in observable behaviour, not interpretations, serve as the basis of monitoring behaviour and the results of treatment.

The outcome of the application of behavioural techniques is *in general* no worse or better than that obtained from a number of other psycho-therapeutic methods. However, behaviour therapy is not as time-consuming and protracted as others. For the most part, it does not require specialist, complex equipment; everyday materials suffice. Reinforcers can be identified and implemented in treatment without segregating the child from his environment.

Children can understand the behaviour therapy explanation of their behaviour, thus aiding insight. They are therefore more inclined to be motivated to change. Behaviour therapy demystifies the treatment of behaviour and turns it into a publicly observable and accountable form of problem-solving. Its techniques are efficient in terms of resources, whether one refers to personnel, time, equipment or materials. It also 'fits in' with the natural order of things – it lends itself to, and can be implemented in, any number of different settings, from the child's own home and school to specialist hospital and other settings. Behaviour therapy allows more than one problem to be tackled, either simultaneously or consecutively. Its techniques do not exclude the use of other parallel measures in conjunction with them (for example, chemotherapy). It is also applicable to practically every group of problem children, from the handicapped to the delinquent.

One of the attractions of behavioural techniques is that many can be implemented by a wide variety of personnel provided that a sound technical base and therapeutic format (a behavioural prescription) have been drawn up. Proponents of behaviour therapy emphasise its scientific and evidence-based orientation, and there is no doubt that a voluminous experimental and research literature exists to support it. Its status is so well established that even the British and American psychiatric associations believe that behaviour therapy procedures have much to offer informed clinicians in the service of modern clinical and social psychiatry; indeed, they advocate instruction in behaviour therapy techniques for psychiatric trainees.

From the viewpoint of a discipline, behaviour modification has the enormous advantage of a clear focus and an accountable process of treatment. The fact that there is by now a large and varied literature on its use with children also helps towards its almost universal applicability and gradual adoption as a sane and ethically defensible approach as a main (but rarely exclusive) plank of treatment.

Unlike the use of medicines, behaviour therapy has no side-effects; unlike the talking therapies, it does not demand high-level verbal ability; and unlike the group and environmental therapies it does not require the involvement of a range of other people or the regulation of wider environmental factors. Its non-diagnostic and non-stigmatising language helps prevent the formation of negative and excusatory self-concepts, particularly among adolescents with deep disorders and who search for ploys which neutralise therapeutic intervention.

The procedures nevertheless continue to engender scepticism in many mental health practitioners, especially those inclined towards the more 'insight' and psychoanalytical therapies. The demystification process, and the wide applicability of behaviour therapy where other treatments have failed, clearly poses some difficulty for traditional psychiatry with its emphasis on disease states, covert mental processes and a combination of drugs and insight to control them. More importantly, certain forms of behaviour modification (such as aversive conditioning and 'time out') can be used and perceived as euphemistic substitutes for straightforward punishment or withholding of 'rights'. Indeed, there are a number of environments in which such terms are used to dress up what are plainly punitive motives (such as in the 'control units' of certain institutions for young offenders).

However, this is no more a reflection on behaviour therapy than the use of drugs or environmental restrictions to control behaviour is on medicine or therapeutic communities. Indeed, given that punishment or negative reinforcement is an indispensable element in shaping critical behaviours, it may be better to use it rigorously in the context of behaviour modification than in other settings. At least in this form its effectiveness can be monitored and, if it fails in its task, it can (and should) be discontinued.

A practical difficulty with behaviour modification techniques is that they frequently require 'finely tuned' systems which are nevertheless robust enough to stand up to necessary human and environmental variability. Much of the reported failure of behaviour modification techniques in use is because they are rarely implemented with rigour and finesse, particularly in group and institutional settings where the previously mentioned problems of 'management' and 'survival' predominate. This difficulty is likely to continue until enough practitioners are persuaded of the efficacy of the techniques and apply them with precision.

Most seriously of all, behaviour modification in one setting may not (and often does not) transfer and generalise to another. Much effort may be expended in changing behaviour which simply reverts to its previous state upon discharge from the treatment setting. This is what accounts for such poor outcomes from behaviour modification with delinquents. Although there is no theoretical reason why the new learning through behaviour modification (BM) should not be generalised and pervasive, in practice most such learning is too shallow and context-bound to be more than a means of survival of the child in an environment bent on securing his conformity. The answer to this problem lies in deeper and more real-life 'conditioning' and the setting up of 'continuation strategies' when the child has returned to his normal habitat.

On balance, the advantages of BM method vastly predominate over its disadvantages, particularly in its modern usage, which acknowledges the importance of other influences and the advisability of combining a range or 'package' of treatment methods in the interests of effectiveness.

Assertiveness training

A technique involving role-play, modelling, coaching, prompting, encouraging, rewarding and behaviour rehearsal, assertiveness training is aimed at getting the child to behave more positively and purposively than he would do otherwise. It trains the child to express himself in a natural, adaptive and 'wholesome' way, including the ability freely to express his opinions and emotions – for example, love, affection, sympathy, admiration, anger, fear, sadness and justifiable criticism. It seeks to promote changes in the child's life-style, especially in social and interpersonal situations, from being a passive (though possibly 'acting-out') child to one who is actively involved in situations that impinge on him.

How does it work?   This technique seeks to inhibit anxiety and fear generated by certain social situations, while simultaneously emphasising that adaptive, assertive responses produce rewarding consequences (such as social recognition, promotion, status and enhancement of self-esteem) for the child. For example, a boy is taught to negotiate for staying up later rather than habitually throwing a temper tantrum at bedtime.

Practice

1   Gather relevant information from records of interview and observation.
2   Determine from the child and others the frequency and pattern of specific social interactions and their associated anxiety level.
3   Ensure (through proper assessment) that you are not confusing *learned* difficulties with an introverted personality pattern.
4   Ask the child to ventilate resentment about apparent injustices; how others ignore him; about what he would have liked to say or do in certain situations but did not or could not. This information can be enhanced by the use of particular assessment instruments.
5   Inform the child that the observable, outward expression of assertive behaviour can inhibit timidity, anxiety and fear and that his current, maladaptive behaviour pattern frustrates his desire for gaining recognition.
6   Role-play (in which the child plays himself and the therapist plays a person to whom the child reacts) in the form of behavioural rehearsal, to show the child how he should act in specific situations.
7   Model to help the child observe how a more assertive person would behave in the same situation.
8   Repeat the process (with variations) and reward until more assertive behaviour is established.

The therapist should outline that, with repeated acts of self-assertion under properly controlled conditions, confidence will increase, and the child's ability to deal appropriately and effectively with difficulties in social situations will improve. Reward and coaching from the therapist are important. Feedback should be provided to facilitate further improvement. Real-life opportunities for practice, both individually and in groups, will reinforce self-assertive behaviour. The therapist's plan should be communicated to other significant adults so that they also encourage the development of relevant behaviour. Other ploys such as keeping a diary of relevant episodes, star charts and self-suggestion are likely to enhance and generalise the newly acquired assertiveness.

Application   Assertiveness training may be indicated for delinquent, timid, embarrassed, inhibited, self-injurious, withdrawn, shy and passive children. Over-aggressive children may also require assertiveness training, to teach them to establish their own rights and wishes without infringing the rights of other people. The therapist should not assume that successful assertiveness training in one situation will generalise to all others. This technique can be used in conjunction with contingency management, covert sensitisation, modelling and shaping. It is not indicated for the very young or for severely mentally handicapped children.

Because assertiveness training is aimed at socially appropriate behaviour, it has no major disadvantages. Most ordinarily intelligent practitioners can grasp the basics of the technique quickly and use it successfully. In terms of resources, therefore, assertiveness training is an efficient technique.

Aversive conditioning (aversion therapy)

Aversive conditioning is a procedure in which aversive (noxious or unpleasant) stimuli are used to suppress or eliminate a maladaptive behaviour. It is a controversial form of behaviour therapy, because the unpleasant stimulus cannot be distinguished from punishment, other than in its different *intention*: punishment being retaliatory hurting, whereas aversive conditioning is meant to be therapeutic. It is employed mainly in the treatment of active behaviours which are damaging to the individual and usually incur social disapproval. As an example, an enuretic child sleeps on a mattress on which a pad with low-voltage wiring (something like an electric blanket) has been placed. When the child wets the bed, the wiring is short-circuited, and a loud bell rings which awakens (and often startles) the child. After several such tries, the unpleasant outcome generalises *backwards* and inhibits the bed-wetting.

How does it work?   The principle is the creation of conditioned dislike and avoidance of unacceptable behaviour by ensuring that it *results* in an unpleasant experience when the act is performed, or by *pairing* an unpleasant stimulus with the cues that evoke the undesirable behaviour. Its rationale is that after a suitable number of such pairings or outcomes the child will become anxious whenever he begins to think of or attempts to undertake that behaviour. This conditioned anxiety is disliked, and the child will therefore avoid the undesirable behaviour in order to avoid the anxiety associated with it. The therapy is designed to bring about a strong connection between undesirable behaviour and some unpleasant experience or to make the unpleasantness a consequence of the undesirable behaviour.

Practice

1   Specify the unacceptable behaviour and the conditions under which it takes place.
2   Determine on the aversive stimulus to be paired with the problem.
3   Provide opportunities for the paired occurrence of the condition and the aversive stimulus.
4   Ensure that no other event comes between the condition and the stimulus, so that one invariably follows the other.
5   Reinforce the link or the experience by appropriate feedback to the child.
6   Ensure that there are no (new) conditions provoking the old problem behaviour.

Application   Aversive conditioning is used generally for conditions which are critical and must be brought under quick control. Major instances are treatment for alcoholism, addictive behaviour (such as drug addiction and smoking), sexual disorders, overeating, head-banging, hyperactivity, self-injury, aggression, stuttering and tics. It can be used in conjunction with desensitisation, massed practice, environmental therapy, modelling, behavioural contracts, relaxation techniques, role-play, assertiveness training, covert sensitisation, speech therapy or self-control techniques, as appropriate. It may be used with children of all ages and conditions.

Limitations include ethical restrictions on the unpleasantness of the stimulus, dependent on the therapist's ability to control the stimulus-response sequence, to make sure that it operates without major interference from inconsistency or opportunity to 'dodge' the unpleasant outcome; the child's perception of the aversive stimulus (some children may find it rewarding – for example, at least it guarantees attention); the child may become habituated; and responses are extinguished quickly by un-reinforced trials. Best results are often obtained by pairing aversive conditioning of the undesirable behaviour with positive reinforcement for normal or socially desirable and incompatible behaviour.

The disadvantages of this technique lie in the difficulty of determining what is unpleasant; in ethical problems of applying unpleasant conditions to children so harshly that they do find the experience unpleasant; in occasional technical difficulties in setting up the conditioning process; and in the problems of generalisation from one setting to another. Given the need for an almost laboratory exactness in the conditioning process, almost invariably the services of a psychologist are required. The strength of the technique lies in its unmatched ability to bring critical behaviour under rapid control.

Chaining

Most behaviour is not just the result of learning separate, discrete stimulus-response units. Rather, it is characterised by a *series* of stimulus-response units linked in a seamless sequence. The process of linking two or more learned stimulus-response units in a sequence is called 'chaining'; it is the process of conditioning a child to perform a series of linked stimulus-response (S-R) units to obtain reinforcement; the response of one S-R unit usually acts as the stimulus (or trigger) for the next.

How does it work?   The connecting of S-R units may be explained by time sequence; that is, because the stimulus is rapidly followed by a response, the two become associated. The response produces stimuli which may serve as a cue for the response that follows; each stimulus produced by a response is referred to as a response-produced cue or stimulus.

The whole process of getting up in time in the morning and eventually going to school provides a common example. The process is made up of getting up, toileting, getting dressed, breakfasting, collecting books, etc., covering the distance to school by appropriate transport and getting through the school gates, each of which is itself a complex behaviour. Although the process is seamless under normal conditions, in cases where it does not occur, the end product has to be achieved through a 'chained' sequence of individually acquired units, where the completion of, for example, getting dressed leads to breakfasting, which in turn triggers off collecting books and so on. The role of response-produced stimuli in learning response chains is clearly demonstrated by the difficulty people have in performing certain learned responses in reverse order – for example, reciting the alphabet backwards. Also, the importance of the response-produced stimuli in cueing each of the S-R units in the chain is shown by the difficulty a person has in starting, say, in the middle of a sequence and performing the remaining responses from that point onwards.

Practice

1   Analyse the behaviour into its constituent parts, as detailed and demanded by the complexity of the task and the learning capacity of the child.
2   Teach the separate S-R units (or links) before attempting to chain them.

3 Practice with the child until each link is executed in the proper sequence.
4 The S-R units (or links) must be performed in close-time association, to minimise interference and to ensure that the links are chained.
5 The sequence must be repeated until the desired learning has been achieved, so that the performance is executed in smooth sequence.
6 Reinforce the learning of chains; execution of the final link must have the proper effect; reinforcement must be immediate.

The important rule in establishing chains is to start with the last response – the one rewarded with primary reinforcement. For example, if you want to teach a dog to fetch your slippers and drop them in front of you, first teach him to drop the slippers and then teach him to fetch them.

Application Chaining is useful in training children in self-help skills such as dressing, toileting and eating correctly. Within reasonable limits, it can be a very useful technique with a very wide range of children, especially where behaviours require building up, as for example with the training of mentally and physically handicapped childre. This is the basis of some of the best-known training schemes for such children. It is also a more basic element in all behaviour therapy, rather than a free-standing technique. Its disadvantage lies in the requirement for a skilled psychologist to break down the tasks and set up the sequence. Its advantage lies in its indispensability for building up any complex skills.

Cognitive behaviour modification

The cognitive view of behaviour assigns primary importance to the self-evident fact that, as people, we think. How and what we think partly determine how we feel and what we do, either when we initiate acts or when we are reacting to others' behaviour. 'Cognition' refers to both the content of thought and the processes involved in thinking – perceiving and processing information. The mechanisms and content of memory and recall, as well as problem-solving styles and strategies, are all aspects of cognition. In short, cognition encompasses the process of knowing as well as its products.

How does it work? Cognitive behaviour therapy seeks to alter or remove views and beliefs that are dysfunctional or maladaptive; it aims to redirect elements of cognition, such as impressions, judgements, opinions and memories, which are counter-productive, so that subsequent behaviours become more adaptive or acceptable. It recognises the three stages whereby children acquire self-control through 'inner speech'. At first the speech of others, usually adults, controls and directs a child's behaviour. Then the child's own overt speech becomes an effective regulator of his behaviour.

Finally the child's covert or inner speech comes to assume a self-governing role. These stages are translated into therapeutic work.

We can see an example of this with a hyperactive child who cannot concentrate on and complete a drawing task. First the teacher does the drawing, speaking to himself aloud about what he should do 'Must go slow round the corner...whoops, I've overshot the line, must come back') until the task is finished. The child then follows, talking himself through the task; later the child only mutters the instruction and eventually goes through the task silently. This procedure uses such tasks as a means of giving the child conscious, cognitive control.

Practice

1 Perform the appropriate task whilst talking out loud, with the child watching or close by (cognitive modelling).
2 Get the child to perform the same task according to your instruction (overt, external guidance).
3 Let the child perform the task while instructing himself aloud (overt self-guidance).
4 Ask the child to whisper instructions to himself as he goes through the task again (faded overt self-guidance).
5 Encourage the child to perform the task while guiding his performance via inaudible or private speech or non-verbal self-direction (covert self-instruction).

Application This technique is more useful with older children who are cognitively intact. It is not ideal for use with intellectually handicapped children; if it is used, tasks must be simpler and given more practice. It is a useful technique in training self-control skills, especially with over-active, impulsive and aggressive children. Other behaviour and scholastic problems treated by self-instructional procedures include resistance to temptation, delay of gratification, problem-solving, reading and creativity. It can be profitably used in conjunction with contracting, assertiveness training, modelling, differential reinforcement, aversive conditioning, positive reinforcement and token reinforcement, as appropriate to particular behavioural goals.

The technique has no disadvantages in ethical or resource terms. Most ordinarily intelligent people can use it, in almost any setting. Its chief merit lies in its emphasis on cognitive self-control. We shall further elaborate this in our discussion of rational-emotive therapy (RET) in Chapter 10.

Contingency contracting

This technique involves a negotiated and signed contract between a child and other person(s), such as parents, teacher or therapist, regulating the actions (rewards or sanctions) that would follow if the child behaved (or failed to behave) in a particular way. In short, the contract is a statement of what will happen to the child depending (contingent) upon his actions. An example would be of a child who is contracted to fulfil certain treatment tasks in return for additional pocket-money.

How does it work?   Contingency contracting relies on learning principles embodying positive reinforcement in the form of material rewards, points and reinforcing events to promote desirable behaviour. These are given depending (contingent) upon fulfilment of target behaviours as agreed upon in writing by relevant parties. It is a means of regulating the exchange of positive reinforcements among two or more people.

Contracting is based upon four basic assumptions: (1) receipt of rewards in interpersonal exchanges is a privilege, rather than a right; (2) effective interpersonal agreements are governed by reciprocation or give-and-take; (3) the value or worth of an interpersonal exchange depends on the range, rate and size of the positive reinforcements which have been made possible by that exchange; (4) interpersonal exchange rules encourage and create genuine personal freedoms.

Practice   Spell out crucial elements, as listed below, in detail. The contract should be arrived at following *negotiation*. It must be accepted willingly by the child, not imposed upon him. It should start with short-range goals, which may be lengthened according to the child's success. The behaviours selected for contracting must be possible and achievable by the child. The rewards selected must be of things/experiences which he likes enough to want to work for. The contract should not be a disguised way of 'trapping' the child and showing by his failure how incorrigible he is. Sometimes a sanction (punishment or loss of privilege) may be included as a penalty clause in the contract, but sanction-based contracts are usually much less effective than strongly reward-based ones. If possible and/or appropriate, behaviours required in the contract should be rehearsed prior to commitment by a child.

The procedures follow the following steps:

1   Give a clear, detailed and unequivocal description, in writing, of the required behaviour, in keeping with the child's capacity to understand and perform.
2   Establish criteria for duration, frequency and quality which will constitute the goal of the contract; that is, state what is to be achieved.
3   Specify the positive reinforcements or rewards contingent upon correct behaviour.
4   Make provision, if appropriate, for some penalties (fine or loss of

privilege) upon non-fulfilment of the contract by either party, stipulated according to the criteria in 2.

5 Include a bonus clause to indicate additional positive reinforcements obtainable if the child exceeds minimal demands of the contract.

6 Specify means by which the contract response is observed, measured and recorded; establish a procedure (for example, by a chart) for giving feedback to the child about his achievements during the term of the contract.

7 Deliver the contingent rewards as soon as possible after the appropriate response.

It is essential that the terms of the contract be adhered to by all parties.

Application Children must be of sufficient age and ability to understand the format of the contract. The technique is useful for 'acting-out' behaviour (such as fighting) or general behaviour disorders (such as lack of self-control), bed-wetting, soiling, hyperactivity, nail-biting, tardiness, lack of motivation, poor school attendance and/or truancy and general non-compliant behaviours (such as refusing to do homework or to maintain personal hygiene). Complemented by time-out procedures, assertiveness training, covert sensitisation, modelling, shaping, relaxation, token economy and self-management techniques, the power of contracting is substantially increased.

The main difficulty with contingency contracting is that the child may be poorly motivated to achieve the objectives. Even if he is well motivated, the child who has difficulty in fulfilling the contract may become disheartened and may resort to cheating or avoiding those who know about the contract. It may thus give rise to unintended consequences, including a poorer relationship with other parties to the contract.

The enormous advantage of contingency contracting is its flexibility in relation to targets, the child's capacity and administrative circumstances. Contracts may be phased to tackle increasingly complex, less overt problems. The above disadvantages can be overcome with careful planning. It is crucial to remember throughout that the contract is intended to bring about positive change in the child, not to create yet another instance of failure.

Covert conditioning

A widely used technique of behaviour modification is 'systematic desensitisation' (discussed later in this chapter), a method of anxiety reduction that uses self-presented imagery as a substitute for reproducing actual conditions under which a child experiences fears. Changes are effected by a graded visual presentation of the feared stimulus. Covert conditioning, on the other hand, relies on visual *imagery*; thoughts and fantasies serve as covert operants (rewards or punishments). It is essentially, in all its forms, a self-reinforcement technique.

How does it work?   Covert conditioning operates according to the principles governing operant conditioning (discussed later). There are four types of covert conditioning: covert sensitisation; covert reinforcement; covert extinction; and covert modelling.

Practice

Covert sensitisation

1 Ask the child to imagine a scene depicting undesirable behaviour that he finds rewarding; exhort the child to imagine the scene with clarity, vividness and intensity.
2 Then ask the child to switch abruptly into imagining a relevant very unpleasant event – physical, familial or social; aversive stimuli are invoked and modified to suit the child's personal history and circumstances.
3 Ask the child to escape the unpleasant situation and the feelings associated with it; after the 'escape', he visualises relief and reduction of discomfort.
4 Give strong and positive reinforcement; thus, the maladaptive behaviour is paired with aversive consequences, and escape is rewarded by the relief experience.

An example from solvent abuse would be relevant. The child is encouraged to imagine a 'sniffing' scene vividly, with his usual companions. When this is achieved, he is asked to imagine being very sick and suffocating and to go on doing so until it becomes unbearable and he is showing signs of distress. He is then asked to imagine dropping the glue bag and walking away to go home, where he breathes freely and has his favourite drink. When he has done this and relief is evident, the therapist congratulates him on the achievement and gives him a chocolate bar.

Covert reinforcement

1 Train the child to imagine a scene that is subjectively experienced as happy or pleasant; an example would be of an enuretic child who is asked to imagine being given a big prize in front of a favourite group of people but eventually to imagine this only when he has been dry the night before.
2 Give him practice in imagining pairing of the target behaviour with the pleasant imagery, until the link is established.
3 Ask the child to practise this pairing by himself.

This practice utilises the same procedures as in the process of extinction (discussed later in this chapter), but imagination is used instead of real-life experience.

1 Determine the target behaviour to be reduced or removed.
2 Train the child to imagine the target behaviour resulting in a neutral feeling or experience.
3 Give enough practice until the link is established.
4 Reinforce with appropriate encouragement.

Covert extinction
Reinforcing one response rather than another changes the probability of its recurrence compared with others which have not been reinforced. Differential reinforcement uses this principle to train the child to respond differently to different situations. For example, to reduce overeating, the child is asked to imagine himself eating food but to find it tasteless and unpleasant.

Covert modelling
This approach uses imaginary people as substitutes for live or filmed models in the reduction of fearful behaviour. It combines covert methods with usual open modelling techniques.

1 Train the child to practise imagining the unpleasant scene in detail for a series of trials.
2 Ask the child to imagine another person – the model – performing the feared behaviour, such as stroking a dog or entering a lift without difficulty.
3 Describe the model in positive terms such as 'confident' and 'determined'.
4 Encourage the child to persist with imagining the model and target behaviour.
5 Ask the child to imagine himself with the characteristics and behaviour of the model.
6 Repeat the associated imagery and reinforce until it is well established.
7 Extend, where appropriate, to real-life practice, with appropriate encouragement.

Application Clinical reports suggest that careful preparation of the child is needed for him to become proficient in imagining the suggested scenes. Not only must the child be intellectually intact and capable of exercising imagination; he must also be highly motivated and co-operative. The technique may prove useful in suppressing or modifying undesirable 'approach' (for example, homosexuality) or avoidance (for example, inhibited behaviour or phobias) tendencies. It may also be used as an adjunct to other techniques for modifying self-concept, smoking, solvent abuse, exhibitionism, voyeurism, fear of public speaking, stuttering, tics and 'bad' habits.

Disadvantages of the approach lie in its complexity and the need for skilled practitioners. In practice also, many children cannot sustain the concentration for repeated pairings of the imagery and feelings. Apart from the intellectual and motivational requirements, these techniques also demand honesty on the child's part and take somewhat longer than comparable overt methods. An advantage of covert techniques is that they are less objectionable than actual aversion therapy. They are effective in promoting self-control of behaviours and may be accompanied by any other treatment.

Differential reinforcement

Differential reinforcement is a form of conditioning or training a child to respond to a specific stimulus rather than to react generally. It is used to help the child discriminate and perform appropriate responses.

How does it work?   Reinforcing one response rather than another changes the probability of its recurrence, compared with others which have not been reinforced. Differential reinforcement uses this principle to train the child to respond differently to different situations. For example, if a child fears a 'real' dog, a furry toy dog may evoke the same fear reaction. The child therefore needs to learn to discriminate between different, yet similar, stimuli. Differential reinforcement is an 'operant' technique which helps achieve this end.

Practice

1   Determine what response you want to achieve.
2   Work out your reinforcements and how (often) you propose to use them.
3   Reinforce the child selectively, when the appropriate response has been produced, and omit reinforcement when an inappropriate response is made.
4   When the child responds regularly as expected, begin to vary/reduce the reinforcement (whether verbal or material) until the response occurs without close dependence on the reinforcement. Phase out the sessions.

Application   Differential reinforcement techniques are useful in teaching children basic educational skills, social skills (such as how to speak with and behave towards familiar and non-familiar peers and adults), modification of particular behaviour patterns (such as an aggressive response to name-calling, or anxiety during examinations), or, indeed, any behaviour in which discrimination is particularly important. Such training procedures work best in conjunction with extinction and prompting.

The limitation lies in the need to monitor the child's behaviour closely and consistently. A further difficulty may be that the target behaviour (for example, inappropriate touching of others) may not be readily or frequently evident or easy to set up. On the other hand, the advantages of the technique lie in its high degree of specificity, ease of operation, relatively low-level skill requirement and applicability to a wide range of conditions.

Extinction

Extinction is a process by which a specific response or behaviour is weakened by the withdrawal of the reinforcement maintaining it.

How does it work? Many deviant or maladaptive behaviours are maintained or strengthened by positive or negative reinforcements. For example, reinforcement in the form of attention (looking at, castigating or shouting) often increases, rather than decreases, disorderly or disruptive behaviour in children. To modify such behaviour, therefore, reinforcement must be withheld, although it may take many non-reinforced trials before the unwanted behaviour is 'extinguished'. The rate at which behaviour is extinguished depends on how well (through what reinforcement schedule) the behaviour was previously learned and/or stimulated. If behaviour has been promoted on a continuous schedule (100 per cent reinforcement), extinction occurs rapidly. However, most responses are learned with variable ratio schedules (less than 100 per cent or unpredictable reinforcement) and take longer to get rid of.

Extinction operates on the basis that the withdrawal of reinforcement reduces the probability of occurrence of a behaviour. Just as reinforcing a behaviour increases the probability of its recurrence, so withholding the reinforcement weakens it. It must be noted, however, that there is often an *increase* in the undesirable behaviour after reinforcement has been removed. This is an attempt to regain the reinforcement by stepping up the behaviour which previously achieved it. A child who previously banged his head until he got his way, when ignored, may bang his head so much as to draw blood. Persistence in withholding reinforcement is essential, and the behaviour will eventually be extinguished.

Practice

1 Conduct systematic observation of the child to collect data on the frequency of problem behaviour and the nature and frequency of naturally occurring reinforcement (such as adult attention for temper tantrums).

2   Instruct relevant others (adults and peers) simply to ignore the behaviour.
3   Encourage them in consistency and persistence and, if necessary, reward them to ensure that they continue to ignore.
4   Ensure co-operation between interested others and warn them of potential initial increase of undesirable behaviour.
5   Supplement extinction of the inappropriate response with positive reinforcement for incompatible or appropriate behaviour.

Application   Extinction procedures are applicable to a wide range of behavioural disorders. Unacceptable behaviours include temper tantrums, tale-telling and models of speech (such as swearing); inappropriate crying and whining; all forms of inappropriate attention-seeking and over-demanding behaviour, and almost all forms of self-injury. The technique is applicable to all age groups.

Limitations of extinction include the 'slowness' with which it effects behavioural changes. It also often results in an immediate increase in the inappropriate behaviours before they begin to weaken. 'Ignoring' disruptive behaviour is always difficult and sometimes (as in the cases of self-injury) not permissible. Possibly also, other children may imitate the inappropriate behaviour, since it appears to them that the miscreant is 'getting away with it'. Furthermore, extinction, as an exclusive technique, is not advisable when behaviour must be stopped immediately because it is harmful to the child or to others (for example, assaults or arson), or when the frustrating effects produced by the lack of reinforcement initiate other, potentially dangerous and uncontrollable behaviours. Its advantages lie in its wide range of application to normally occurring behaviour in natural settings, its absence of 'technology' and the relatively permanent nature of the treatment effect.

Fading

Fading is a procedure for gradually reducing the control of a child's behaviour by a particular stimulus. As one stimulus is reduced, so another one takes its place, until the child's behaviour is maintained by the cues that exist in the normal environment.

How does it work?   Behavioural changes which occur in one situation may not necessarily generalise to other, equally relevant situations. For example, a child trained to be sociable in the classroom may continue to be aggressive in the playground or at home. Effective treatment should therefore aim to accomplish maximum applicability of change. Fading relies on the gradual transition to other stimuli which will ensure that the child continues to behave appropriately over a wide range of conditions.

For example, a 'school-phobic' child may go to school again when prompted or rewarded. Gradually the prompts and the rewards given by the parents are withdrawn, whilst the teacher makes an increasing effort to make the child's return pleasant and rewarding. The withdrawal of parental reward is called 'fading out', and the teacher's reward 'fading in'. The basic principle is stimulus generalisation through 'pairing'.

Practice

1 Work out the time scale of fading and whether any new, specific rewards are to take the place of the old ones.
2 Start the process. Ensure that it is not so vapid as to extinguish the desired behaviour because it is not being 'properly' reinforced.
3 Continue to encourage the child verbally and by other non-specific rewards which may be found in the normal environment.
4 Ensure that parents and others continue to encourage the child.

Application Fading is a useful technique for 'weaning' a child off a particular treatment measure, from drugs to token economies, and establishing normal behaviour. In this respect it can be regarded as a necessary and indispensable requirement of all treatments which are achieved through stimulus or contingency control. It is more an adjunct to other treatments than a treatment technique by itself. It can be used with all age groups and in all treatment conditions. It can be used by a wide range of people without specialist knowledge, in any treatment setting.

Fading has no disadvantages, apart from the careful planning required to effect transition from one setting to another.

Flooding (or implosive therapy)

Flooding is a technique, whereby the child is confronted in imagination or reality with the most feared situation and encouraged to remain in contact with that situation until his anxiety subsides. The aim of the treatment is the extinction of anxiety by non-reinforced practice. It is called 'flooding' to liken it to swamping the subject with anxiety and thereby reducing susceptibility to it. A child with an intense fear of dogs is encouraged to sit (or imagine sitting) next to and stroke a dog until such time as his fear becomes manageable.

How does it work? Implosive therapy relies on principles derived from both learning theory and psychodynamic theory. Flooding assumes that fears and their associated anxiety are learned and can be best unlearned by using extinction procedures. It also recognises, however, the importance of internal 'events' such as thoughts and impulses which become associated with anxiety and thereafter serve as anxiety-provoking cues. 'Implosive' refers to the massive surge of internal anxiety when the person is brought face to face with a feared object or event.

Practice

1   Identify, through a structured interview, both internal and external cues which evoke anxiety and avoidance responses.
2   Construct an avoidance 'cue' hierarchy. The low-ranking cues are usually those of which the subject is most aware, and the higher-ranking cues are the more serious and less conscious ones (such as aggressive and sexual conflicts).
3   Start the treatment (after due preliminaries such as building up proper rapport and explaining the procedure) by asking the child to imagine, as vividly as possible, the feared situation and to experience all the associated emotions.
4   Maintain the child's anxiety level at maximum by describing progressively more fearful scenes, including those higher up the cue hierarchy.
5   Present low-hierarchy cues first and move up the scale only when the child's apparent anxiety level falls.
6   Encourage the child to 'live' the scenes with genuine emotion and feeling.
7   End the session when anxiety is reduced; encourage the child to re-enact his anxiety with therapist, parents or other trusted people until it is reduced.

Application   This technique is useful for the treatment of phobias, fears (such as of examination), ritualistic behaviour associated with anxiety, and panic attacks. It is useful in conjunction with relaxation training, systematic desensitisation, modelling and paradoxical intention. It should not be used as a first choice of treatment until other relevant techniques such as desensitisation have been tried. Neither should it be used with very young children or, indeed, others who may be debilitated by an increase in anxiety. The potential for worsening the situation is the major shortcoming of this technique. Also, given the amount of skilled time taken, there are more focally useful techniques available.

Modelling

Modelling is a process by which a child learns the response or behaviour of a model by observing and imitating the model's performance. For example, a child is shown how to make a request or ask a favour instead of making an aggressive demand.

How does it work? Several theories attempt to explain modelling. The associative and classical conditioning view suggests that modelling occurs when the relevant behaviour and its consequences are observed to occur as 'paired' or in a short interval of time. Another theory suggests that modelling results from a well-motivated observer being positively re-inforced for closely matching the appropriate behaviour of a model in a situation initially based on trial and error. Yet another theory suggests that modelling involves two processes and/or systems: imaginal and verbal. Images of the model's responses form as a result of sensory conditioning – that is, a picture is built up of what the model does; this picture persists and can be retrieved later. Simultaneously, it is suggested, a type of verbal coding of the observed stimulus-response chain occurs.

Practice The acquisition of modelled responses involves four basic steps:

1 Encourage the child to attend to and observe the appropriate behaviour as modelled by the therapist (or another person).
2 Ask the child to describe the behaviour and to try to remember it.
3 Give the child repeated opportunity to reproduce or rehearse the appropriate behaviour by both imagining and describing it.
4 Provide appropriate incentive or reinforcing conditions to ensure that the child will, in fact, perform the desired (modelled) behaviour.

Application Characteristics of the model and the learner determine the extent of learning. Performance is enhanced when the learner (a) has a previous history of successfully imitating others' behaviour; (b) accepts the competence, prestige and status of the model; (c) considers the modelled behaviour exemplary; (d) has low self-esteem; (e) is dependent; (f) has been previously incompetent. Desirable characteristics of the model which influence the extent to which modelling occurs are (a) similarity in sex, age, race and attitudes; (b) prestige; (c) warmth and support; (d) competence; (e) reward value.

This technique is useful for all ages and intellectual levels, and in combination with any other technique. It is used extensively in the treatment of fear-related behaviour – for example, phobias, children facing surgery, dental treatment or hospitalisation, socially incompetent children, withdrawn and shy children. It is especially useful with the mentally handicapped in teaching self-help survival skills. Basic verbal and motor skills can be acquired by autistic children who observe adult/peer models. It is of some use with aggressive children to teach them new, constructive and socially acceptable alternative behaviours in provocative situations. It is a cornerstone of social skills training.

The technique has no disadvantages and hardly any limitation, given that it is a basic medium of everyday learning. It has the supreme advantage of low cost, openness to expert use by parents and others and quick results.

Negative practice

Negative practice is the repetitive and massed execution of an undesirable response for the purpose of decreasing or eliminating it. For example, a child who jerks his neck (as a 'tic') is asked to keep on jerking it until he is so tired or fed up that he stops.

How does it work? There are at least three reasons for the effectiveness of this technique: the response is extinguished because anxiety (which is a motive for continuing it) is no longer present; the fatigue that accumulates by repetition makes performance of the response painful and/or unpleasant; the child may, via repetition, be made more aware of the successive steps involved in the performance of the behaviour and is able to interrupt the sequence.

Practice

1 Ask the child repeatedly to perform the undesirable behaviour; continue for a given period of time, at pre-set intervals or at repeated sessions.
2 End each session when the child is no longer willing or able to continue.
3 Repeat the sessions to ensure 'over-learning'.
4 Stop when the necessary 'clear' period of time has been achieved.

Application Useful for children of all ages and abilities, to reduce or eliminate such behaviour as tics, eye-blinking, stammering, disruptive 'imitations' in class, smoking and overeating. It can be used in isolation or with other techniques. Care must be taken to avoid damage to the child and to find means of retaining contact in what can become an increasingly unpleasant experience. The advantages lie in specificity and relatively rapid therapeutic outcome, which persists over a period of time.

Negative reinforcement

Negative reinforcement refers to the termination or removal of an aversive, unpleasant stimulus following the performance of a desired response. It is any stimulus which, by its removal, strengthens the response that follows it. For example, an adolescent child-molester is given a mild but unpleasant electric shock all the time he is viewing slides of little children; the shock is stopped when he presses a button to change the slide to young women.

How does it work? If a person is subjected to aversive (that is, unpleasant or painful) stimulation, any action which results in stopping that stimulation is reinforced and thus made more probable. Unpleasant stimuli are terminated for the purpose of strengthening desirable avoidance responses – for example, learning to give up smoking, drinking, fattening foods or molesting little children. It is a variant of operant conditioning.

Practice

1 Pair the undesirable behaviour with an unpleasant experience (aversive stimulus).
2 When using negative reinforcement, provide an incompatible alternative positive response.
3 The termination of the aversive stimulus should be contingent, immediate and consistent.
4 The time between escape or avoidance trials must not be too brief; the aversive stimulus should be off long enough to make relief enjoyable.
5 Repeat the sessions for long enough to achieve over-learning.

Application The technique can be used to promote escape and avoidance behaviours but is also helpful in enhancing desirable behaviour. Its power is substantially increased in combination with positive reinforcement for the desirable response. This technique is not widely used because it is difficult to justify using stimuli which both are unpleasant enough and yet can be ethically used with children. It is potentially a powerful conditioning technique, particularly with the more anxious child or one whose deviant behaviour is not so rewarding as to demand repetition despite such unpleasant treatment. These same reasons also render it of dubious value, particularly when less ethically problematic treatments are available.

Operant conditioning

Operant conditioning is a process by which a response is strengthened or weakened by the consequences that follow it. The importance of the procedure lies in emphasising the fact that it is the consequence of acts which determine the probability of their recurrence under similar conditions at a later time. As an example, a child is more likely to throw a temper tantrum if the tantrum is followed by sweeties and a cuddle than by his being put in another room or missing his favourite TV programme.

How does it work? Operant conditioning relies on the theory that the major determinant of response frequency is the consequence of the behaviour. If the consequences are positive or rewarding, the behaviour will tend to increase in frequency or be maintained at a high rate; if the consequences are absent, neutral or unpleasant, the behaviour will tend to decrease in frequency and disappear. Two types of positive consequence tend to increase the response frequency: presentation of a reward (positive reinforcement); and removal of an aversive stimulus (negative reinforcement). When a neutral consequence or no consequence follows a response, the behaviour tends to decrease in frequency until it is no longer evident.

Two types of negative consequence serve to decrease response frequency: namely, punishment (discussed later in this chapter), where an unpleasant stimulus (such as spanking) follows the behaviour; and 'time out' (discussed later), where a pleasant stimulus, or the opportunity to obtain one, is removed.

Practice   Six basic procedures are considered essential in conditioning operant behaviour:

1 Define and state operationally the behaviour to be changed; the target behaviour should be defined in terms of what is observable, the criteria by which the behaviour is considered acceptable and the conditions under which the behaviour is expected to occur.
2 Obtain a 'baseline' of the behaviour to be promoted or discouraged; the frequency, magnitude and severity of the behaviour should be determined before treatment; thus, it becomes possible to determine treatment effects and whether treatment procedures require modification.
3 Arrange the environment to maximise the probability that the desirable behaviour will occur; before reinforcements are administered, it is necessary to determine whether the child can actually perform the desired response in the appropriate manner; it is pointless setting targets which are impossible for the child to attain.
4 Identify potential and potent reinforcers; before most children will do something, they must want something; apart from possibly 'primary reinforcers' (such as food) and some unpleasant experiences, a stimulus has no inherent reinforcement value; it is therefore necessary to determine the reinforcement property of a stimulus – that is, its capacity to increase the probability that a response will occur; in other words, it is essential to discover what the child likes – this can be done by observing a child, by listening to his comments or, more formally, by asking the child to complete a 'reinforcement survey schedule', selecting from a detailed list the order of his likes and dislikes, both material and social.
5 Reinforce the target behaviour; if the child can perform the desired response, reinforce it on its first and every subsequent appearance until it is established; modify the reinforcement schedule thereafter to maintain the behaviour, bearing in mind that variable ratio and variable interval reinforcements promote long-term learning; if the child is unable to perform the terminal, desired response, successive approximations of the behaviour should be identified and reinforced appropriately (see the section on shaping).
6 Monitor accurately the reinforced behaviour to determine whether the response strength and/or frequency has changed; longitudinal records

allow for a comparison between the level of 'treatment' response and the baseline rate and thus indicate whether the reinforcement contingencies have been effective; if the reinforcement is not producing the desired result, it is necessary to analyse the pertinent conditions, determine why and make appropriate modifications.

Application Operant conditioning can be used in practically every aspect of the management and treatment of problem children, whether the problem results from deficient or from deviant learning. The techniques are particularly effective in training mentally handicapped children for self-help skills such as feeding, walking, dressing and toileting, as well as building up speech, communication and other skills in 'autistic' children.

The limitations of the approach lie in its skill requirements, in analysis of behaviour as well as determination and application of reinforcements. The more complex the behaviour, the more difficult the conditioning process will be. Its strength lies in its focus and applicability to virtually all aspects of children's behaviour. This is such a potent and pervasive technique that it can be regarded as the cornerstone of all behaviour modification.

Paradoxical intention

Paradoxical intention is a technique whereby the therapist expresses agreement with the child's irrationality and exaggerates his distortion(s). It often entails a concrete, literal or bizarre intervention. For example, consider a child who persistently complains and whines about minor physical ailments; the therapist will reply, 'Yes, I agree with you; you are virtually at death's door. We had better arrange an emergency bed in hospital for you.'

How does it work? Paradoxical techniques cut across theoretical and diagnostic boundaries and draw on methods as diverse as psychoanalysis, existentialism and behaviour therapy. They tend to rely on intuition and a bullish, 'common-sense' approach to interpersonsal communication. Many people, including children, fail to recognise the irrationality of their opinions, feelings and behaviours, but when it is 'reflected' back at them they often recognise its inappropriateness. In behavioural terms, therefore, it may be hypothesised that maladaptive responses are not being reinforced or are, alternatively, negatively reinforced.

Practice

1   When the child expresses an irrational opinion, feeling or behaviour, exaggerate and distort his statements, as indicated in the above example.

2 Take care to retain a poker face so that the child does not perceive the procedure as either a game or a contest with a mad and malevolent person.

3 Whilst exaggerating the child's comments or behaviour, draw out the inherent contradictions or untenableness of the views and behaviours expressed.

4 Attempt to give the child a more realistic perception of his state.

Application   This is a useful technique for older children who engage in irrational ruminations, allusions or seemingly immutable behaviours. The technique is useful as a means of reorientating, for example, distorted self-perceptions. (For example: 'I am useless; I can't do anything right', says the child. The therapist replies, 'You are quite correct. That's why you are so good at your schoolwork, and popular, and such a good all-round sportsman.') The difficulties lie in the time, effort and skill it takes to maintain communication whilst giving such contrary feedback to the child. The technique's value lies in the jolt and shock which the unexpected agreement by the therapist engenders. It cannot be used effectively as a long-term ploy but is worthwhile as an adjunct to other behavioural or talking and group therapies.

Positive reinforcement

The procedure of positive reinforcement entails giving a reward following the performance of a desired response. Defined operationally, a positive reinforcer is any stimulus that strengthens the response it follows. As an example, a child who is rewarded for being co-operative and prosocial will tend to behave more in this manner than a child who is not.

How does it work?   With this procedure, the response is strengthened by the addition of something positive that follows its occurrence. Three types of positive reinforcer exist:

(a) social reinforcers, such as praise, approval, affection and recognition;
(b) tokens and material reinforcers: tokens may be check marks, ticks, points, marks or plastic strips; food, drink, toys and sweets are examples of tangible reinforcers;
(c) intrinsic reinforcers, including satisfactions which are gained from an activity such as playing games and doing puzzles, and a feeling of well-being and pride in a job well done.

Practice

1 Identify appropriate reinforcers by observing their effects on behaviour for the individual child; that is, do not assume that what you (or others)

find rewarding applies equally to the child with whom you are dealing.
2 Identify appropriate reinforcers across and within a variety of natural settings.
3 Deliver the reinforcers immediately, but only when the behaviour has been shown consistently.
4 Reinforce the behaviour at the highest constant level, then gradually modify the frequency and intensity of reinforcement.
5 Pair social reinforcers with material ones and gradually phase out the latter until social reinforcers have taken over; occasionally reinforce with tangible rewards to maintain the behaviour across settings.

Application Positive reinforcement techniques are especially useful and effective in establishing, strengthening or maintaining a whole range of desirable behaviours from simple acts such as maintaining eye contact to higher-level responses such as attitudes or complex behaviour patterns. It is one of the most widely applied, potent and versatile techniques in the realm of behaviour change. Its limitations lie in the level of skills required to analyse behaviour, set reinforcement schedules and apply and monitor them. The advantages lie in the range of application with regard to both the child's condition and his age and capacity. Being positive, it is also ethically on the side of the angels.

Prompting

Prompts are behavioural interventions which direct the learner's attention to the task to be learned and its requirements. For example, a child is reminded to ask for the salt pot rather than stretch across the table to get it.

How does it work? Adequate adjustment to an ever-changing environment calls for quick and accurate tuning in to appropriate cues that signal expected forms of behaviour; for example, 'Say "please" if you are asking for something', or 'Talk in whispers in a library.' Subtler social signals dictate how we approach, converse with and relate to other people – friends, strangers, family and authority figures. Maladaptive behaviour is often the result of responding to an inappropriate stimulus or a failure to respond to an appropriate one. If the responses can be brought under the influence of verbal or non-verbal signals (hints, cues, prompts, directions or requests), then appropriate responses can be more efficiently managed and set the stage for generalisation and maintenance.

Practice There are three ways of prompting:
1 Issue simple, unequivocal instructions; for example, 'Put that on there', or 'Put your sweater on' – this is termed 'verbal prompting'.

2   Use gestures; for example, point to something, or beckon someone
    – this is 'gestural prompting'.
3   Physically guide someone's movements; for example, turn them round
    to look at you – this is 'physical prompting'.

Gradually fade out the prompts. Provide gradually fewer cues so that
the child eventually learns to respond on his own. Remember, as with
fading, to start by removing the last part of the prompt first.

Application   This is a useful technique for all age groups to teach motor,
academic and social skills. There are no limitations. Its advantages lie
in its wide applicability across both problems and capacities, the common-
sense nature of prompting, the lack of cost and the relatively low skill
requirement. It is particularly useful when employed by parents and other
non-specialists who are seeking a way of helping a problem child.

Punishment

Punishment is the presentation of an unpleasant stimulus or the removal
of a positive reinforcer immediately following a piece of behaviour. Its
aim is to stop or suppress undesirable behaviour. For example, the back
of a child's hand is slapped every time he touches an electric socket.
Punishment is intended to suppress or remove undesirable behaviour. In
this context, however, it is not meant to be retaliatory or a means of 'getting
even' with the child.

How does it work?   Numerous studies have addressed themselves to the
effects of punishment on behaviour. The findings suggest that the extent
to which punishment is effective in suppressing undesirable behaviour
depends on (a) the intensity, duration, frequency and dispensation of the
aversive (unpleasant) consequences; (b) how soon after the act punishment is administered; (c) the strength of the behaviour to be punished;
(d) the availability of alternative responses; (e) the extent to which the
opposite or desired behaviour is rewarded. To be effective, therefore,
the punishment must be sufficiently harsh and last long enough to be
experienced by the child as unpleasant and thus to be avoided. However,
it must not last so long that the child simply gets used to it. It must be
administered on each occasion during or immediately after the undesired
behaviour occurs. It is more effective to administer punishment as soon
as the undesirable behaviour begins than to wait until it is completed. Well-
established undesirable behaviours warrant greater intensity and frequency
of punishment. To achieve better results, concurrent and more desirable
alternative responses should be available and frequently reinforced. Threats
of punishment do not, on the whole, affect behaviour.

Practice

1 Use punishment as a last resort, infrequently and never as the only method for controlling or eliminating undesirable behaviour.
2 Specify clearly the acceptable and unacceptable behaviours and the consequences of each; when a child is punished, the reasons should be given so that a cause-and-effect connection can be established.
3 Punish the undesirable behaviour as soon as it appears; do not wait until the behaviour has run its course.
4 Provide desirable and attainable alternatives for the child.
5 While punishing undesirable behaviour, reinforce desirable behaviour.
6 Be consistent in punishing behaviour; inconsistencies may enhance and strengthen undesirable behaviour.

Application Punishment may be used to suppress or eliminate almost any undesirable behaviour from early childhood onwards. Its limitations lie in its unpleasantness and the hurt it inflicts by an adult on a weaker child. It also has a number of seriously undesirable side-effects which include generalisation from the undesirable to similar desirable behaviours (for example, punishing aggression may also suppress other, socially desirable assertiveness); it leads to avoidance of the punishing adult and so removes or reduces the opportunity for positive reinforcement of the child; it may lead to a range of undesirable avoidance reactions, such as lying to avoid detection, or running away; and it provides an aggressive model which may be imitated by the child.

To avoid these undesirable side-effects the punishable behaviour must be clearly identified and explained. Even in the case of a verbally handicapped child, the explanations eventually become a secondary and more permanent source of learning. The unintended consequences may also be avoided in the case of older children, if the boundaries of punishment are subjected to some sort of contractual agreement and the punishing agent is still seen, on balance, as a source of general reward and positive reinforcement.

Though this is not an advantage, punishment is so deeply ingrained in the social control of undesirable behaviour that it is usually accepted without difficulty, provided the delicate balance between necessary harshness and even more necessary fairness is maintained. In a behaviour therapy context, punishment is best used to modify those behaviours which place the child or others in immediate danger and where a quick result is urgently required. It should not be used as a first resort, nor when it is clearly failing to achieve the desired end rapidly. Its continued application will simply immunise the child against effective future use.

Relaxation training

Relaxation training refers to a set of procedures used to train a child to produce a state of muscle relaxation through the alternate tensing and relaxing of specific muscle groups.

How does it work?   The sympathetic branch of the autonomic nervous system prepares the body for 'fight or flight' in 'dangerous' situations. It is also responsible for such anxiety symptoms as palpitations, faster breathing, increased sweating, feelings of nausea, sickness, mental confusion and panic. The parasympathetic branch of the autonomic nervous system, however, is antagonistic to the sympathetic branch and limits its effects, thereby encouraging anxiety reduction. Relaxation helps the parasympathetic nervous system to restore 'balance' without unwanted side-effects; it is, in short, an antidote to tension and anxiety.

Practice

1   Use a quiet, warm, slightly darkened room; ask the child to loosen any tight clothing and lie back on chair, bed or couch, with his legs uncrossed and his arms allowed to flop by his side.
2   Go through all the major muscle groups in turn, asking the child alternately to tense and relax his muscles to recognise the difference between tension and relaxation; the session starts with the muscles of the hands and arms: 'For about five seconds, clench both fists as tightly as you can and feel the tension; now relax them completely; note the difference between tension and relaxation; continue to relax the muscles of your hands and arms for about a minute.'
3   Apply this procedure to the muscles of the upper arms (biceps and triceps), the neck, shoulders, eyes and eyebrows, forehead and scalp, mouth, jaw, throat, chest, stomach, legs and hips, in turn.
4   Demonstrate to the child the above tensing/relaxing sequences.
5   Because tension is frequently shown most in the face, you may usefully engage in massaging the child's face through gentle 'kneading' or circular motions, starting with the chin and ending on the forehead.

Alternatively, and specifically for older children, other variants of the technique are useful, namely:

Breathing: 'I want to teach you how to breathe, so you can become relaxed and cool. Take a deep breath, as though you are playing a trumpet. Let out your breath very slowly. Do it very slowly and, as you breathe out, make a sound like "Aaah" – see how long you can keep it going. Let's do it again, really slowly. Fill your lungs and breathe out very slowly. It is helpful when you run or ride your bike or swim. Just breathe away tension. Breathing slowly, just like you have done, is the key to relaxation.

As you breathe out, let out a sigh of relief. Then you feel better, and you can keep calm and relaxed. Use this whenever you feel tense or uptight.'

Self-sentences: 'The idea is to tell yourself some sentences which will help to calm you. What can you tell yourself? (Allow child to respond.) OK. Good. Let's use these two (three, etc.). No worries. Everything is calm. I'm in control and relaxed. These are your special sentences for keeping control.'

Application   This technique is useful with problems in which the anxiety component plays a large part, or in settings in which a child requires to behave calmly and retain control, such as hyperactivity and insomnia; and with generalised or specific anxiety-producing situations and phobias (as part of systematic desensitisation). In short, relaxation training can be used to treat any condition in which the elimination of anxiety is required. It may be used in conjunction with any other techniques. It has no limitations or disadvantages, although it is often most useful as part of a more complex treatment package. Its virtues lie in its simplicity, pleasantness, low cost, wide-ranging applicability and the sense of trust and well-being it creates in the child.

Self-management

Self-management is a process by which an individual learns to regulate his own behaviour in a manner maximally rewarding or satisfying. For example, a diabetic child is trained to regulate his own food intake in the correct manner, administer insulin injections and take other protective measures as necessary.

How does it work?   Self-management techniques rely on the following rationale: (1) Many behaviours are inaccessible for modification by anyone but the client (for example, sexual behaviour or timidity); they can produce discomfort not apparent to an observer. The participation of the child as his own agent of change is essential in such cases. (2) Maladaptive behaviours are often inextricably bound up with one's own reactions to them and, importantly, with such processes as thinking, engaging in fantasy, imagining and planning. These processes are inaccessible to direct observation; but because children think, and their thoughts influence their behaviour, responsibility and answerability for thoughts and related action can be reasonably shifted towards the child. (3) Modification of behaviour often proves onerous and occasionally unpleasant. In seeking or being given assistance, many children are motivated not so much to change as to avoid censure, threats of discomforts, preferably without altering their behaviour or life-style. Convincing the child that behaviour change is desirable, feasible and worthwhile is a basic motivational requirement and constitutes a critical target in self-management. (4) The usefulness of a modification programme lies not only in removing situation-specific problems or enhancing situation-specific defects; it should also include a whole repertoire of generalisable skills, such as coping responses and wide-ranging behavioural rules, for common use, so that the child can avoid or handle future problems more effectively than in the past.

Practice   For effective self-management programmes, the following steps should be taken:

1   Conduct a behavioural analysis, including a description of specific problem behaviours, positive and negative reinforcers appropriate to the child's abilities and the resources in the child's environment that can be enlisted to aid behavioural change.
2   Observe and monitor target behaviour.
3   Develop a plan for behaviour change, negotiate a contract that includes specific goals to be achieved, over what time period and the consequences of achieving them, as well as the methods for producing the behaviour change.
4   Discuss with the child the underlying assumptions and rationale of the techniques to be used.
5   Model and/or role-play the desired behaviours.
6   Frequently verify progress (or lack of it); provide feedback and if necessary redraft the contract.
7   Record and inspect qualitative and quantitative data describing change(s); extend the behaviour to different areas and situations.
8   Continue to discuss the child's self-reinforcement programme in terms of his views (what he feels and thinks about it) about his behaviour.
9   Encourage demonstrations of new, overt learned behaviour in his natural environment, with discussion and correction as required.
10   Frequently verbalise the procedures, their effects, how they are achieved and the extent to which they can be applied in the future.
11   Support the child as he assumes more personal responsibility for his behaviour; emphasise that *he* is doing it, not the technique or the therapist.
12   Summarise what has been learned in the change process and prepare the child for transferring his new knowledge and skills to future situations.

Application   Self-management strategies are particularly useful for dealing with any behaviours which reflect self-control deficits. Systematic feedback coupled with positive reinforcement increases self-control. Extensive evidence suggests that individuals, even seriously problematic ones, have a much greater capacity for self-management than has been assumed.

The limitation of the technique lies in its high skill content and the time it takes to set up, implement and monitor a self-management programme. It is also not very productive with younger children or those who have extensive and severe problems. Its attractions lie in its wide applicability; the fact that it treats the child as a powerful agent of change; and its ethical probity. It can also be used in conjunction with many other techniques. Its chief merit lies in that it is directed towards the ultimate therapeutic goal of individual choice and self-direction.

Shaping

Shaping refers to the process of gradually transforming a deficient piece of behaviour into one that is adequate. For example, a child who refuses to make eye contact is gradually conditioned so as to maintain it.

How does it work? Shaping is achieved through response differentiation. An already existing but deficient behaviour is built up by increments until it reaches the desired level and standard. New behaviours are produced by reinforcing improved variants of existing behaviours while simultaneously withdrawing rewards from all other levels. The application of reinforcement to new behaviour(s) systematically to move the behaviour in a planned direction is termed 'shaping'. Each new and reinforced form of behaviour is an approximation to the target behaviour. In the example of eye contact, the child is first reinforced for turning his head in the right direction; then reinforced for looking up; then for looking at the treatment agent and eventually only for making and maintaining eye contact.

Practice

1   Observe the child whose behavioural repertoire is considered deficient. Identify the antecedent and consequent events associated with observed high-frequency behaviour that you want to change. Note the variability in form, strength and duration of available responses.
2   Based on 1, decide whether a desired end behaviour can be differentiated out of existing behaviours and, if so, what a first approximation to the target behaviour could be.
3   Establish criteria for the first approximation; tend towards low and achievable criteria.
4   Arrange the environment to maximise the probability of a behaviour occurring.
5   Differentially reinforce (with powerful reinforcers, such as food, praise and affection) variants of the behaviour that are crude approximations

of the ultimate target behaviour; withdraw reinforcements from variants that are incompatible with the target behaviour.

6   Observe the shift in the direction of the target behaviour: if repeated reinforcement fails to establish a response, criteria may need to be lowered; when a behaviour is established at a high, stable rate, shift criteria in the direction of the desired response; alter reinforcement schedules from constant and predictable to variable, so as to strengthen behaviour.

7   Use verbal or gestural cues or instructions at all stages in conjunction with the reward, to elicit the behaviour being shaped.

Application   The technique can be used to enhance academic (reading, writing, paying attention) and social (talking, approaching and co-operating) skills and complex motor behaviour. It is often used to establish single behaviours, such as feeding oneself or making eye contact. When the goal is the establishment of behaviour sequences (such as getting dressed, toileting and setting a table) it is used in conjunction with chaining. Its power is substantially increased, as with other forms of behaviour therapy, when used in conjunction with verbal encouragement and cues. It can be used in a wide range of settings to ameliorate deficient behaviours with children of all ages and intellectual levels. It is, indeed, the basis of much ordinary social training. Both the principles and the practice are sufficiently simple to be usable by a wide range of workers in any number of settings. Because it is largely reward-based and aimed at building up competence, it does not present any important ethical difficulties.

Systematic desensitisation

Systematic desensitisation is a procedure used to reduce or eliminate phobias and anxiety by the gradual presentation of the anxiety-eliciting stimuli while the client is in a state of relaxation. A child who is so terrified of dogs that he will not go to school is, for example, treated by this technique until he is able to pat a dog, however gingerly, without swooning in terror.

How does it work?   The basic assumption of this technique is that anxiety and fear (for example, of heights, water or the dark) are learned or conditioned. They can be inhibited by an activity that is antagonistic to (or 'acts against') the fear response. The most typical target of treatment in the use of this technique is anxiety, and the response frequently substituted for it is relaxation and calmness. Since fear and calmness are mutually exclusive, if the child can be taught to be calm in the presence of fearful objects or experiences, he will not be afraid. In other words, he will be 'counter-conditioned' or 'desensitised'. The principle underlying the desensitisation process is termed 'reciprocal inhibition'.

Practice Systematic desensitisation is accomplished by exposing the child in small, graduated steps to the feared situation while he is performing the activity that is antagonistic to anxiety. The gradual exposure to the fear can occur either in the child's fantasy (where he is asked to imagine being in various fear-related situations) or in real life. The procedure comprises the following steps:

1 Train the child in deep muscle relaxation.
2 Take a detailed history, particularly in relation to those aspects and circumstances which arouse the greatest fear; for example, for a child with a pathological fear of wasps, such features may turn out to be size (the larger the wasp, the greater the anxiety), proximity (the nearer the wasp, the more fear evoked); these dimensions provide the basis for constructing a list of graded items, known as an 'anxiety hierarchy'.
3 Write the items on separate slips of paper and ask the child to rank them in order from the least to the most fear-arousing.
4 Keep the child relaxed throughout this initial interview; ensure he remembers how to induce deep relaxation.
5 Ask the child to relax in the way he has learned, to imagine a neutral scene and to signal by raising his index finger whenever he is disturbed.
6 Ask him to imagine the weakest fear-arousing item on the list; if his relaxation remains unimpaired, proceed to the next item, asking the child to imagine it, explore around it and mull it over, reassuring him and telling him to indicate when he is anxious.
7 At the slightest sign of anxiety, ask the child to stop imagining the stimulus and relax deeply, including thinking about something pleasant.
8 Repeat the two steps above until the list is exhausted and the child can freely imagine the fearful stimulus and remain relaxed about it.
9 Maintain deep relaxation throughout, lest the process of treatment itself becomes anxiety-provoking.
10 Never end a session with an anxiety item; it is best to end the session with the presentation of an 'easy' item.

The duration of scene presentations is a matter of a few seconds for the first few items, and the time is gradually increased as the treatment progresses; the availability of time and endurance of the child are the main determining factors. The interval between the presentation of individual scenes is again a matter of a few seconds when no disturbance is indicated;

otherwise, the duration is determined by the time taken to reinduce deep relaxation. Desensitisation is usually carried out in imagination, but the technique can be adapted to accommodate graded retraining *in vivo* – that is, desensitisation under relaxation with the presentation of real stimuli such as pictures, sounds and real creatures.

Application   Systematic desensitisation is useful in helping children overcome their fear of situations, other people, animals or objects. It is especially useful in the treatment of phobias or any circumstances producing irrational, heightened anxiety. Its limitations lie in the high skill content and the difficulties of maintaining motivation for continued treatment; with some children, the 'fear' masks a deeper problem. The advantage of the technique lies in its sharp focus, rigour and ability to produce fast results. It is one of the 'purest' applications of psychological principles to alleviating a problem. For phobias it is almost the only effective treatment.

Time out (TO)

Time out entails removal of the child (for a short period of time) from a reinforcing situation to decrease or eliminate an undesirable behaviour. The two major TO procedures are:

(a) removing the reinforcer from the individual;
(b) removing the individual from the reinforcing system.

For example, an obstreperous child is sent to his room and thus deprived of company or other desirable experiences.

How does it work?   TO procedures assume that a decrease in a particular behaviour can be achieved if the opportunity to obtain positive reinforcement is denied to the child. Just as the presence of reinforcement increases the probability of recurrence of a behaviour, so removal of (or from) the reinforcement reduces the probability of recurrence.

Practice

1 Identify the positive reinforcement maintaining the behaviour.
2 Ensure that the interruption of positive reinforcement is immediate and precisely contingent on the behaviour you want to change (the target behaviour).
3 Determine the duration the child will spend in TO on the basis of practical, administrative and behavioural criteria. In general a child should remain in TO until he has lost several reinforcement opportunities, and the undesirable behaviour has stopped.

4 Provide explanation to establish cause-and-effect relationships.
5 Ensure that the time out does not give access to other or more desirable rewards; guard against manipulation by the child. For example, the teacher who removes an aggressive child from a class and subject which the child dislikes is not depriving the child of pleasure. Also, if the child is sent to the headteacher's office and becomes the target of attention, undesirable behaviour may increase rather than decrease. Being sent off the football field when this is the child's favourite game is a more suitable example of the purpose of TO.

Application   TO is a useful technique to help eliminate acting-out behaviour (such as fighting), problems of self-control (such as temper tantrums and overactivity), obscene behaviour or language, excessive talking, 'clowning' in a formal setting and general misbehaviours. It has no serious disadvantages apart from requiring care in administration. Its advantages lie in its quickness, relatively low cost, 'obvious' legitimacy and reasonable effectiveness. It is best used with children who are well enough motivated towards the therapist and the activity setting to mind the deprivation and indignity.

Token economy (TE)

Token economy is a system of reinforcement in which tokens (chips, marks, paper money, points and so on) are administered as the immediate reward and later exchanged for more substantial, tangible 'back-up' reinforcers. It is a set of procedures for systematically using tokens to reinforce desired behaviour until that behaviour is established. It is a good and more effective alternative to attempting to manage or shape children's behaviour through fear of punishment. It is not a magic technique to be used to replace more usual methods of care and control; rather, it is an adjunct to be used to increase the range of measures concerned with improving the behaviour of children. For example, a child is rewarded whenever he acts in a helpful manner, until his helpfulness becomes habitual and not dependent on the rewards.

How does it work?   The content and quality of behaviour is largely determined by its consequences. Those consequences that strengthen responding are called reinforcers. Token economy systems, therefore, rely on behavioural principles, the most important of which are: (1) *reinforcement* – responses followed closely in time by rewards tend to be strengthened; (2) *establishing conditioned reinforcers* – initially neutral stimuli repeatedly followed by reinforcers tend to acquire reinforcing properties; (3) *differential reinforcement* in discrimination learning – a response repeatedly reinforced in the presence of one kind of stimulus but not in another will occur more often in the future when that stimulus is presented; (4) *prompting* – to elicit a previously acquired response to occur in a new situation, previously acquired signals must be used as prompts and then gradually faded out; (5) *shaping* – new behaviour can be promoted by reinforcing only ever-closer approximation to the desired behaviour.

Practice   In simple terms, operating a TE consists of a predetermined behaviour, followed by a token reinforcer, which is exchanged for a 'back-up' reinforcer in a systematic process.

1   Specify behaviours which will earn tokens in a way that will be straightforward to determine if they have occurred or not; ensure that:
   • behaviours are specified quantitatively and qualitatively;
   • bits of behaviour-earning reinforcers are gradually increased;
   • schedules of reinforcement are varied appropriately;
   • the number of tokens available for each behaviour is specified;
   • individual daily targets are set;
   • opportunities and circumstances for the occurrence of required behaviours are maximised;
   • children are kept informed about their progress.
2   Determine what the back-up reinforcers will be. These may include activities (such as watching TV), locations (under more or less restrictive conditions), consumables (such as sweets), possessions (such as a bike), use of time (doing nothing) and so on.
3   Avoid monotony by introducing new items frequently; crucially, determine what is reinforcing for each individual child; this may be facilitated by using a reinforcement survey schedule.
4   Determine the 'tariff' (that is, 'earnings and prices'). Specify how much each item in the 'menu' will cost. Display in a prominent position. Adjust 'earnings and prices' appropriate to your 'inflation rate'.
5   Decide what to use as tokens. Durable plastic discs or foreign coins are useful, especially if various denominations can be obtained.
6   Decide how you propose to fade out the tokens so that their place is taken by cues in the natural environment.
7   Verbally praise behaviour immediately before awarding tokens.
8   Avoid haggling about tokens.
9   Keep a book, monitoring exactly the flow of tokens for each behaviour for each child.
10   Make the exchange times (paying in of tokens and 'buying' back-ups) important and open events, laced with praise, feedback and a generally positive air. Establish two kinds of aversive (unpleasant) consequences (contingencies) to cover misbehaviour: (a) define behaviours that warrant a 'fine' and specify the size of the fine,

ensuring that the child knows the rules; (b) 'time out' from positive reinforcement consists of placing the child in a dull, quiet room for a specified period – this prevents the child earning tokens, but should be used only for highly disruptive behaviour such as tantrums or fighting.
11 If you deal with groups, tie up their rewards with those of individual members. This requires that all group members meet a certain criterion to earn tokens, which serves to foster group cohesion.
12 Maintain accurate 'bank' and balance books and monitor the token flow.

Application   Token economies have proved useful with mentally handi-capped disruptive children, delinquents, drug addicts, problem drinkers, stutterers and those with serious language and mental disorders. Specific behaviours which respond favourably to TE include academic performance, disruptive behaviour, over-compliant behaviour, speech, social behaviour, problems of self-concept, self-care procedures, personal chores, attending and participating in activities, language skills, on-task behaviour, adaptive behaviours, over- and undereating, smoking and many others.

The limitations of TE lie in the time taken to set it up and the effort needed to maintain consistency and alertness in response to changing 'market conditions'. Also, TE is often used to control behaviour (that is, 'manage' it) rather than to achieve long-term amelioration. Because of difficulties in satisfactory transition to natural reinforcers, the long-term impact of TE is suspect.

The advantages of TE lie in its wide-ranging applicability both to problems and to children's conditions and capacities. Because it is reward based, it creates a positive atmosphere which brings other benefits. The provision of verbal feedback and praise further encourages self-control. It is one of the best positive methods of achieving behavioural boundary-setting and ameliorating otherwise intractable problems. It is best used in conjunction with cognitive, talking and group therapy techniques.

Further reading

Bandura, A. (1969) *Principles of Behaviour Modification*. London: Holt, Rinehart & Winston.
Blackham, G.J. and Silberman, A. *Modification of Child and Adolescent Behavior*, 2nd edn. Belmont, CA.: Wadsworth.
Browning, R.M. and Stoves, D.O. (1971) *Behavior Modification in Child Treatment*. Chicago: Aldine.
Gardner, W.I. (1971) *Behaviour Modification in Mental Retardation*. London: University of London Press.
Graziano, A.M. (ed.) (1971) *Behavior Therapy with Children*. New York: Aldine.
Graziano, A.M. and Mooney, K. (1984) *Children and Behavior Therapy*. New York: Aldine.
Herbert, M. (1981) *Behavioural Treatment of Problem Children: A Practice Manual*. London: Academic Press.

Hudson, B.L. and Macdonald, G.M. (1986) *Behavioural Social Work*. London: Macmillan.

Karoly, P. and Kanfer, F.H. (eds) (1982) *Self-Management and Behavior Change*. New York: Pergamon.

Kazdin, A.E. (1977) *The Token Economy: A Review and Evaluation*. New York: Plenum.

Lazarus, A.A. (1972) *Behavior Therapy and Beyond*. New York: McGraw-Hill.

Leitenberg, H. (ed.) (1976) *Handbook of Behavior Modification and Behavior Therapy*. Englewood Cliffs, NJ: Prentice-Hall.

Lovaas, O.I. and Bucher, B.D. (eds) (1974) *Perspectives in Behavior Modification with Deviant Children*. Englewood Cliffs, NJ: Prentice-Hall.

McAuley, R. and McAuley, P. (1977) *Child Behavioural Problems: An Empirical Approach in Management*. London: Macmillan.

Meichenbaum, D.H. (1979) 'Teaching children self-control', in B.B. Lahey and A.E. Kazdin (eds), *Advances in Clinical Child Psychology*, Vol. 2. New York: Plenum.

Pavlov, I.P. (1927) *Conditioned Reflexes: An Investigation of the Physiological Activity of the Cerebral Cortex*. London: Oxford University Press.

Russo, D.C. and Varri, J.W. (eds) (1982) *Behavioral Pediatrics: Research and Practice*. New York: Plenum.

Skinner, B.F. (1938) *The Behavior of Organisms: An Experimental Analysis*. New York: Appleton Century Crofts.

Skinner, B.F. (1953) *Science and Human Behavior*. New York: Macmillan.

Stumphauser, J.S. (ed.) (1973) *Behavior Therapy with Delinquents*. Springfield, IL: Charles C. Thomas.

Thomas, E.J. (ed.) (1974) *Behavior Modification Procedure – a Sourcebook*. New York: Aldine.

Vargas, J.S. (1972) *Writing Worthwhile Behavioral Objectives*. New York: Harper & Row.

Walker, H.M. and Buckley, N.K. (1974) *Token Reinforcement Techniques*. Eugene, OR: EB Press.

Watson, D.L. and Tharp, R.G. (1972) *Self-Directed Behavior: Self-Modification for Personal Adjustment*. Belmont, CA: Brooks/Cole.

Watson, L.S. (1972) *How to Use Behavior Modification in Mentally Retarded Autistic Children*. Libertyville, IL: BMT.

Yates, A.J. (1970) *Behavior Therapy*. New York: Wiley.

Yule, W. (1985) 'Behavioural approaches', in M. Rutter and L. Hersov (eds), *Child and Adolescent Psychiatry*. Oxford: Blackwell.

Yule, W. and Carr, J. (eds) (1982) *Behaviour Modification for the Mentally Handicapped*. London: Croom Helm.

9

Cognitive Methods

All human beings must acquire certain skills to achieve successful maturity. In developed societies, chief among these are scholastic and social skills. Both are essentially the results of successful problem-solving. The child learns little by little about reading, writing and arithmetic. Similarly he learns about appropriate modes of relating to a wide diversity of people – from his age mates to adults. Deficiencies and distortions in these skills give rise to difficulties which demand intervention. The chief method of intervention is cognitive, not least because the intellect and its individual modes of operation are the chief medium of human problem-solving. In this chapter we shall deal with feedback, certain basic forms of remedial education and social skills training. A number of other techniques, currently called cognitive (such as rational-emotive therapy), are treated elsewhere in this book.

Theoretical basis

'Cognition' is a broad term referring to all modes of knowing, perceiving, remembering, imagining, thinking, reasoning and evaluating. Cognitions embrace both the content of thoughts and the processes involved in problem-solving. Thus, how a person perceives and processes external events, how he utilises the mechanisms and content of memory and recall and how he develops problem-solving attitudes and strategies are all aspects of cognition. These forms of cognition are transformed into statements, codes and labels – that is, some sort of language. The communicative aspects of language are important, and so the relationships between cognition and inner language (or self-verbalisation) are extensive and intimate.

A major limiting factor in all problem-solving, whether scholastic or social, is intellectual potential. Clearly, a mentally handicapped youngster is less able to assimilate complex cognitive skills than a bright one. The role of intellectual potential in problem-solving is influenced by cognitive structure (or 'schemata'), namely inner statements, codes and labels, which tend to be relatively enduring characteristics of a person's thinking style. They reflect the influences of prior experiences, which are recalled, organised and utilised through different schemata. Such a concept can be used to explain why different youngsters react differently to similar situations, and sometimes behave less competently than may be expected purely from their intellectual potential.

Theoretically, human beings are regarded as problem-solving organisms who require the basic ability to solve problems. Although most children acquire social and scholastic skills to an acceptable level, some do not. This is because of either limited intellectual potential or faulty socialisation, including poor teaching. Whatever the cause, the child's problem-solving ability has to be engaged, faults corrected and new skills inculcated.

Cognitive learning, so far as is known, is no different from other forms of learning, based as they all are on association, outcome and recognition of correct sequences of behaviour, whether scholastic or social. To this extent, cognitive techniques are involved in almost all other forms of treatment. The exceptions are perhaps surgery and medication, where the child is a wholly passive subject and is not required to participate in the treatment. Otherwise, we cannot think of *any* treatment in which the child does not have to form concepts and acquire appropriate responses to diverse demands.

The difference between cognitive and other treatments, therefore, lies in the emphasis on correct problem-solving through the guided application of intelligence as well as the areas of difficulty.

Status

The cognitive approach to maladaptive behaviour differs from other psychological approaches which may overemphasise motivational, adaptational or analytical concepts whose empirical validation remains elusive. The main ideas in cognitive treatments are testable, and many have been supported by empirical evidence. The approach does not assume that a well-adjusted individual is one who invariably thinks logically and solves problems rationally. What it recognises is that to identify, understand and correct deficient scholastic and social skills a child must focus on the problem, recognise what is required of him, acquire rules to apply and have feedback on his performance. The therapist's task is therefore to identify the deficit, enable the child to attend to the problems and give opportunity for the acquisition of general rules of responding, reinforcing the acquired competence until a response pattern appropriate to the child's intellectual potential has been achieved would not be considered maladaptive.

As with all other treatments, the more extensive and serious the deficit, the more specialised will be the treatment requirements. However, compared with other specialisms, remedial teachers are reasonably easy to find, and their services are generally available through normal, and free, educational provision. Social skills training, though also potentially highly specialised, draws on competencies which most 'ordinary' people, such as parents and main grade staffs of specialist services, possess.

The advantages of cognitive treatments are so great and essential to the adequate social functioning of children that they cannot be overestimated. Over and above this, these treatments do not demand any specialised equipment and are wholly benevolent and thus free of ethical constraints.

Feedback

Originally used in engineering, a feedback refers to information about how your own objective is being achieved or how a system is operating at a particular time. In psychology, and specifically in learning theory and practice, feedback refers to information about the correctness, appropriateness or inappropriateness of an action or response which acts as a basis for future action. For example, a star chart for a child's dry nights is seen as 'feedback' by the cognitive theorist and as 'reinforcement' by the learning theorist. In practice, however, the chart fulfils the criteria for both feedback and reinforcement. In general terms, then, feedback (which can assume a multiplicity of forms such as nodding/shaking of the head, brief comments, points and star charts) refers to any information about the functioning or performance of an individual that leads to a modification of that individual's behaviour. It is an inescapable part of all social interaction.

How does it work? Feedback, in itself or in terms of its effect, relies on the fundamental learning principle that we learn to perform a particular response or modify existing responses when we receive appropriate information about the consequences of that response. Thus, in the light of feedback, we either (a) continue to respond as before or (b) make appropriate changes. Such changes may alter any one or combination of beliefs, feelings or behavioural intentions.

Practice For optimum effect, feedback should be immediate and direct, and preferably positive and constructive in content. It often assumes the form of a verbal comment accompanied by a gesture. For example, successful completion of a task or an appropriate action should be instantly recognised by a 'well done' or 'thank you' or 'that was splendid', possibly reinforced with a show of delight and a pat on the back. Conversely, an undesirable behaviour may warrant an instant censure, such as 'that kind of behaviour won't do', a scowl, wagging of the finger and suchlike. Feedback may also be through star charts, graphs or other visual displays.

Feedback itself should be supplemented by corrective advice, such as 'now, this is how it is done', perhaps supported by a demonstration. Video, either live or in recorded form, is particularly helpful with older children for both demonstration and discussion. 'Mirroring' or mimicking a child is also useful as instant feedback, particularly in such cases as tics, grimaces, twitches or peculiar body postures. The more serious behaviours warrant concerted feedback by a whole group, preferably encompassing both adults and peers.

Application   Any behaviour which is deemed 'unacceptable' or 'undesirable' can respond to feedback. Its very commonness makes it difficult to separate from normal social behaviour and to utilise as a specific treatment tool. Since a knowledge of results or performance is essential to the development, improvement and modification of a skill, feedback can be used in a wide variety of situations where learning is essential. It has the advantage of being a 'normal' way of dealing with interactions; and since it focuses on observable behaviour, rather than the person, it can be detailed and specific. It is a wholly individualised measure, which rarely requires unusual resources and can be used by non-professionals with equal productiveness. It has no ethical costs.

Remedial education

The term 'remedial' implies that something is to be remedied. In this sense, it is useful to separate it from the term 'special' education. Under the Education Act 1981, formal procedures apply to those whose special educational needs arise from complex or severe learning difficulties which require provision additional to, or different from, facilities or resources generally available within mainstream education. Normal resources include special units or remedial classes for pupils. In the context of this book, therefore, remedial education refers to provision whose aim is to enable the child to return to appropriate mainstream curriculum or, for those above the age of statutory education, to possess at least the basic attainments that will allow them to cope with the appropriate demands of daily living, such as reading notices and calculating wages. Remedial and special education are among the best developed of the non-physical approaches to children's problems. The diagnostic and assessment systems utilised are complex and on the whole reliable. The field of remedial education is vast and primarily of specialist interest – somewhat akin to medication and surgery. Our treatment will therefore be only brief.

Theoretical basis
This issue can be approached from several angles, depending on the particular deficit to be remedied and its 'causes' as revealed through skilled assessment. Each of the three major 'Rs' – reading, writing (or spelling) and arithmetic – is acquired by relatively 'normal' children in the course of their 'normal' schooling. Some children, however, show deficits and aberrations due to factors ranging from mental handicap to specific disorders

of memory or visuo-motor co-ordination. The specific remedial treatment used will seek to tackle the roots and manifestations of the disorder. The general theoretical view is that cognitive deficits and distortions can be remedied, given appropriate stimulation, shaping and reinforcement of new and appropriate learning. In this respect, remedial education has no unifying and exclusive theoretical basis but, rather, one that draws on the general theory of treatment, on the one hand, and the theoretical view of the disorder, on the other.

Status
As borne out by the huge and pervasive provision of remedial education in all schools, this approach commands the widest possible support among politicians, administrators, professionals and parents. Everyone recognises that a child with deficient scholastic skills is socially handicapped, and so considerable effort is made to remedy the deficiency.

In principle, remedial education has no major disadvantages, apart from its relatively high cost, its demand for specialist practitioners and the possible stigmatising effects of its practice. The advantages should, however, outweigh these. If successful, remedial education ameliorates a deficit or corrects a distortion of learning and enables the child, at least cognitively, to partake fully of social opportunities.

General guidelines for practice
When attempting to teach basic literary or numeracy skills using remedial programmes, the following general principles should be borne in mind:

1 Adopt a systematic, practicable approach.
2 Present a learning task by breaking down the stages involved into discretely graded steps.
3 Ensure that each step falls well within the child's capabilities so that you increase the probability that he will succeed.
4 Provide reward and reinforcement, not only by making the individual 'feel good' but by also providing positive praise and encouragement.
5 Provide the individual with the means to chart his own progress, thus giving visual evidence of improvement.
6 Encourage active involvement in tasks, thus increasing attention.
7 Teach to the point of over-learning; that is, teach and revise beyond the point at which an idea or skill is initially grasped.

Reading
In planning treatment for reading difficulties, it is important to be realistic regarding what the future potential of any individual child might be. Clearly a very dull child would not be expected to reach the same level of proficiency in the subject as a bright one, and the implications of this statement are that a full intellectual assessment by a qualified psychologist is a prerequisite

of a good remedial reading programme for an individual child. All too often children are judged in the classroom by their verbal skills, and those children with retarded verbal development may often be mistakenly labelled as 'dull', even though may be above average at practical tasks.

1 The whole-word or 'look–say' approach

How does it work? This approach requires a good visual memory, since the child has to memorise different word 'shapes'. Most people have the capacity to do this, but for some children this complex task becomes particularly difficult, due to either poor innate capacity or deficient teaching.

Practice Teach a chosen number of 'keywords', perhaps 500 in number, to give the child a basic sight vocabularly together with some self-confidence. Basic words needed by children of infant age (4 to 8) at primary school are available in systematic programmes such as 'Starter Word Splits', a programme of over 250 words in a game form. Keywords needed in the junior age (8 to 11) are available in such programmes as 'Junior Word Splits', which feature more than 500 words.

Application The whole-word approach is not suitable for children with poor visual memory, who will probably learn more quickly via a phonic approach. Initial progress, however, is quicker with the whole-word approach. This results in increased confidence and feelings of success at an earlier stage, which is rewarding to the child and thus encourages further progress.

2 The phonic approach

This is a method for proving the raw materials for reading – the sounds of vowels and consonants. Learning the sounds of letters and syllables allows the individual subsequently to recognise and pronounce whole words of varying length and complexity.

How does it work? The phonic approach depends upon auditory skills, since words are built up systematically through syllables and letters, which are 'blended' together using 'pure' letter sounds as the basis.

Practice Teach the 'pure' letter sounds of the alphabet, without the 'u' (voiced) sound. Thus, or example, in the word 'span', the letter sounds 's' and 'p' have no voiced component, being made by blowing through the tongue (s) and with the lips only (p). This makes blending the sounds much easier and avoids the results sounding 'su-pu-a-ner', which sounds nothing like the word 'span'.

Computer letter-recognition games aid learning of the basic alphabet letter, as for example 'Alpha Chopper', where a helicopter is steered on to letters which are then lifted out, and 'Snakebiter', where they are hunted with a snake.

Application The phonic approach can be used with all ages of children. There are three main categories of usage: (a) with infant children as the main teaching method; (b) with infant children as a complement to the whole-word approach; (c) with older children who have found difficulty with the whole-word approach.

The phonic approach gives slower initial progress. It depends upon auditory skills and is therefore not suitable for children with poor auditory memory. It requires particularly high-level skills, specially where the child may have serious mental handicap or speech disorders. On the other hand, once mastery of phonic analysis and blending has been achieved, phonic approaches may be more effective, especially in dealing with longer words.

3 'Miscue analysis'
Miscue analysis is a recent approach to the teaching of reading and stresses the importance of making reading more meaningful.

How does it work? This approach enables the child to recognise words in context, utilising a variety of signals for this purpose. Because of emphasis on 'meaning', the child can use past experience and probability of word experiences to identify words.

Practice Teach the child to learn to pick up cues from the context of the reading matter, such that the word shape can be matched to a guessed probability of what the word actually is. Make sure the material is interesting and well graded to encourage the child to persevere.

Application This is a useful approach in all stages of reading, from basic words and sentences to quite complex ones. It requires more thought than mechanistic approaches, and slow learners may experience some difficulty with it as a result. On the other hand, it teaches both reading and comprehension, whereas other approaches may not develop the two skills together, often teaching reading at the expense of comprehension. It can also be used by parents and non-expert helpers.

Spelling
Spelling problems are often overlooked, and emphasis may be placed upon reading and number work, to the apparent exclusion of spelling. An analysis of the nature of the spelling errors will often point the way to the type of treatment approach required. If words are phonically constructed

yet incorrect (for example, 'benefishal') the remedial task is likely to prove reasonably straightforward. In other cases, however, specific difficulties of a 'dyslexic' nature are evident, where letters are frequently written down in incorrect order (for example, 'paln' for 'plan') or, rarely, where complete 'mirror writing' of a word or words is evident. In such cases a full psychological assessment is recommended in order that the appropriate treatment can be prescribed.

1   The phonic approach
This approach is based on pairing sounds with shapes or letters and words.

How does it work?   The phonic approach is systematic in building up words from their component parts. Letters and syllables are blended together to form words. Phonic rules are applied, since only a small proportion of English words are totally irregular.

Practice   Teach letter sounds, then teach sounds which result from common combinations of letters, such as 'th' (consonant digraphs). From these letters and sounds construct syllables. Finally, build words. To avoid confusion of letters such as 'b', 'a', 'd', 'p', and 'q', add a visual cue to the letter. ('Pictograms', available commercially, use this approach whereby letters are made into picture cues. Thus, for example, the letter 's' is made into a snake, and so on.) Because spelling can be intrinsically boring, colourful and stimulating new computer programs have much to commend them. Many such programs are now available. Examples are 'Starspell', for older children, which is a practice program covering 800 words and 115 spelling rules. For younger children the 'Spellbound' series provides four simpler spelling programs featuring irregular or difficult spellings.

Application   Materials are available or can be constructed right across the age and ability range. The phonic approach can successfully be used only with fairly regular words; rules become complex if the approach is to be applied to most words. Initial progress is slow. It is not suitable as a method for children with a poor auditory memory. It is also not particularly useful with specific spelling problems.

2   The whole-word approach
How does it work?   The whole-word approach relies on visual imagery and memory to enable the child to recreate whole word shapes from memory, by memorising each discrete word as an entity in itself. Although this may require the separate memorising of some thousands of words, innate abilities enable many children to cope successfully with this approach.

Practice   Use visual reinforcement. Present the words repeatedly in visual form, for example in stories, in much the same way as in reading. Computer programs are available, as for the phonic approach, 1 above.

Application   The approach is applicable to the full age and ability range. This approach to spelling is less systematic then the phonic approach. It may result in a faster rate of learning to read, but at the expense of progress in spelling. It is not recommended for children with poor visual memory. Communication skills may initially develop more quickly than by the whole-word approach. This results in greater early confidence and possible faster subsequent progress.

Mathematics

The subject of remedial mathematics has received less attention regarding specific techniques than either reading or spelling. Because numerical skills tend to be cumulative, children who have missed out on previous steps cannot learn new skills. Thus, children who have not mastered the basic skills will become increasingly retarded and in need of remedial help.

Motivation is often a key problem in the area of number work, because the subject-matter is intrinsically dull. The use of bright and stimulating materials is often a key factor to success, and this has in recent years been realized, with several successful remedial approaches being available in both book and computer program form. 'Discovery' methods are increasingly being used.

How does it work?   Since mathematics is a cumulative skill, more so than reading, remedial programmes often have to return to quite basic concepts. They must therefore be carefully sequenced and structured, based on a good profile of the child's skills.

Practice   Ascertain the starting baseline, then gradually teach successive, sequenced skills in the basic operations. Provide immediate corrective feedback to encourage learning and to prevent errors from turning into a habit. As new skills are learned, consolidate previously learned skills and review them to ensure retention. There are a number of good computer programs and educational 'toys' available which, linked with other ever-popular computer games, can make learning mathematics a pleasurable activity.

Application   Remedial programmes are available for all age ranges and ability levels. Older children can become averse to mathematics because its cumulative nature often results in long-term failure. For this reason, it is important to detect problems and give help early on.

The only disadvantages lie in the use of unimaginative, mechanistic remedial help in number work, which can easily have the effect of reinforcing past failures. Depending on the level of deficit, it may require specialist help. The advantages lie in imparting competence to the child, even though, with increasing computerisation, basic numerical ability has lost much of its earlier significance for many (particularly low-achieving) children.

Social skills training (SST)

Many children experience serious problems in basic social interactions. Poor social skills can lead to major difficulties in social living and result in a child's isolation and stigmatisation as 'odd' and socially disordered. Such children often present and experience other major difficulties which point to the need for treatment of deficient or inappropriate social skills. These may include an inability to make or refuse requests, to initiate and carry on conversations, to relate to a person of the opposite sex, to stand up for one's own rights and numerous other essential elements in effective social living.

Theoretical basis

During the last two decades there has been a burgeoning of interest in social skills and their role in social adaptation. For a long time success in social functioning was held to be the result of socioeconomic and personality variables. The work of Argyle and his colleagues and extensive subsequent research have shown that, while these factors are important, social know-how is a significant factor in gaining social success.

This research has suggested that, as the term implies, social 'skills' are learned patterns of successfully manipulating the environment to the person's greatest benefit without negative consequences for others. They comprise specific verbal and non-verbal behaviours towards other people and in particular social settings. These are interactive and are affected both by the child's condition and by characteristics of the environment. The theoretical basis of social learning is thus similar to that of other skill acquisition, as in school subjects. The difference lies in greater emphasis on social experiences, learning from models and situational feedback. Indeed, basic components of SST comprise *instruction and discussion, modelling, practice and role-play, feedback, social reinforcement* and the adoption of appropriate techniques for *generalising* the learned skills to a wider social setting. We have covered a number of these components in other chapters. This, by itself, shows that SST is not a 'pure' treatment modality, but it is all the stronger for this meshing with other approaches. In this section we shall cover only instruction, practice and generalisation techniques.

Status

This mode of intervention with disordered children has now become an enormously influential element in any serious treatment programme. This is because of the self-evident difficulties of such children in getting on with their peers and adults and drawing the greatest benefit from social interactions. SST can be and has been used with the full age range, from 4-year-olds to young adults. Whilst the forms and content of SST change with each age group, the importance and the structure of the procedures remain constant.

As with all other forms of clinical intervention, careful assessment is necessary to identify the areas of deficit, taking care that maladaptive responses to stress and institutional rules are not interpreted as social skill deficits. SST has no inherent disadvantages, in either resource or ethical terms, any more than other general issues we have earlier considered. Although a skilled specialist may be more efficient in gaining the desired ends, all the techniques are regularly practised by good parents (even if implicitly) and can be easily acquired by a wide range of professionals. This is, indeed, one of the main reasons for the increasing popularity of SST.

General guidelines for practice

1 Determine the size of your group; the more serious the difficulties, the smaller the group size should be.
2 Decide whether you want a co-trainer; younger children often need an additional person to keep them in order and attentive to the training.
3 Choose a quiet area free from a lot of traffic and distractions; arrange the seating in a horseshoe shape so that everyone can see and hear the others.
4 Define carefully the problem situation to be remedied and specify what the expected goals for the participants and the session are to be.
5 Be encouraging and generous in suggesting alternative ways a problem may be tackled.
6 Give plenty of practice, but ensure that the sessions are not so frequent as to bore the participating.
7 Give plenty of positive feedback, particularly in the early stages, even when the gains are small.
8 Use as many games as possible during each session to create variety, give practice and make the point in a way particularly effective to children.
9 Train other workers and parents to give the child opportunities for practice and reinforcement in identified skill areas; the wider the range of such practice opportunities, the more durable the outcome of SST is likely to be.

The role of discussion

Rather than telling the children about skills deficits, it is often preferable to encourage them to discuss the general topic to be covered during the session.

How does it work?   Before a child can remedy a deficit, he needs to be aware of it. Discussion allows this to happen, from a variety of perspectives, as other group members air their views and recount experiences.

Practice

1 Define the problem area and draw out each child's experiences.
2 Draw out and discuss what are better alternatives and why.
3 Encourage the children to identify and voice alternative and better coping skills in a problem area.
4 Emphasise the better consequences for the children if they behave differently; get them to debate the issues and the consequences among themselves; a 'debating society' with rewards for the best discussions, the use of a 'jury' and similar games would help make the point.

Application   Discussion is a most common medium of communication. Everyone can do it; it does not need any specialised resources, costs nothing and, if properly conducted, can be a most potent element in any behaviour change. It is, however, rarely enough by itself to bring about such change.

Practice
The ability to use and repeat a newly learned skill is an essential element in ensuring that the learning does not disappear.

How does it work?   Simply by providing an opportunity for repeating the same stimulus-response sequence, with appropriate rewards, ensuring that the learning is well established.

Practice

1 Set targets for each group member.
2 Ensure that these targets reflect both the severity of the deficit and the child's ability to reach the target.
3 Praise and otherwise reward successful achievement initially every time and, as the habit is established, only periodically.
4 Gradually make the targets more difficult until the goal skill is reached (see also shaping).
5 Encourage the children to set their own targets at even higher levels, if appropriate.

Application   Practice is an essential element in every form of learning across the age group from potty training to complex social situations. As such it is a universally accepted element, devoid of any special cost or ethical considerations. As a specific technique it is particularly suitable for the simplest skills, such as eye contact, head movements and standing still while talking.

Generalisation
Generalisation is not so much a technique as the ultimate aim of all education and treatment – that it should be applicable in a range of other settings and with other people than the trainer and other social skills trainees.

How does it work? The processes are complex, involving cognitive, emotional and behavioural elements. Essentially, significant elements of the stimulus and response are gradually changed, in small enough measures to keep them recognisable. The change, however, is big enough to demand some readjustment. If the learning is rewarded or is otherwise successful, the essential cause-and-effect relationship is learned in a most 'general' form applicable to a wide variety of settings.

Practice   Much generalisation occurs naturally, because of normal variations in the SST setting, the trainer and the child. There are, however, a number of measures which will enhance it:

1   Teach behaviours that occur or are required in the child's normal environment; this will ensure that normally available social rewards will support the child's behaviour.
2   Adopt a variety of training styles and conditions to ensure that the child is not conditioned to just a few stimuli. A degree of 'controlled chaos' is desirable, but only when the child is interested enough to continue attending and has gained the rudiments of the skill.
3   Encourage multiplicity of responses and emphasise that more than one response is appropriate in any situation; give practice in these and reward as appropriate.
4   Gradually phase out your rewards and allow 'natural' and social rewards (such as a smile, saying 'well done' and other forms of approbation) to take over.
5   Use other people, such as peers and parents, in the training; the greater the diversity of trainers, the more generalised the learning will be.
6   Encourage the child to monitor and evaluate his own performance; reward accurate self-appraisals and teach the child self-reinforcement: 'I did that well' (see also rational-emotive therapy in Chapter 10). The more 'real life' the practice of newly acquired skills is, the better they will generalise.

Application   Generalisation should be the planned aim of every training session, irrespective of the problem being tackled or the age and ability of the children. Without it, all the training effort is at best short-lived and at worst a total waste.

Further reading

Alberti, R.E. and Emmons, M.L. (1970) *Your Perfect Right: A Guide to Assertive Behaviour*. London: Impact.

Argyle, M. (1969) *Social Interaction*. London: Methuen.

Argyle, M. (ed.) (1981) *Social Skills and Work*. London: Methuen.

Argyle, M., Furnham, A. and Graham, J.A. (1980) *Social Situations*. London: Cambridge University Press.

Barton, L. and Tomlinson, S. (1981) *Special Education: Policy, Practice and Social Issues*. London: Harper & Row.

Brennan, W. (1982) *Changing Special Education*. Milton Keynes: Open University Press.

Clarke, M.M. (1974) *Teaching Left-Handed Children*. London: University of London Press.

Cooper, C.L. (1981) *Improving Interpersonal Relations*. Aldershot: Gower.

Ellis, R. and Whittington, D. (1981) *A Guide to Social Skills Training*. London: Croom Helm.

Feldman, P. and Orford, J. (eds) (1980) *Psychological Problems: The Social Context*. Chichester: Wiley.

Gillingham, A. and Stillman, B. (1940) *Remedial Training for Children with Specific Disability in Reading, Spelling and Penmanship*. New York: Sackett & Wilhelms. Also subsequent manual by S. Childs.

Gittleman, R. (1983) 'Treatment of reading disorders', in M. Rutter (ed.), *Developmental Neuropsychiatry*. New York: Guilford Press.

Goodman, Y. (1972) *Reading Miscue Inventory: Procedure for Diagnosis and Evaluation*. New York: Macmillan.

Haring, N. and Brown, L. (eds) (1976) *Teaching Severely/Profoundly Handicapped Individuals*. New York: Grune & Stratton.

Hollin, C.R. and Trower, P. (eds) (1986) *Handbook of Social Skills Training*, Vol. 2. Oxford: Pergamon.

Jastak J. and Jastak S. (1978) *Wide Range Achievement Test: Manual*. Wilmington, DE: Jastak Associates.

Johnson, D.J. and Myklebust, H. (1967) *Learning Disabilities: Educational Principles and Practice*. New York: Grune & Stratton.

Kazdin, A.E. (1975) *Behavior Modification in Applied Settings*. Homewood, IL: Dorsey Press.

Kendall, P.C. and Holton, S.D. (eds) (1981) *Assessment Strategies for Cognitive-Behavioral Interventions*. New York: Academic Press.

Lange, A. and Jakubowski, P. (1976) *Responsible Assertive Behavior*. Champaign, IL: Research Press.

Levis, D.J. (ed.) (1970) *Learning Approaches to Therapeutic Behavior Change*. Chicago: Aldine.

Melnik, A. and Merritt, J. (eds) (1972) *Reading Today and Tomorrow*. London: University of London Press.

Michelson, L., Sugai, D.P., Wood, R.P. and Kazdin, A.E. (1983) *Social Skills Assessment and Training with Children*. New York: Plenum.

Moyle, D. (1976) *The Teaching of Reading*. London: Ward Lock.

Ollendick, T.H. and Hersen, M. (1979) 'Social skills training for juvenile delinquents', *Behavior Research and Therapy*, 17.

Pellegrini, D.S. (1985) 'Training in social problem solving', in M. Rutter and L. Hersov (eds), *Child and Adolescent Psychiatry*. Oxford: Blackwell.

Peters, M. (1967) *Spelling: Caught or Taught?* London: Routledge & Kegan Paul.

Priestley, P., McGuire, J., Flegg, D., Hemsley, V. and Welham, D. (1978) *Social Skills and Personal Problem Solving: A Handbook of Methods*. London: Tavistock.

Reid, J.F. (eds.) (1973) *Reading Problems and Practices*. London: Ward Lock.

Spivack, G. and Shure, M.B. (1976) *The Problem Solving Approach to Adjustment*. San Francisco: Jossey Bass.

Swann, W. (ed.) (1981) *The Practice of Special Education*. Oxford: Blackwell/Open University Press.

Trower, P., Bryant, B. and Argyle, M. (1978) *Social Skills and Mental Health*. London: Methuen.

Wallace, G. and McLoughlin, J.A. (1979) *Learning Disabilities: Concepts and Characteristics*, 2nd edn. Colombo, OH: Charles E. Merrill.

Wendon, L. (1986) *The Pictogram System*. Barton, Camb.: Pictogram Supplies.

Wine, J.D. and Smye, M.D. (eds) (1981) *Social Competence*. New York: Guilford Press.

Wolman, B. (ed.) (1972) *Manual of Child Psychopathology*. New York: McGraw-Hill.

Youniss, J. (1980) *Parents and Peers in Social Development*. Chicago: University of Chicago Press.

Yule, W. and Carr, J. (eds) (1981) *Behaviour Modification for the Mentally Handicapped*. London: Croom Helm.

10
Talking Therapies

Talking is probably the most pervasive medium of treatment. It is also most lay people's idea of what goes on between a therapist and the client. Indeed, the term 'therapist', used by itself, usually pigeonholes the treatment agent as being a practitioner of talking therapies. In this chapter we present five prominent techniques of talking therapy: *counselling*; *Gestalt therapy*; *psychoanalytic therapy*; *rational-emotive therapy*; and *transactional analysis*.

Talking is also the most common, yet unique, human activity, particularly as a means of communicating and reducing distress. Though the activity increases in range and complexity as a person gets older, it is not unreasonable to use it as a means of understanding and resolving children's difficulties.

The major influence on talking therapies comes from the ideas of Sigmund Freud, who saw the root of problems as unresolved conflicts in the course of a child's development. Though he was himself less interested in children than in adults, some of his most significant followers, such as Melanie Klein, Karen Horney and Anna Freud, did their major work on children's problems. Despite the heated debates amongst practitioners regarding the finer points of their theories, their similarities vastly exceed their differences. Practitioners of these therapies also believe, in varying degrees, in a particular view of personality, the existence of the 'unconscious' and 'defence mechanisms' as a means of coping with anxiety (with the arguable exception of rational-emotive therapists). These defences are believed to become manifest in various maladaptive responses that can be cleared up only through certain forms of 'psychotherapy' – principally free association, dream analysis, analysis of defences and, more in the case of children, playing, drawing and story-telling.

Distilled to their essence, talking therapies use focused conversation as a medium of helping. The client's verbal and non-verbal communications are interpreted as a means of understanding the source of difficulty. The interpretation is intended to provide insights which are meant to unravel and resolve conflicts and thereby lead to better-adjusted behaviour. This is why talking therapies are also sometimes referred to as 'insight therapies'. This approach is meant to apply to the widest range of difficulties, from asthma and bed-wetting to antisocial behaviour and phobias.

Psychotherapy has been in high fashion since the beginning of this century. However, other forms of talking therapy, under a broadly Freudian influence, also began to proliferate in the 1960s and 1970s due to the growth of humanistic psychology, which emphasised the integrity and primacy of the client – even a disordered child – and asserted that talking through problems was the only ethical and effective way of resolving 'psychological' problems.

Theoretical basis

Given the diversity of talking therapies, it is not possible to find a common theoretical basis which stands up to rigorous scrutiny. Furthermore, proponents of each school or method of practice claim distinctions for their own brand of treatment which are more evident in argument than in practice. We would not, therefore, pretend that our brief description of the theoretical bases of talking therapies would be wholly acceptable to specialists.

The core element of all talking therapies is that, in the context of a 'therapeutic relationship', talking can be used to give the client insight into his difficulties and thereby help overcome them. The 'therapeutic relationship' possesses particular characteristics, of which the most important are: regard for the child; consistency between what the therapist says and what he does; genuineness towards the child; and empathy. It takes time to build up such a relationship, which, though sensitive to change, must be robust enough to withstand crises in the circumstances of the child and pressures on the therapeutic relationship.

A particular difficulty, to be noted in passing, is the emphasis in the literature on the term 'client' – that is, someone who seeks help. However, in reality, children with difficulties rarely *seek* help but rather have forms of help suggested for or imposed upon them. This can potentially distort the therapeutic relationship. Of necessity, the relationship between the child and the therapist is not an equal one; the latter has, in every important sense, more power and is frequently required by other people than the child to engage in therapy. For these reasons, although in talking therapies no less effort is made to establish a therapeutic relationship with the child, it is recognised that this relationship may not conform to the ideal in all respects.

So much emphasis has been laid, both in theoretical writings and in empirical research, on therapeutic relationships that the relationship itself has been held to be at least as important as the use of talking, which is its medium. Clearly language has to be used in the process of establishing the relationship, which in turn will affect what language is used and how either party will interpret and respond to it. This raises logical problems of interpreting the special roles of language and relationship in achieving treatment. In turn, this also has implications for the practice of talking therapy. However, because the issue has not been satisfactorily analysed and does not in any case seem unduly to hinder practitioners, we shall also leave it alone.

The special characteristic of therapeutic language is that it is the medium for enabling the (child) clients to gain 'insight' into the motives, beliefs and other underlying 'causes' of their actions. Inadequate understanding of these causes is believed to underlie disordered behaviour (including such problems as bed-wetting and asthma). Greater insight will therefore increase control over the behaviour and thus lead to improvement in the problem condition. Unlike behaviour therapy, emphasis is less on active behaviour change than on uncovering hidden causes and thereby *facilitating* change.

Focus on 'insight' is central to all talking therapies, even though it is given different degrees of emphasis in the different techniques. Furthermore, all these therapies, with the exception of rational-emotive therapy, are based on an implicit acceptance of psychodynamic views of personality which derive, more or less, from the work of Freud. Rational-emotive therapy is regarded by its proponents as either a 'cognitive' or a behaviour modification technique. Its theoretical basis lies predominantly in experimental psychology, and unlike the other talking therapy techniques it has a firm empirical foundation and good-quality evidence to support it.

The differing emphases in the techniques might warn against lumping them together as 'talking therapies'. Also, these and other techniques have often been promoted as 'group therapies'. This is particularly true of counselling and transactional analysis. However, we believe that bringing them together in the present chapter is legitimate on the grounds that talking is the main medium of treatment. Although their power may be enhanced by the addition of group pressure, the main emphasis in the writings (either theoretically or practically) is on verbal interaction rather than on group pressure.

Status

We comment in each section on the theoretical status and practice issues related to each technique. Suffice it to say here that in general the popularity and widespread use of the general method is in inverse ratio to satisfactory empirical evidence of its effectiveness with troubled children. Empirical paucity does not seem to deter continued use of these techniques, particularly with troubled adolescents. This reflects the central importance of 'talking' as a means of sharing and alleviating problems. It also reflects the spirit of the times in demanding that we should attempt to 'understand' children's problems in a gentle and non-authoritarian manner. Of all methods of treatment, talking is the easiest and least 'mechanistic', and it is therefore not surprising that it should command such widespread usage.

Counselling

Counselling is much more a collection of approaches than a specific technique, in the sense illustrated in the other chapters. The core of the approach is an attempt to help people explore their own problems as an aid to resolving them. For example, a youngster has been referred for help after a homosexual episode has come to light. He is distressed and confused about whether his preferences are primarily homosexual or heterosexual. The counsellor provides the trusting relationship in the context of which the youngster can explore his sexual identity and come to an acceptable resolution of his conflict. The most widely known and practised form of counselling is associated with the name of Carl Rogers.

As is evident even from the above example, counselling is an activity that is undertaken in a wide variety of settings and in the context of many other relationships than those of 'counsellor' and child. It is legitimately practised by parents, teachers, family friends and even the child's peers, though they may not be aware that their activity would be termed 'counselling'.

Such counselling can take place either with an individual child, as in the example, or with groups of children who have similar difficulties. The choice is determined by the availability of resources, the specificity of the problem and the evaluation of effort needed to establish the appropriate therapeutic rapport with a potentially diverse group.

Group counselling is more often practised where the objective is to facilitate *client development*. So, for example, a teacher may run a session during which he explores with the class the difficulties of growing up, the conflicts that have to be resolved and choices that have to be made. To do this he will impart and elicit information, attempt to teach problem-solving skills, draw attention to possible consequences and generally enable and enhance social growth.

Individual counselling, on the other hand, is more often undertaken in *crises*. Although the above steps are still taken, they are more finely tuned to the problems of the individual child in his particular context, rather than to a general problem and general modes of resolution. We shall deal with group counselling in Chapter 11.

How does it work? As has already been indicated, counselling is more an orientation and a cluster of approaches than a specific technique. There is no unitary theoretical or explanatory system underlying counselling approaches. The place of theory is taken by a series of therapeutic prescriptions which are more in the nature of humanistic and moral exhortations than technical guidelines. The idea is that such prescriptions will help create a therapeutic relationship which is self-evidently an aid to the open sharing of problems, unimpeded exploration of alternative solutions and eventual healthy decision-making. The core requirements of such therapeutic relationships are considered to be the following:

1   *Unconditional acceptance* of the child, in a positive, affirmative manner; the counsellor conveys to the child that whatever his problem, he is a decent person entitled to respect and dignity which the counsellor recognises and, by the way he treats the child, confirms. Another view of the requirement is that the counsellor must be 'non-judgemental' in terms of assigning 'good' and 'bad' labels to the child and his behaviour.

2   *Openness* demands that the counsellor should allow the child to perceive his feelings and attitudes and should not leave the child in a state of uncertainty concerning these.

3   *Genuineness* of the counsellor's attitudes and values in the exchanges with the child is a prerequisite of the child responding in a similar manner; this demands the removal of any 'professional façade' or setting oneself up as 'expert'.

4   *Empathy* enables the child to recognise that the counsellor understands him and his problems, and the resolutions reached are therefore likely to be valid and relevant.

It is not evident from the above – or, indeed, from the voluminous writing on the subject – what particular processes take place in achieving the therapeutic change. The issue becomes further complicated when we recognise that there are different 'schools' of counselling, each using a different theoretical focus. Some of these, such as psychoanalytic therapy and transactional analysis, are techniques in their own right and will be discussed later. However, there is a tendency in the literature to lump them all together as 'schools of counselling', in which case the subject-matter becomes so all-inclusive as to be vacuous.

In so far as talking is used as the main medium of counselling, some practitioners emphasise the need to understand past events in resolving present conflicts (psychoanalytic); the need to understand the accumulation of pain and distress and the means of discharging them (affective); the particular styles of thinking as a source of personal difficulty (cognitive); maladaptive learning as a source of personal difficulties (behavioural); and the essential goodness of human beings and the need to force personal potential towards optimal fulfilment (client-centred therapy). Of these, perhaps the last one, associated with the name of Carl Rogers, is the one most frequently thought of as 'counselling'.

Client-centred counselling is based on Rogers's premise that the best forms of human communication and learning take place where people are not anxious about the other party's approval. The therapist should therefore create an accepting, non-directive atmosphere in which the client can explore the alternatives open to him in any difficulty. There is greater emphasis on 'healthy psychological growth' than on problem-solving. The counsellor's role is to enable the client to discover the best path to personal satisfaction and 'self-actualisation'. The therapeutic relationship enables the individual gradually to open up and explore the difficulties that are blocking his satisfactory adjustment. As these are mirrored back to the individual without moral judgement, he is gradually able to accept them and move towards greater self-fulfilment. From massively emphasising the 'non-directive' nature of counselling, Rogers now accepts that no therapeutic relationship is ever 'non-directive' or value free, but rather that these aspects are subjugated to the interests of the client.

Practice There is great reluctance on the part of writers on this subject to specify guidelines for practice. It seems that each individual counsellor should practise the core requirements of acceptance, openness, genuineness and empathy in a personally 'authentic' manner. However, in so far as practice guidelines can be discerned, they are practised in the following sequence:

1 Identify the reasons for referral (whether by the child or by others).
2 Explain the 'helping relationship' and how it works.
3 Create a permissive climate in which the child is capable of talking without fear of adverse consequences.
4 Rehearse back to the child the problems identified, attempting to discover their wider ramifications and the child's perception of these and their impact.
5 Enable the child, through reinforcing the positive relationship, to explore alternative approaches to the difficulty being experienced and their probable costs and benefits.
6 If necessary, guide the child's thinking towards the implications of different solutions to the problem.
7 Encourage positive feelings in the child about himself; label, elaborate and return these feelings as an aid to the child's search for self-fulfilment; encourage self-acceptance.
8 Enable the child to remain focused on the problems at issue and draw attention to partial and incomplete analyses.
9 Evolve, if necessary, a self-directed action programme by and for the child; encourage positive action.
10 Begin to wean the child from therapeutic dependence towards autonomous, self-fulfilling action.

Application Counselling can be used as a means of alleviating developmental problems of adolescence (such as sexual identity and conflict with parents) as well as crises (such as solvent abuse and anorexia). It is more useful with those problems over which the child's beliefs and feelings have some impact, and this is clearly age-related. Older adolescents, with their greater verbal facility and emerging ideas of what they want to be, are more likely than smaller children to benefit from the therapeutic exploration of their feelings and options with a trustworthy adult.

Considerable work in this area has largely failed to find either a clear theoretical basis or much empirical support for the efficacy of 'formal' counselling, particularly with children. As our previous frequent use of the term 'client' rather than 'child' has indicated, much of the work in this area has been done with volunteering adults rather than children. Children have usually little coherent idea of what they are or should be, and notions of 'self-actualisation' undergo profound change during adolescent development.

The approach is, by its generality and time-consumingness, more appropriate to mild than severe problems. The latter, being more urgent, cannot await the uncertain outcome of such slow dawning of insight, and demands more immediate results. The use of counselling is also questionable in the case of those children who express the wish to persist with their unacceptable behaviour – as happens, for example, in the earlier stages of drug taking, sexual promiscuity and criminal behaviour, where need and potential for effective help are greatest. Simply to repeat that these children must be helped to find their 'essential goodness' ignores the impact of external factors which lock the children on to a self-defeating course of action.

Associated with this is the fact that most children are referred for help, rather than seeking it voluntarily. This projects the counsellor as part of a probably coercive system, which comes into serious conflict with such essential tenets of counselling as acceptance and genuineness. The counsellor may be accepting of and non-judgemental towards the child, but he cannot adopt the same attitude to the child's behaviour. Furthermore, in practice, many even full-time counsellors can be seen to balk at total personal 'openness' and dropping of their professional garb. They consider that it is possible to be 'client centred' (indeed, which treatment is not?) and therapeutic without adopting Rogers's full panoply of core requirements.

For these reasons, full-blown and prolonged (of necessity) Rogerian counselling cannot sensibly be the sole treatment for serious problems in children. Indeed, it appears too imbued with much of the 'permissive' 'growth' preoccupation of the 1960s and 1970s, mainly in the United States, to offer anything but a generally benevolent orientation to treating problem children.

On the other hand, counselling is, in fact, a much more common form of helping than is realised. Despite attempts at mystification by various practitioners, there is no mystery in the process of helping children to explore their difficulties, considering alternatives and resolving them. Because it is such a familiar activity, it can be used to considerable advantage in a wide variety of settings, where the use of more formal techniques may be deemed inappropriate. It can be used to augment other treatments where it may enhance their impact.

Because it is a common practice, almost everyone who can encourage a child to talk can be taught the skills for more focused counselling using the above guidelines, without any grandiose training programmes, even though such programmes are available and may be useful. There is much writing on the subject that is intelligible to ordinary people. A further advantage is that counselling does not require any specialised equipment or setting. Given the benevolent attitude of the counsellor to the child, the use of the technique is free from ethical objections and can therefore be practised without close supervision. Perhaps for these reasons it is almost impossible to imagine any setting or form of child treatment in which counselling does not take place.

Gestalt therapy

Gestalt means 'whole' or 'configuration', and Gestalt therapy emphasises the need for integration of thought, feeling and action as a means of maintaining the whole person. It highlights awareness, the 'whole self' being in touch with itself and the external environment, recognising those aspects of self which are 'blocked out' in order to cope better with problems of living.

Like client-centred counselling, Gestalt therapy is also based on an essentially positive view of human potential and the belief that open expressiveness helps achieve it. As developed by Perls, it is predominantly a group activity, where the use of insight-giving talk augments group pressure to bring about therapeutic change.

How does it work?   The basic assumption of Gestalt therapy is that we bring our own feelings and needs to any new situation we meet. This is where it is associated with Lewin's 'Gestalt psychology', in which people are seen to interpret ambiguous events or incomplete experiences in ways which have personal significance. Thus, in Gestalt therapy a person is said to bring his past experiences to bear on the present and distort it in unhelpful ways. However, unlike psychoanalytic therapy, Gestalt therapists do not spend time delving into the past but, rather, concentrate on the central significance of 'here and now' as determinants of behaviour.

The theoretical basis consists of the assumptions that (1) the patient/client is asked to express what he is feeling at that moment; (2) his attention is drawn to hesitations and other signs that he is blocking his expressions, and he is encouraged to explore other ways of expressing himself; (3) he is encouraged to voice the changes that he desires in himself; and thus (4) through increased awareness enhance his capacity for living. The core belief here is that 'awareness of the whole' is critical to proper functioning, and an attempt should be made to achieve it. When achieved, awareness is thought to be therapeutic – a person who is aware of his feelings and sensations is able to put them into perspective and achieve a chance for the better.

As is evident, the above collection of premises hardly amounts to a rigorous theory. However, as with other humanistic perspectives, this does not bother the practitioners, who, on the contrary, seem to adopt an anti-theory approach. Unlike other humanistic perspectives, however, Gestalt therapy uses a wide range of standard procedures, although latter-day proponents insist that the Gestalt attitude of openness to experience and the spontaneous creativity of 'letting it all hang out' are more important. The most important of the standard procedures are:

1   Insistence on personal experience and the translation of 'it' into 'I'. So instead of 'It would be nice to give up glue sniffing', the statement becomes 'I would like to give up. . .' This insistence demands that the client accepts 'ownership' and responsibility for his actions and desires.
2   The 'hot seat' allows the person to project himself to a whole group and to receive feedback, often critical, about his behaviour.
3   The 'empty-chair' procedure asks the client to place some disliked person or experience in an empty chair opposite him and talk to the person/experience as if it were alive. So a child who hates his father is asked to put the father in the chair and talk to him about his feelings 'here and now'. The child is then asked to adopt the position of the father and speak to himself as an adversary.
4   'Opposites' demand that the client behave in an opposite way to what he feels. So an aggressive child may be asked to behave as if he were a gentle one.
5   'Dreamwork' entails interpreting dreams, not as the key to the 'unconscious', but rather as a reporting of symbols which represent alienated and disliked portions of the self. So a child who has dreams of being chased by a terrifying dog is asked to imagine becoming that dog and to say why it is chasing the child, thus giving clues to the child's anxieties about unacceptable features of himself.

In Gestalt therapy considerable attention is paid to non-verbal cues that might alert the therapist to stresses which are not being voiced. Thus, changes in tone of voice, posture, eye contact and similar events are used to open up sources of self-awareness and emotional blocking.

All the above procedures and many others are regarded as means of sorting out 'unfinished business'. According to Perls, we conduct much of our lives with unresolved conflict which we take into new experiences, and thus distort them. Sorting out 'unfinished business' should release energies which can be used to enhance creative living.

Practice In view of the 'creative variability' of Gestalt procedures, it is difficult to specify steps which the therapist has to follow. The procedures used are based on the therapist's perception of the client and his stage of treatment. All Gestalt interventions, however, contain the following elements:

1 Ascertain 'where the child is at' by asking questions about what he thinks, feels and senses about himself and significant portions of his experience 'now'.
2 'Confront' the child with his behaviour and its implications.
3 Give feedback regarding the behaviour; interpret it and say what it represents by way of unfinished business.
4 Encourage the child to interpret his own behaviour by using some of the procedures outlined above.
5 As the client improves, encourage increasing self-reliance and acceptance of responsibility for his own behaviour.
6 Throughout, remain cautious about the limitations of the child and about possible damage through over-zealous 'confronting' and interpreting.

Application Given the demands of Gestalt therapy on personal insight, expressive ability and comprehension of life experiences, it is clear that it is at best suitable for older adolescents. Such adolescents must have considerable resilience to withstand the onslaught of their own opened-up feelings and the interpretations that may flow from them. As such, Gestalt therapy does not seem to be particularly suitable for seriously disordered children who are incapable of setting and observing behavioural boundaries based on the perception of personal feelings and 'unfinished business'.

Despite it fame and good fortune, Gestalt therapy is devoid of any coherent, rigorous, testable theoretical foundation. As with other similar approaches, it has relied much more on the benevolent impact of some practitioners, and the use of evocative language, than on empirical evidence to underpin its continued use.

Given the material available, almost anybody could set up shop to carry out Gestalt therapy. Apart from preferred accreditation through working with other therapists, no other qualification seems necessary. Yet, unless the practitioner is very sensitive to possible damage and centrally concerned with the impact of his practice, he is likely to do substantial damage by opening up feelings which neither he nor the child can channel or control. Given the current low demands on therapist accountability and monitoring of competence, we would consider Gestalt procedures to be best used as part of a wider array of carefully controlled therapeutic interventions.

On the other hand, Gestalt therapy has made a significant impact by drawing attention to 'here and now' and 'unfinished business' in the genesis of problems. Its procedures aimed at drawing out feelings and expressing them are significant additions to the other techniques available for gaining access to such material. Carefully used, in conjunction with other techniques, they can be of considerable help.

Psychoanalytic therapy

Psychoanalysis is perhaps the most famous of all therapies for children. Its fame is more widespread than its usage, however, certainly in a pure form by a duly accredited psychoanalyst. The ideas of psychoanalysis are so deeply embedded in both the culture and the training of people who work with children that, regardless of their orientation, almost all make use of it in a more or less explicit way.

Psychoanalytic therapy (or psychoanalysis for short) is a form of treatment which employs the patient's statements as a means of drawing out hidden motives and anxieties to illuminate the causes of current conflicts and difficulties. When insight has been achieved, work can begin on replacing the 'pathological' manifestations with more adaptive responses. For example, a child's fire setting may be traced to infantile experiences of being separated from his mother, feeling cold and lonely in her absence and wanting to conjure her up again through a recreation of heat and excitement in later life. Though to the 'uninitiated' this may sound far-fetched, the literature is strewn with case histories which place infinitely more demand on credibility.

Psychoanalysis is associated with the name of Sigmund Freud. Although certain of his followers, such as Melanie Klein, Karen Horney, Erik Erikson, Anna Freud and Donald Winnicott, have made significant contributions to analytic child therapy, their work arguably complements that of Freud, and their particular emphases are of interest mainly to specialists. There are also other significant contributors to this field, such as Jung and Sullivan, with quite different emphases in both theory and practice. We shall, however, not refer to these because theirs are tangential and (judging by the literature) infrequently used therapies.

How does it work?   Through his work with neurotics and other people with psychological problems, Freud came to believe that personality developed sequentially and was eventually made up of three parts: *id, ego* and *superego*. The 'id' is present at birth and is the source of all psychological (or, in his terms, 'psychic') energy operating at the 'unconscious' or ('below-awareness') level of the mind. The main force within the id is 'libido', which is primarily sexual. The id operates through the 'pleasure principle', seeking immediate (sexual) gratification; when this is not forthcoming, tension is built up which must be released through either actual acts (such as eating) or symbolic ones (such as fantasy). The id is seen as an ever-hungry life force which is only marginally tamed by the social growth.

'Ego', the second part of personality, which operates at the conscious level, is the result of a child's growing-up experiences. Through these experiences the child learns of demands of living in a real (as opposed to fantasy) world which will not allow him to do just what he wants when he wants it. The ego therefore operates through the 'reality principle'.

The 'superego' emerges from the child's recognition of the concepts of 'right and wrong' when he is old enough to realise that fulfilling certain desires (such as possessing his mother) is likely to have unpleasant outcomes (such as being castrated).

The three parts of personality are in constant turmoil, each seeking individual fulfilment that comes into conflict with the others. This creates the 'psychodynamics' of personality, which is also the name by which a whole spectrum of therapeutic techniques is known.

Many of the pressures, frustrations and conflicts which give rise to anxiety are dealt with by the child at the conscious level. However, some of the conflicts (for example, love for one's father and wanting to get rid of him at the same time) are so disturbing that they cannot be dealt with at the conscious level. They are therefore 'repressed' (that is, pushed beneath consciousness) but continue in turmoil so that eventually they give rise to other problems, such as delinquent or self-destructive behaviour. Conflict of motives gives rise to anxiety. To cope with the anxiety, the person develops a number of 'defence mechanisms'. Freud proposes a long list of defences, such as denial, projection, rationalisation, reaction-formation, regression and sublimation, to illustrate the many forms that deviant adaptation to anxiety and conflict can take. There is hardly any aspect or form of behaviour which is immune from such adaptation. Almost every form of talking therapy, implicitly or otherwise, makes use of these concepts.

Psychoanalytic therapy seeks to unravel the tangle of past conflicts which have caused the current difficulties. This is done through a process of releasing and interpreting the old, repressed material.

Practice Next to physical medicine, psychoanalysis is the oldest formal treatment of children's clinical disorders. Unlike physical medicine, however, psychoanalysis has always demanded a strict and wholesale acceptance of Freud's ideas and 'authorised' variations. For this reason, the only 'proper' psychoanalysts were deemed to be medically qualified people who had undergone personal analysis in the course of being trained to practise it. Both these ideas have been somewhat modified over time, so that 'lay analysts' are now tolerated, and 'brief analysis' is used for training the majority of those who are not going to practise psychoanalysis full-time.

The implication is that psychoanalysis may be practised only by 'properly trained' and accredited analysts, very much as is the case with medicine.

Although posing as an analyst without appropriate training will not get the practitioner into trouble with the law (as it would with unaccredited medical practice), it is unlikely to be professionally acceptable. For this reason it would be improper to set out guidelines for the practice of psychoanalysis in this book. The following outline of main techniques is intended to inform those dealing with children who may be subject to analysis and wish to know what the treatment entails.

The most important technique for unravelling the conflicting motives and anxieties of the past is *free association*. The child, reclining on a couch, is encouraged to say anything that comes into his head. Earlier sessions are taken up with building the *therapeutic relationship* through which the child is encouraged to trust the analyst so as not to censor the ideas and feelings that come into his head. Particular emphasis is laid on not being afraid or ashamed of coming out with material which the child has had to suppress in the past. Each set of ideas and feelings is traced back to earlier ones until the child reaches his earliest memories. Some people have, indeed, claimed that the child has anxiety-provoking memories of being in the womb and experiencing a rude shock during delivery. The attempt is therefore made to take the child back to *relive* his unpleasant experiences and, through that, to purge the festering anxieties underlying his difficulties.

Dreams provide what Freud regarded as the 'royal road to the uncon-scious', which harbours all the unpleasant material. The child is encouraged to recount his dreams, which provide another view of his difficulties. In dreams, Freud and his followers believe, things are not as they seem; perfectly innocent objects and experiences (as well as more notable ones) have a significance which goes beyond the appearance. It requires the skills of the therapist to bring out their true significance.

In the course of both free association and dream analysis, the therapist notices that the child may be hesitant to recount a particular dream or complains of 'forgetting' some detail of the past. This is regarded as a form of 'resistance' which alerts the therapist to the possible significance of the cause of hesitation and forgetting, to be confirmed when, after skilful probing, the material is eventually brought to light.

In the course of therapy, the child may develop strong feelings of like or dislike for the analyst, which in turn may help or hinder the treatment process. These feelings are transferred from the child's past to his present. This process is termed 'transference' and, according to its content, may be regarded as 'positive' or 'negative'.

In addition to the above, and particularly with younger children, *drawing, story-telling* and *play* are used as means of getting at the child's unconscious and attempting to resolve conflicts.

The core and culmination of all the above (and many other related) activities is the analyst's *interpretation* of the significance of the material that has been exposed. The task of the analyst is to sift through the material; discard the irrelevant; bring together those items which matter; interpret their significance; relate them both to past experiences and to current difficulties; and ensure that the child understands the interpretation (however intuitively) so that an alternative adaptation may be made.

It is taken for granted that the analyst's interpretation is 'right', and the patient's acceptance simply confirms it. However, if the patient believes the interpretation to be wrong, then that is equally taken as confirmation of the rightness of the interpretation – another aspect of 'resistance' and possible 'negative transference' that must be further worked through.

Application   There is a massive literature concerning the psychoanalytic treatment of difficult children, everything from bed-wetting, asthma and fits to family conflict, antisocial behaviour, drug taking and suicide attempts. As soon as a child is able to play, draw or talk, he becomes eligible for psychoanalytic treatment, although there is much more reluctance now, particularly in the United Kingdom, to refer younger children or those without obvious 'psychological' abnormalities for such treatment, in so far as this can be controlled. The literature gives no guidance as to what type of problem child would best benefit from psychoanalytic therapy. However, given the length and complexity of analysis and its demands on the ability to communicate, the protractedness of its process would rule out any critical problems which demand urgent control and amelioration.

The practice of psychoanalysis is mainly illustrated by detailed case histories provided in the literature. Such case histories contain so many variables and potentially different pointers to practice that it is almost impossible to consider or develop them into a rigorous set of prescriptions. Further to complicate the issue, there are many variations in emphasis among psychoanalytic child therapists.

The most damaging weakness of this form of treatment is the absence of good evidence concerning either the validity of the approach or the benefits of its outcome. No study with adequate controls has yet demonstrated the efficacy of psychoanalytic techniques for treating disordered children, or its superiority over other, much cheaper and more readily available techniques. Indeed, there is some evidence to suggest that, for example, 'conduct-disordered' children become worse after such treatment.

At the resource end, psychoanalysts are relatively scarce, particularly in the public sector. A course of analysis can run to years and, because of its individual nature, is highly resource intensive. So it is unsuitable for common (and therefore plentiful) problems or those which require urgent amelioration. The fact that the outcome of treatment (whether positive or negative) can itself be analysed in a multiplicity of ways does not enhance confidence in the accountability of the therapists for their work.

This matter is not helped by the mystifying terminology of psychoanalysis or by its practice, which is often cloaked in secrecy.

On the other hand, if the 'appropriate' child and the resources can be found, a course of psychoanalytic therapy (or its variants) is likely to ameliorate his problems. Additionally, he is likely to acquire deep insight into his past. Exposure to psychoanalysis may give him evocative and often intriguing concepts which may help elucidate his self-understanding and provide one coherent interpretation of his life experiences.

Rational-emotive therapy (RET)

RET is a relatively new form of treatment which emphasises the importance of thinking style and content (cognition) in the genesis and resolution of emotional problems. For example, an adolescent boy who is frequently in serious trouble with his parents is helped to see that his inappropriate and unrealistic beliefs about parents underlie his conflicts with them. Although RET is usually bracketed with cognitive or behaviour therapies, we have here classified it as a talking therapy because it primarily (though not exclusively) uses talking as a medium of change. The title 'rational-emotive' is intended to draw attention to the inseparable links between reasoning ('rational') and feeling ('emotive') elements in human action. Although this seems both obvious and age-old, it was not until the 1950s that its main underlying ideas were rigorously formulated by Albert Ellis and developed into well-articulated practice. There is by now, an extensive and high-quality list of publications supporting the use of RET and allied approaches to problem children.

The allied approaches, which include principally *interpersonal cognitive problem-solving (ICPS)*, *stress inoculation training* and *self-instruction training (SIT)*, place the same weight on the importance of beliefs as precursors of behaviour, but emphasise slightly different aspects and objectives. They are best seen as variants of the same technique; and, indeed, in practice it is difficult not to stray from one into the other. Although we shall briefly outline each of them, we believe they are best used in conjunction with each other – and also with other methods, where appropriate.

How does it work?   There is a considerable body of psychological research into cognitive processes: perceiving, recognising, construing, reasoning, judging, imagining, problem-solving and other 'symbolic' processes. Although recognised as fundamental psychological processes in human beings, it is only recently that they have been given due prominence in the treatment of problems of adaptation.

The fundamental tenet of RET and allied approaches is that human behaviour and emotional reactions are guided by the beliefs which people hold. The process of social growth inculcates many beliefs and values which are not conscious and articulated, such as those about freedom, fairness and individual rights. However, many other important beliefs are held explicitly and used in order both to initiate and to justify action.

Research has shown that, in certain forms of problem-solving, most people, particularly children, use a form of 'inner speech'. Clinical evidence has suggested that such inner speech is used by many people with emotional problems. Closer examination shows that the inner speech contains beliefs which are faulty and irrational and thus lead to maladaptive responses. The internal articulation of such beliefs is called 'self-talk'. It fulfils two functions: expressive and instrumental. 'Expressive' functions are concerned with feelings, emotions and attitudes; 'instrumental' beliefs are those which are used for purposes of guiding oneself and planning one's life. So, for example, a child's beliefs about his own incompetence or the infallibility of his parents are of the expressive kind, and those which concern his academic goals and how he should achieve them, the instrumental kind. It should, however, be emphasised that in practice and in children's minds the two are fused and in constant turmoil.

The linkage of faulty beliefs and maladaptive actions is symbolised as 'ABC', where 'C' is the *consequence* or maladaptive behaviour, 'A' the *activating event* and 'B' the faulty *belief*. The assessment process uncovers the above elements. Treatment takes the form of actively *disputing* 'D' the faulty beliefs, through which process new and sounder beliefs are created giving rise to better *behavioural effects* 'E'. Thus 'ABCDE' encapsulates both the theory and practice of rational-emotive therapy. (Care should be taken not to confuse the above with the more commonly used and accepted social learning analysis of behaviour as 'A' *antecedent*, 'B' *behaviour* and 'C' its *consequence*.)

Faulty beliefs which lead to adverse emotional and behavioural consequences fall into three main categories, with many variants:

1   'I must do well and win approval for my performances, or else I rate as a rotten person.'
2   'Others must treat me considerately and kindly in precisely the way I want them to treat me; if they don't society and the universe should severely blame, damn and punish them for their inconsiderateness.'
3   'Conditions under which I live must be arranged so that I get practically everything I want comfortably, quickly and easily and get virtually nothing that I don't want.'

These, in turn, lead to three irrational belief systems which focus on an adverse view of events and experiences: negativism ('It's awful; this shouldn't be happening to me'); intolerance ('I can't stand it; this can't go on any more') and self-derogation ('Everyone will think I'm useless if I don't do this').

The other allied approaches mentioned above use a combination of theoretical assumptions shared by behaviour modification (see Chapter 9) and others as elaborated for RET above. There is, in general terms, less concern with developing practice based on rigorous theory than with generating theory from clinical practice, very much as in the work of Freud, although there is substantial experimental evidence for the main ideas set out in RET.

Practice   In contrast to the other talking therapies outlined so far, RET emphasises the importance of assessment and proper hypothesis formation before treatment is undertaken. The focus of treatment is determined after probing by the therapist of four main areas:

1   Do the child's beliefs distort reality?
2   Does the child evaluate situations in a self-defeating way?
3   Does the child lack the appropriate beliefs about the relevant situations?
4   Does the child lack necessary and sufficient problem-solving skills?

Given the heavy emphasis on language and cognitive skills, therapists must take account of the child's age, developmental stage and other individual characteristics in arriving at the best 'package' of treatment measures. Here, as in every other form of treatment, the need for rapport is emphasised, although the absence of rapport and child hostility can themselves be used as part of therapy to point out a faulty 'ABC'.

The broad developmental profile of the child must suggest how far the therapist will use 'D' 'disputation' as a means of giving the child insight into his faulty cognitive functioning. Clearly, disputation is more appropriate to the verbally skilled and generally older adolescent, who has relatively better developed belief systems. On the other hand, with younger children considerably more imagery and other cognitive and illustrative aids must be used to bring out the child's beliefs.

The following steps provide a framework for carrying out RET with problem children and adolescents. Appropriate adjustments should be made for both the developmental state of the child and the severity and urgency of problems. Having carried out the appropriate assessment:

1   Separate which feelings the child wishes to keep from those he is prepared to discard; point out the consequences of each.
2   Teach the child how to record the occurrence, frequency and effects of his emotional reactions to each set of beliefs.
3   Challenge and dispute the child's irrational and maladaptive self-talk.
4   Enable the child to recognise how his unrealistic expectations of self and others, tendency to exaggerate disadvantages and adversities, intolerance and condemnation are self-defeating.

5 Develop and, through practice and reinforcement, inculcate rational and adaptive beliefs and self-talk; use imagery and role-playing to show that this is achievable.

6 Encourage the child to articulate how rational and irrational beliefs are likely to affect him and what their emotional consequences will be.

7 Explore at length with the child the different ways of responding to the same situation; show him how to observe other people's reactions and learn from them.

8 Encourage the child to reward himself for coping well with adverse emotions and experiences.

9 Teach the child necessary coping skills for the problem situation he is most likely to encounter.

As is evident from the above list, there is heavy emphasis on teaching the child new positive beliefs as well as more positive, paired emotional reactions.

Interpersonal cognitive problem-solving (ICPS)

The ICPS technique (developed by Spivack and colleagues) also highlights the cognitive elements of maladaptive behaviour. It emphasises that in the course of treatment the child's attention should be drawn to the practice given in:

1 *Causal thinking* about events and their emotional consequences, as an aid to identifying the child's sources of possible difficulty.

2 *Consequential thinking* through the costs and benefits of each alternative course of action.

3 *Means–end thinking* to enable the child to acquire the skills of how to achieve goals.

4 *Sensitivity training* or *perspective taking* to enable the child to recognise that different people have different views of issues and problems and what steps should be taken.

5 *Alternative thinking* to enable the child to see that there are a number of different ways of dealing with the same problem.

Stress inoculation training

The following steps are taken in the course of giving the youngster skills for coping with stress (adapted from Novaco):

1 *Prepare for provocation* – teach the child how to anticipate difficult situations, by telling himself not to be provoked into an adverse reaction.

2 *Confront the difficulty* – teach the child how to confront the provocation but remain in control of the situation; use imagery, play-acting and rehearsal to make a positive response probable.

3 *Cope with provocation* – extend the above to make the child aware of his physical response to confrontation (such as a tightening of the muscles and rising fear or anger); teach simple tricks, such as 'count to twenty before you say or do anything', as coping skills.

4 *Reflect on consequences* – teach the child to think about the outcome of handling the provocation, whether negative or positive; encourage him to become more reflective about himself, others' responses and other consequences by keeping a diary, talking to a friend, parent or therapist and generally becoming more aware of the possibilities of self-control.

Self-instruction training (SIT)

The practice of SIT is not dramatically different from the other techniques outlined above. The training undertaken with children focuses on the development of four major skill areas (Meichenbaum and colleagues), emphasising internal 'self-talking' responses. The teaching of these skills can be planned to cover a number of sessions as required to enable the child to engage competently in the necessary overt or covert verbal self-instruction:

1 Teach problem-identification and self-interrogation skills ('What is the problem? What am I supposed to do?').

2 Teach attention-focusing and appropriate responding skills ('Pay attention. What is the right thing to do? What are the alternatives? What are the consequences for me and the others?').

3 Teach self-reinforcement skills, so that the youngster evaluates his own responses and rewards the adaptive ones ('Good, I'm doing well. If I keep at it I'll be able to sort this out properly').

4 Self-correction and coping options enable the youngster continuously to monitor his behaviour, evaluate alternatives and arrive at optimal solutions ('I didn't do so well then. I should not have raised my voice. Perhaps I'd better stop interrupting until he's finished and I can then answer him calmly').

Application   Rational-emotive therapy and allied techniques are relevant to children from the time they become able to think and deliberate on how they should respond to circumstances. The literature contains case histories of RET and other techniques with children as young as 4 years old. Nevertheless, the older the child and the greater the verbal and cognitive skills, the more likely the child is to engage effectively in cognitive restructuring.

RET and allied techniques have also been used with a wide variety of problems, such as addiction, sensitivity training, antisocial behaviour and a range of personal psychological difficulties. It is clear, however, that such techniques are most useful when the pattern of behaviour is not so well established as to have become habitual and therefore prone to relegating cognitive problem-solving to a low rank among the determinants of behaviour.

The above point constitutes the major limitation of RET and similar techniques. It is evident from the empirical evidence that such techniques have little success (either by themselves or as the primary treatment) in dealing with entrenched behaviour patterns. Such patterns as habitual antisocial behaviour, drug abuse and violent outbursts are triggered off by a wide variety of stimuli and maintained by a range of internal and environmental conditions. The response is too readily and diversely activated to be susceptible to such cognitive intervention. Clearly the sensitive, challenging and highly skilled practitioners required for such treatments do not grow on trees. Nor can all children cope with confrontation and the disputational element in the treatment.

A further limitation of the technique is its heavy dependence on cognitive skills. This makes it less productive with many of the most problematic children who, in addition to their other difficulties, have poorly developed cognitive skills. Although the development of these skills is one of the primary aims of such treatment, there are too many cultural impediments to a child's independent use of such cognitive skills in an unsympathetic subculture to warrant the effort entailed in the treatment.

The same limitation applies to the subculture limitations and propensities which engender a sense of fatalism in such children and tramline them into 'adaptive' thoughtlessness. Nothing we have seen in the published literature contradicts this.

Despite the above weaknesses, we have devoted this space to RET and allied techniques because they represent one of the most powerful and widely usable treatment methods. Already there is a substantial and high-quality literature on the theoretical assumptions, procedures and practices of these techniques to demand serious attention from *all* child therapists. The supreme strength of these techniques is that they give due prominence to the importance of cognitive problem-solving and appropriate self-instruction in both the genesis and the resolution of young people's difficulties. Other treatment methods also pay some attention to this area, but only scantily and inconsistently.

The central involvement of the youngster in examining and adapting the structure and content of irrational and unhelpful beliefs has a wider benefit than just the specific problem resolution. No aspect of the practice of these techniques gives rise to ethical difficulties. The emphasis on reasoning is an antidote to authoritarian claims to special insight and expertise, so often evident in other talking therapies. For the same reason, the use of these techniques does not require long and convoluted training. Indeed, the available material is easily understandable and capable of being used by any number of moderately skilled workers with children, from parents and nurses to teachers, psychiatrists and psychologists. They do not require any special setting or materials. Even when their sole use may not be appropriate, they provide a powerful and, we would claim, indispensable adjunct to the treatment of any but the 'pure' physical problems.

Transactional analysis (TA)

Transactional analysis is a therapeutic technique which concentrates on identifying and changing the habitual response patterns which cause interpersonal difficulties. Through the treatment's providing insight into these patterns and enabling the acquisition of alternatives, the child will achieve an adaptive, mature and realistic attitude towards life. A youngster, for example, habitually provokes parental anger in discussion of his behaviour. He is helped to see that this is like a self-defeating and unnecessary game he plays. He is taught alternative responses; and when the difficulty is no longer apparent, treatment is terminated. The aim of all TA is to enable the person to recognise and accept his own weaknesses and strengths and those of others in a realistic way – abbreviated in the catchphrase 'I'm OK, you're OK'.

How does it work? Transactional analysis is associated with the name of the psychologist Eric Berne. Berne considers personality to comprise three 'ego states': 'parent', 'adult' and 'child' ('PAC'), in the reverse developmental order. The 'child' ego state develops in early infancy and is characterised by a person's feeling, wanting, playing and manipulating. Such 'childlike' behaviour can manifest itself at any age.

The 'adult' is the thinking and rational part of a person, dealing with reality and arriving at the best possible choice of alternatives. The term applies more to a state of awareness and functioning than to age, and therefore applies to younger children as well.

The 'parent' is learned from one's own parents and significant others. It is concerned with issues of right and wrong and the ethics of dealings with others. It is the controlling, criticising and punishing aspect of personality as well as the protective and nurturing one. It is easy to see the parallel between Berne's postulation of the 'PAC' and Freud's id, ego and superego. In the TA literature, considerable emphasis is laid on divisions and subcategories within each ego state (such as 'nurturing parent'/'critical parent') to take account of the complexity of human interaction.

These ego states coexist in any person. A healthy person can activate (or 'cathect') the state which is appropriate to the circumstances in hand. So each of us can use any of our three ego states to address any of the three that the other person possesses. If the child in us addresses the child in another (for example, 'Give me a cuddle'), and the reply is 'Of course, come on, I'll give you a cuddle', there is no problem. But if the same suggestion provokes 'Don't be silly; you're too grown up to have a cuddle', then the transaction is from a 'child' to a 'parent' and is thus 'crossed'. Furthermore, the above response snubs the 'child' and makes him feel devalued. Any action or statement which provokes feelings in another person is called a 'stroke'. TA places much emphasis on positive and negative stroking. Positive strokes are the best and collected by 'winners', who acquire the motivation and skills for collecting positive strokes in the course of their upbringing. Yet others are brought up to believe that it is wrong to collect positive strokes. The child learns either to do without positive strokes or to collect negative ones. These are the 'losers'.

There are considered to be six ways of structuring our time to collect strokes: withdrawal, rituals, pastimes, activities and work, games, and intimacy. The best known of these are the 'games' people play, of which Berne has delineated over a hundred. Games are regarded as a rich source of negative strokes, and 'intimacy' a source of positive ones. As with Gestalt therapy (see earlier in this chapter), TA emphasises the here and now and seeks to discover the hidden 'scripts' in faulty interactions.

The therapeutic aspect of TA has no unitary theoretical basis and draws upon many concepts and techniques from other therapies.

Practice As indicated above, TA relies on a wide range of therapeutic practices and procedures, few of which can be identified as purely TA. Nor is it easy to discover how TA procedures may be used in a rigorous professional setting. The basic steps in the practice of TA may be summarised as follows:

1 Teach the basic concepts and principles of transactional analysis; these include the 'PAC', 'winners' and 'losers' and the notion that there are no 'born losers' and that patterns of interaction can be beneficially changed.
2 Draw attention to types of transaction; types of stroke; the tendency for some people to collect positive or negative strokes for subsequent transaction ('collecting trading stamps'); different games that may be played; and the scripts to which the child appears to be acting.
3 Draw up contracts. This is a critical element of TA and encapsulates what the child and therapist set out to achieve together. This would start with simple contracts about, for example, 'learn about TA', but will eventually extend to all the changes that the child and the therapist hope to achieve.
4 Continue bringing out the faulty interactions; ensure that the child understands and internalises the material brought out; play games, engage in exercises and rehearse interactions until the child has acquired the necessary transactional skills, and then terminate treatment.

As with other talking therapies, TA places considerable emphasis on the context and ambience of treatment. The most important elements in enabling the treatment are 'potency' (the therapist's ability to make the appropriate interventions), 'permission' (enabling the client to defy previous parental restrictions placed on behaviour) and 'protection' (the therapeutic atmosphere in which the child feels safe to accept and respond to permissions).

Application   TA has been used with children as young as 5 and more extensively with adolescents and well into adulthood. The younger the age group the greater the emphasis on symbolic game playing rather than verbal discourse, which becomes more appropriate as children grow older. In general terms, TA demands clients with a reasonably good conceptual ability to understand, pursue and apply TA concepts.

The necessary emphasis on transactions renders TA particularly relevant to family, social skills, antisocial and some personal problems. The technique's demands, however, would rule out problems that require urgent resolution (such as propensity to violence). Similarly, its reliance on contracting would exclude the application of TA for those children who are incapable of or unwilling to engage in contracting or in those areas where the child is responding (appropriately) to the provocative and negative transactions of others, such as an abusive parent.

The above limitations narrow down the use of TA to relatively mild interpersonal problems of moderately well-integrated and articulate children, leaving out the many who have multiple problems of some severity and who see little pay-off in the TA contracts.

The theoretical basis of TA is dubious, bearing many of the same criticisms that have already been voiced in relation to other talking therapies. There is a considerable body of unnecessary jargon which makes the practice of TA cultish, although many of the words bear similar meanings to those in standard English. It involves mastery of complex concepts, games and relevant exercises, for both rehearsal and interpretation. This demands specialised training and therefore restricts the utility of TA. Above all, there is little evidence of systematic, effective use of TA with disordered children. Despite the relatively long period of exposure it has enjoyed, it remains a minority practice in limited use.

On the other hand, the theoretical basis and imagery adopted by TA are evocative and highly fruitful as an analytical tool. It retains good face validity until it begins to postulate such entities as 'ego states'. Its discourse can be most effectively seen as a series of helpful, heuristic images, allowing a window on to maladaptive transactions. TA also places welcome emphasis on the importance of the 'self-concept' in determining modes of interaction between children and others.

Because of a similar emphasis on cognitions and alterable beliefs, it encourages the development of assertiveness and personal power over interactions. It does not require any particular setting for its practice, which can be undertaken with a wide range of children's ages and problems, both individually and in a group setting. Its practice, even in comparison with other talking therapies, does not arouse any ethical or professional anxieties.

Further reading

Bernard, M.E. and Joyce, M.R. (1984) *Rational-Emotive Therapy with Children and Adolescents*. New York: Wiley.

Berne, E. (1961) *Transactional Analysis in Psychotherapy*. London: Souvenir Press.

Berne, E. (1964) *Games People Play*. Harmondsworth: Penguin.

Berne, E. (1972) *What do You Say after You Say Hello?* London: Corgi Books.

Brammer, L.M. and Shostrom, E.L. (1977) *Therapeutic Psychology*, 3rd edn. Englewood Cliffs, NJ: Prentice-Hall.

Burks, H.M. and Steffloe, B. (1979) *Theories of Counselling*, 3rd edn. New York: McGraw-Hill.

Carkhuff, R.R. (1969) *Helping and Human Relations*. New York: Holt, Rinehart & Winston.

Dare, C. (1985) 'Psychoanalytic theories of development', in M. Rutter and L. Hersov (eds), *Child and Adolescent Psychiatry*. Oxford: Blackwell.

Dryden, W. (ed.) (1984) *Individual Therapy in Britain*. London: Harper & Row.

Ellis, A. (1962) *Reason and Emotion in Psychotherapy*. New York: Lyle Stuart.

Ellis, A. and Bernard, M.E. (eds) (1983a) *Rational-Emotive Approaches to the Problems of Childhood*. New York: Plenum.

Ellis, A. and Bernard, M.E. (1983b) 'An overview of rational-emotive approaches to the problems of childhood', in Ellis and Bernard (1983a).

Ellis, R. and Whittington, D. (eds) (1983) *New Directions in Social Skills Training*. London: Croom Helm.

Erickson, E. (1950) *Childhood and Society*. New York: Norton.

Freud, A. (1946) *The Psychoanalytic Treatment of Children*, London: Imago.

Freud, S. (1909) *Analysis of a Phobia in a Five Year Old Boy*. London: Hogarth Press.

Freud, S. (1926/1962) 'The question of lay analysis', in *Two Short Accounts of Psychoanalysis*. Harmondsworth: Penguin.

Freud, S. (1986) *The Essentials of Psychoanalysis* (selected with introduction and comments by Anna Freud). Harmondsworth: Penguin.

Garfield, S.L. (1980) *Group Psychotherapy with Children*. New York: Wiley.

Garfield, S.L. and Bergin, A.E. (eds) (1978) *Handbook of Psychotherapy and Behavior Change: An Empirical Analysis*, 2nd edn. New York: Wiley.

Glasser, W. (1965) *Reality Therapy: A New Approach to Psychiatry*. New York: Harper & Row.

Glenn, J. (ed.) (1978) *Child Analysis and Therapy*. New York: Aronson.

Harris, T. (1967) *I'm OK – You're OK*. London: Pan Books.

Herbert, M. (ed.) (1981) *Psychology for Social Workers*. London: British Psychological Society/Macmillan.

Hopson, B. (1981) 'Counselling and helping', in Herbert (1981).

Horney, K. (1942) *Self-Analysis*. New York: Norton.

James, M. and Jongeward, D. (1971) *Born to Win*. London: Signet Books.

Klein, M. (1930) *The Psychoanalysis of Children*. London: Hogarth Press.

Krunboltz, J.D. and Thoresen, C.E. (eds) (1965) *Behavioral Counselling: Cases and Techniques*. New York: Holt, Rinehart & Winston.

Lewin, K. (1951) *Field Theory in Social Science*. New York: Harper.

Lubarovsky, L. and Spence, D. (1978) 'Quantitative research on psychoanalytic therapy', in Garfield and Bergin (1978).

Meichenbaum, D.H. (1977) *Cognitive Behavior Modification: An Integrative Approach*. New York: Plenum.

Meichenbaum, D.H. (1983) *Coping with Stress*. London: Century.

Meichenbaum, D.H. and Asarnov, J. (1979) 'Cognitive behavioral modifications and metacognitive development', in P.C. Kendall and S.D. Holton (eds), *Cognitive Behavioral Intervention: Theory, Research and Procedures*. New York: Academic Press.

Meyers, A.W. and Craighead, W.E. (eds) (1984) *Cognitive Behavior Therapy with Children*, New York: Plenum.

Midgley, D. (1983) *Taking Charge of Your Own Life*. Middlesbrough, Cleveland: TA.

Murgatroyd, S. (1985) *Counselling and Helping*. London: British Psychological Society/ Methuen.

Murgatroyd, S. and Woolfe, R. (1982) *Coping with Crisis – Understanding and Helping Persons in Need*. London: Harper & Row.

Nelson-Jones, R. (1982) *The Theory and Practice of Counselling Psychology*. London: Holt, Rinehart & Winston.

Novaco, R.W. (1979) 'The cognitive regulation of anger and stress', in P.C. Kendall and S.D. Holton (eds), *Cognitive Behavioral Intervention: Theory, Research and Procedures*. New York: Academic Press.

Ollendick, J.H. and Hersov, M. (eds) (1985) *Handbook of Child Psychotherapy*. New York: Plenum.

Perls, F. (1969) *Ego, Hunger and Aggression*. New York: Random House.

Perls, F.S., Hefferline, R.F. and Goodman, P. (1974) *Gestalt Therapy*. Harmondsworth: Penguin.

Priestley, P. and McGuire, J. (1983) *Learning to Help*. London: Tavistock.

Prochaska, J.O. (1979) *Systems of Psychotherapy*. Homewood, IL: Dorsey Press.

Proctor, B. (1978) *Counselling Shop*. London: Burnett Books.

Rogers, C.R. (1961) *On Becoming a Person*. Boston, MA: Houghton Mifflin.

Spivack, G., Platt, J. and Shure, M. (1976) *The Problem-Solving Approach to Adjustment*. San Francisco: Jossey Bass.

Tough, A. (1982) *Intentional Changes – a Fresh Approach to Helping People Change*. Chicago: Follet.

Walens, S., DiGiuseppe, R. and Wessler, P. (1980) *Practitioners Guide to Rational-Emotive Therapy*. New York: Oxford University Press.

Waters, V. (1982) 'Theories for children's rational emotive therapy', in C.R. Reynold and T.B. Gustkin (eds), *Handbook of School Psychology*, New York: Wiley.

Winnicott, D.G. (1971) *Therapeutic Consultations in Child Psychiatry*. London: Hogarth Press.

11

Group Therapies

Most people live in groups, experience their problems in groups and have to rely on groups to accept and define them as social entities. It is therefore not surprising that group therapies have been universally employed in the treatment of problem children. A considerable literature has grown around the topic of group therapies, and many forms of group practice have been claimed to be therapeutic. In this chapter we shall briefly describe family therapy, group behaviour modification, group counselling, positive peer culture, psychodrama and role-play.

Groups are used for a variety of purposes, even in specialist settings for children. These include gatherings for the purpose of exchanging information, providing support, joint decision-making and problem-solving, as well as for sharing normal life activities.

Group therapies, however, are different from these, because they involve the application of therapeutic techniques to groups for purposes of ameliorating the difficulties of group members. For example, a group of solvent misusers are brought together for counselling as a means of helping them to stop the habit. Or a group of antisocial children are brought together and subjected to mutual scrutiny and pressure, in the context of a positive peer culture, to modify their attitudes and behaviour. In both of these instances, groups are being used as both a medium and a focus of treatment, with a view to changing individual behaviour patterns. This is different from the (accidental) therapeutic effects of group living, where, in order simply to survive, children have to moderate some of their more outlandish propensities.

Theoretical basis

The power of group therapies derives from two sources: the group dimension of some problems and group dynamics. As we have already indicated, every problem must be identified as such. This takes place either in a group setting (such as classroom or family) or according to group-related norms, as with bed-wetting or depression. There are, indeed, very few problems from which we can remove all group-related elements. This becomes the more important when we consider the prevalent view that certain behaviours are generated by faulty system (or group) functioning. This is the basis of all family therapy and much group counselling.

Whereas family-related problems such as attempted suicide or anorexia nervosa may be manifested alone or in the family, certain other problems become obvious only in groups. These include social skills problems (such as insensitivity or uncooperativeness) and aspects of personal development (such as emotional immaturity or 'immoral behaviour'). Such problems are best resolved in a group setting. Thus, theoretically, groups must be used to tap both the 'causation' of the problem and the context in which it is manifested and maintained.

Much socialisation takes place through group processes, first in the family and subsequently in school and a widening social environment. Every civilised and well-behaved citizen is a walking testimony to the power of groups to shape individual behaviour, from the family to the more amorphous social groupings. Group power is exercised through its much greater ability to identify unacceptable behaviour; lay it out for public scrutiny; shape it through positive or negative feedback; provide a range of appropriate or alternative methods of adaptation and do so with sufficient diversity to make it withstand changes in the child's physical and social conditions.

The topic concerned with the power of the group is encompassed by 'group dynamics'. It includes such elements of group influence as group size, climate, the composition of group members, communication media, task and leadership. Much more is known about the power of these elements in the experimental and industrial settings than in clinical contexts, particularly in relation to children.

We can now consider the role of the two main elements of group origins of problems and group dynamics in the therapies to be described in this chapter. *Family therapy* is firmly based on the notion of the family as a system of interacting members and functions which, in disarray, causes problems for one or more of its members. A variety of techniques are used to create and utilise group pressure to enable the family members to gain insight into and control over their aberrant members and functions.

Group counselling makes little use of groups as an explanation of problem behaviour but uses the group as a medium for highlighting and sharing problems and discovering common means of resolving them. The same is done in *group behaviour modification*, apart from the change-over from insight-giving to the use of behaviour modification techniques in a group setting. The propensity of group members to give feedback and reinforcement is used as a major medium of shaping behaviour.

A similar theoretical conception underlies *positive peer culture*, only here greater emphasis is laid on the peer-group origins of much antisocial behaviour. Therapeutic work therefore concentrates on transforming the usual pressure towards antisocial behaviour into a powerful dynamic for emphasising prosocial and positive aspects of individual functioning.

Psychodrama and *role-play* have theoretical roots in Freudian psychology as well as in the group genesis of problems. The acting out of conflicts relates to group dynamics mainly in the tendency of other group members to react to each other's behaviour and thus provide both feedback and means of shaping it.

General practice issues

The effectiveness of group therapy derives from the competence of the leader/therapist, the composition of the group and the operation of its dynamics.

The group therapist must have the basic qualities of all therapists, to which we have earlier drawn attention. He should also know what he wants to achieve from his group session in both general (for example, creating a co-operative atmosphere) and specific terms (for example, to give Johnny a powerful message about what people think of him). He should also know enough about group dynamics to make good use of silences, outbursts, alliances and scapegoating. He should be capable of varying his style from the democratic to *laissez-faire* or directive, according to his objectives.

The composition of the group depends on the number, age, sex and intellectual and personality characteristics of the group members, their problem profiles and their condition at any given time. Depending on the task and therapeutic technique, workers have claimed that anything from three to thirty youngsters can produce good dynamics. However, given the objective of intensifying interaction among group members to bring out and resolve problems, most workers have tended to adopt group sizes of between six and sixteen. It is difficult to generate much *group* pressure with fewer than about six members; and with more than sixteen, there are potentially too many sources to be able to control the dynamics. These are nevertheless broad rules-of-thumb, which should be evaluated in the particular context of the therapist. Family therapists usually ignore the family size and deal with groups as small as just mother and child or as large as extended families.

Age is not a significant factor in group therapies, though adolescents are more susceptible to group pressure than very young children. Nor is the child's gender a significant factor, according to the published literature, unless group therapy concerns such issues as premenstrual tension or wet dreams, which affect only one gender.

Intellectual and personality factors clearly affect the group process and its outcome because they are fundamentally involved not only in determining how members will behave in the group, but also in the degree to which they will benefit from groupwork. Intellectual potential is no more relevant to group therapies than it is to individual treatment. Personality dimensions, on the other hand, are much more significant because of the impact they have on group harmony. Experimental results are not conclusive in terms of the best type of personality for groupwork. Some authors claim that introverted and anxious children benefit more; others that extroverted, impulsive and morally primitive youngsters do better. Whilst in an ideal world it would be nice to be able to choose the composition of the group, in reality this is rarely possible, and so the question of group composition becomes academic. We just have to do the best we can with groups of varying hue.

The same cannot be said of the children's problem profile and condition. We clearly do have some choice over whom we select for group therapy and when. In general terms, group therapy can concentrate at any one time on a particular *problem area*. Thus, it is sensible to attempt group treatment of family-related problems, or social skills deficits, or antisocial behaviour, or personality problems, whether it is done consecutively during the same session or tackled at different times. What is not practicable is to attempt to deal with one youngster's anxieties about excessive drinking and another's temper tantrums at the same time, unless they are treated as instances of poor self-control.

The dynamics of the group, in so far as therapy is concerned, are manifested in terms of readiness to reveal problems and providing negative or positive reinforcement for the problem. Such factors as communication patterns, affiliation and withdrawal, group pressure and reward can facilitate or impede group effectiveness.

In general terms, groups are most effective when the group (1) has some idea of its objective; (2) is aware that its operation can bring about the objective; (3) allows all members to feel part of the group and contribute to its functioning; (4) allows good communication between members; (5) can cope with the conflicts that arise; (6) has worked out its decision-making guidelines; and (7) can respond flexibly to its own shifting dynamics.

Status

There is so much writing on group therapies of one sort or another, and so much is claimed for their univeral applicability and efficacy, that it is difficult to know what to cite as a limitation. A generally accepted limitation is that group therapies are less useful with very young children than with teenagers. There are also limits in the type of problem for which it is used. Broadly speaking, physical and intellectual problems are not susceptible to group therapy. Thus, while there are numerous studies of group therapy with, for example, drug abusers or psychotics, the therapeutic work is directed more at changing the cognitive and emotional components of the behaviour than the condition itself.

The most significant limitation of this therapy derives from the high level of skill that is required for its effective practice. People who can conduct productive group therapeutic sessions must have considerable training and experience, and these are not easy to come by. Also, depending on the particular form of group therapy used, the child can be subjected to intense and unacceptable group pressure to change. Neither children nor adults are able to leave behind the feelings aroused during the therapy session and they sometimes ventilate their anger and anguish on themselves and others subsequently. The therapist must therefore be vigilant towards such consequences.

Even allowing for the limitations on the problem conditions to which they can be applied, group therapies still have a commendably wide application. In any case, such limitation is more than outweighed by the immense power of group dynamics to change the beliefs, feelings and behaviour patterns of the participants. It is not surprising that religious evangelists and political demagogues use large group settings in which to make their maximum impact. The greatest appeal of group therapy is in its efficiency. The effort of one therapist can be much more economically utilised in ameliorating the problems of a whole group than of one youngster alone. This efficiency is further extended when we consider that, because of the greater numbers of other youngsters in the group, they can act as prompters and reinforcers more frequently than the therapist can alone.

Moreover, the therapist would find it difficult to generate the same pressure towards change that can result from the effective management of a group therapy session. This is particularly the case with family therapy (where the members must learn to function adaptively together) and with group behaviour modification and positive peer culture, where group pressure is the main instrument of change.

While there are undoubtedly high skill requirements of group therapists, dealing with groups is also a fairly common experience for most workers with children. Depending on the particular form of group therapy to be used, the skill requirements can be acquired in anything from a few days to a few months, though almost everyone benefits from longer practice. These therapies are not immune from attempts to mystify and mythologise the group process and its outcome. However, given the basic personal and professional requirements of all therapists, it is difficult to see why group management and therapy skills cannot be reasonably achieved.

This is much aided by the wide availability of writings and audio-visual materials concerned with group therapies. Although the claims of effectiveness are not often borne out by published evidence, the spread of the practice indicates a degree of face validity which, often combined with inescapable necessity, makes groupwork an attractive therapeutic option.

Family therapy

Family therapy is the treatment of the total family group rather than of its individual members. For example, when a girl has been admitted to hospital with a severe eating disorder, the attempt is made to treat her problem in the total family context rather than in isolation and on her own.

Although formal 'family therapy' dates only from the early 1950s, it has emerged as one of the most powerful and popular forms of treatment. A huge literature has developed around it, and different 'schools' of practice have already emerged. Family therapy started as the application of psychoanalytic ideas to family groups, but it has gradually moved away from that and incorporated a range of other ideas, particularly from 'systems theory', cybernetics and behavioural psychology. Different practitioners emphasise different aspects of the process, techniques or particular client groups. Thus, almost anything that is said about family therapy is likely to be partial.

How does it work?   The cornerstone of modern family therapy is the idea of the family as a system. 'Systems theory' was initially proposed as a general theory of the organisation of parts into wholes, particularly in computers and machines. Its application to families has enabled therapists to identify the way family members relate to each other to carry out the corporate tasks of the family. Families operate through the transactions of members, which eventually become established as habitual patterns or systems.

Systems can be open or closed. *Closed systems* do not interact with their environment, and their elements quickly reach a state of equilibrium which is resistant to change. *Open systems*, such as most families, on the other hand, interact with their environments and are changed by them. The open/closed characteristics in families are a matter of degree rather than of either/or.

The main implications of systems thinking for family therapy are:

1   Families are *purposive*, functional systems whose operations can be best understood in terms of the purposes they fulfil for members and the whole system.
2   Families as a system comprise *subsystems* such as 'parent subsystem', 'spouse subsystem' and 'sibling subsystem'. Families themselves are parts of supra-systems such as neighbourhood, ethnic or religious groups.
3   Families, like all systems, operate by certain general *rules*, myths or established patterns which regulate the conduct of their members.
4   There are *boundaries* and *hierarchies* within systems and subsystems of the family, some of which are more adaptive than others (for example, parents' position as decision-makers). These must be identified as a means of understanding family problems.
5   Changes in boundaries and hierarchies are not always dysfunctional and are a necessary response to changes within or outside the family.
6   Families, like all other systems, tend towards *equilibrium* and are, to varying degrees, resistant to change; indeed, even problems can be seen as serving a 'homeostatic' or balancing function.

7 The ease and quality of *communication* and *feedback* are major determinants of how well the family and its members will adjust to changes in circumstances.
8 The behaviour of family members is interdependent. They therefore operate in a *'circular' causal chain* rather than a linear one.

Each of the above elements has been elaborated by a variety of family therapists and used in their practice with implicit claim for the self-evident truth of the theorising. Apart from the above core elements, there is little that is generally accepted as the theoretical basis of family therapy.

Practice   Given the many 'schools' of family therapy and the essentially 'try it and see' orientation of therapists (in practice, even if not in theory), it is difficult to discern the steps in treatment which are both comprehensive and yet detailed enough to enable adequate practice. More importantly, family therapy is at least as much about *how* the therapist goes about his task as *what* he does, unlike surgery or behaviour modification.

The *general* elements of practice are as follows:

1 Establish rapport with the family; 'join' them.
2 Accept the family's initial definition of the problem and the problem person.
3 Assess the family's state and problems by determining (a) its 'structure' or the established ways in which members interact; (b) its functioning in such areas as communications, problem-solving capability and emotional responsiveness and involvement; (c) the particular area of dysfunction whether in the family's development or the interaction of its subsystems or arising from interactions within the wider context; (d) what purpose the particular problem serves in maintaining the family balance.
4 Set out a plan of action, including the list of priorities and how they are to be tackled; goals of treatment should be articulated in both 'systemic' (for example, to give the parents better skills of communicating with their child) and outcome/behavioural terms (for example, Mary to stop taking overdoses).
5 Discuss your plan with the family, as a whole or in stages, as appropriate.
6 Arrive at an agreement or 'contract' for the contributions that members are to make, if appropriate.
7 Accelerate the process of treatment which will already have started in the assessment stage; use the technique that seems most appropriate to the task in hand. Of the numerous practices the most frequently used are:
   (a) *focusing* – bringing the family back to the outstanding problem;
   (b) *enactment* – family members act out a scene to illustrate a particular problem;

(c) *intensification* – emphasising or exaggerating a point to bring it forcefully home;

(d) *task giving* – to maintain motivation from one session to another, to give practice and to ensure participation;

(e) *directives* – intended to give the members some idea of what they should do or refrain from doing or do in a different order;

(f) *paradoxical directives* – given as a means of 'throwing' a family who have a chronic problem and are resistant to change;

(g) *family sculpting* – getting family members to adopt particular postures to illustrate particular problems or aspects of family functioning;

(h) *circular questioning* – asking family members questions about how another member is likely to respond to a third member in a variety of ways; an attempt to provide fresh perspectives and to increase interpersonal sensitivity.

8   Attempt to change the family structure, if appropriate, by exploring and modifying its hierarchies, internal and external 'boundaries' and forming alliances to shift the balance of power and thus to promote change.

9   Explore family problems sequentially, at each turn reinforcing the family's greater insight and ability to cope with its problems.

10   Bring the treatment to a conclusion, having set up appropriate support systems for the family and provided guidelines for how they may deal with relapses and other related contingencies.

Application   Family therapy may be used with all age groups and problem profiles. The literature contains accounts of family therapy with problem children as young as 4 years, although there is generally more interest in adolescents and their problems. These problems encompass all the six problem areas enumerated in this book (see Chapter 2). In the physical area there has been much work on alcohol and solvent misuse as well as eating and sleep disorders. School-related (cognitive) problems have also been tackled, though not as much as home and family problems, which are the core of family therapy. Social skills problems do not feature much in the literature. Antisocial behaviour is, however, often seen as a symptom of family dysfunction, as are many personality and other psychological problems. Equally important, the literature contains significant contributions to working both with intact families and with those whose children are in residential establishments.

Despite considerable writing on the subject, there is some ambiguity about which subjects or families are suitable for treatment and which are not. On the whole, family therapy is indicated where there are disorders of family structure, relationships or functions. On the other hand, such treatment is not indicated when the disorder seems to be due to major socioeconomic factors, serious physical or other individual difficulties, or when the problem is so severe as to require immediate curbing.

The disadvantages of family therapy are manifest at a variety of levels. At the most basic, although the literature is by now voluminous, it is full of wholly unnecessary jargon, for which there are perfectly sound, common English alternatives available. Although this imparts an evocative and almost poetic quality to much of the writing, it does not aid clear identification of what is being talked about. This is not helped by the many minute variations of emphasis which are presented as radically different alternatives. Indeed, the analyses of transcripts of sessions of therapists from different 'schools' (which are frequently reproduced) show remarkable similarities.

Equally, much of the literature is couched in such terms as to suggest that some mysterious healing process is taking place. In this respect, family therapy is very much like psychoanalysis and related therapies which are also suffused with intimations of special insights and processes. This orientation also places substantial demands on the therapist, who must be a person of exceptional insight and competence. High-quality family therapists as practitioners (rather than people who say they do family therapy) are hard to come by.

Most fundamentally, however, there is scant evidence of the effectiveness of family therapy in either general or specific terms. The few studies attempted have found little evidence of external validity of the therapy, the efficacy of the treatment process or appropriate changes and durability of outcomes. This is not to say that some therapists do not appear to have an almost magic effect on their clients. But that seems to be attributable at least as much to them as people as it is to what they are practising.

The strengths of family therapy derive primarily from the unique position of the family in the genesis of most problems, either because of its direct impact or because of its failure to provide adequate inoculation against problems. Once the genesis of the problem in the family has been analysed and set out, given the family's basic motivation to do the best for its members, it is likely to become a powerful medium of treatment. This is, of course, provided that the family's competencies are sufficiently great to overcome counteracting pressures which generate and maintain children's problems. If this is achieved then, even in economic terms, family therapy must be deemed cost effective.

A further advantage is the wide range of problems that fall within the purview of family therapy and the relatively long-term effects of any benefits that may result from fundamental changes in family functioning. This is a further commendation for family therapy. In the present spirit of the times, families are seen as a core institution, and anything that helps them to remain intact and cope with their children's problems is ethically laudable.

Group behaviour modification

Group methods as major treatments came to prominence in the late 1960s and early 1970s. 'Growth centres', marathons, T-groups, encounter groups and others abounded. Their ill-defined processes were an amalgam of philosophy, psychology and mysticism as people attempted to 'get in touch with their feelings' or 'achieve self-realisation'. Most of the methods employed (induced fatigue, heightened anxiety, submission to a 'guru', personal attacks, persuasion and so on) are not entirely dissimilar to brain-washing. Some positive changes were occasionally achieved, but it was far more common for some people to emerge emotionally battered. For many, the only outcome was a short-lived state of euphoria or despair; real, positive carry-over effects were conspicuous by their absence. In an effort to incorporate the positive aspects of groupwork and behavioural approaches within a social learning framework into an integrated and systematic format, group behaviour modification emerged as a treatment method. This approach has the happy advantage of being both a therapy and a training. The treatment of self-defeating and/or antisocial behaviours and the acquisition of prosocial, life-enhancing skills are seen as con-stituting a continuum rather than a disease/health dichotomy.

With group behaviour modification, the important role that environmental, as well as cognitive, influence plays in shaping and maintaining behaviour patterns is emphasised. Both adaptive and maladaptive behavioural and emotional responses are viewed as learned. Specific techniques include desensitisation, assertiveness training, observational learning (modelling) and cognitive restructuring. Rather than focusing on personality or motiva-tional factors the main targets are behavioural and attitudinal change.

How does it work?   As with other group therapies, the technique derives its power from both the use of group pressure and also the efficacy of social learning. The former has been described in the general introduction to this chapter. Social learning is the application of learning principles to social interactions. A considerable body of research and clinical writings has shown that human behaviour is shaped by both its antecedents and its consequences, as already set out in Chapter 8. This technique particularly emphasises the 'A' (antecedent) → 'B' (behaviour) → 'C' (consequences) causal connection of the behavioural chain. Modification of behaviour is through the manipulation of both 'A' and 'C', particularly the latter.

Practice

1 Carry out a comprehensive assessment of the individuals' behavioural deficits, excesses or deviations (including their strengths).
2 State the above in specific behavioural terms; for example, 'John responds to innocent teasing by attacking his classmates.'

Such resolution in turn demands frequent reviews of costs and benefits in an open, publicly accountable manner.

The merits of security lie in its unmatched power to provide an appropriate environment for the most rigorous forms of behaviour change. By reducing a child's exposure to previous patterns of deviant behaviour, it provides an opportunity for growing out of maladaptive behaviour patterns so that normal maturational processes can assert themselves. Paradoxically, a secure environment can provide the most 'normal' and growth-promoting set of conditions for severely damaged children. In the last resort, the minimum yet critically important advantage of security is that it provides an environment in which high-risk children who cannot be let loose on the public or themselves may be kept. It is, however, important to remember that security may help temporarily curb a problem, but hardly ever achieves its longer-term amelioration by itself.

Further reading

Balbernie, R. (1972) *Residential Work with Children*. London: Chaucer Publishing.

Bettelheim, B. (1974) *A Home for the Heart*. London: Thames & Hudson.

Bridgeland, M. (1971) *Pioneer Work with Maladjusted Children*. London: Staples Press.

Cawson, P. and Martell, M. (1979) *Children Referred to Closed Units*. London: HMSO.

Clarke, D.H. (1981) *Social Therapy in Psychiatry*. London: Churchill Livingstone.

Cornish, D.B. and Clarke, R.V.G. (1975) *Residential Treatment and its Effects on Delinquency*. London: HMSO.

Cross, J. (1975) 'Therapeutic communities', *Journal of the Association of Workers for Maladjusted Children*, 3 (1).

DHSS (1977) *Intermediate Treatment – Planning for Action*. London: Department of Health and Social Security.

Foudrain, J. (1974) *Not Made of Wood*. London: Quartet.

Foulkes, S.H. (1975) *Group Analytic Psychotherapy: Method and Principles*. London: Gordon & Breach.

Hinshelwood, R.D. and Manning, N. (1979) *Therapeutic Communities: Reflections and Progress*. London: Routledge & Kegan Paul.

Hoghughi, M.S. (1978) *Troubled and Troublesome*. London: Burnett Books/ Deutsch.

Hoghughi, M.S. 'Lock ups for Youngsters', *New Society*, 40, 767.

Jones, M. (1968) *Social Psychiatry in Practice: The Idea of Therapeutic Community*. Harmondsworth: Penguin.

Jones, M. (1976) *The Maturation of the Therapeutic Community*. New York: Human Sciences Press.

Jones, M. (1982) *The Process of Change*. London: Routledge & Kegan Paul.

Millham, S., Bullock, R. and Hosie, K. (1978) *Locking Up Children*. Farnborough, Hants: Saxon House.

Righton, P. (1975) 'Planned environment therapy: a reappraisal', *Journal of the Association of Workers for Maladjusted Children*, 3 (1).

Rose, M. (1978) 'Residential treatment – a total therapy', *Journal of the Association of Workers for Maladjusted Children*, 6 (1).

Rose, M. (1980) 'The context for psychological change in a therapeutic community for adolescents', paper delivered to Liverpool and Newcastle universities, mimeo; private circulation.

3 Specify the treatment goal(s) in precise terms; for example, 'John will shrug off innocent teasing by keeping calm and smiling at his tormentor(s).

4 Select group members carefully; decide whether to set up a group whose members share a common problem (such as fear of flying) or to form a group that comprises an admixture of problems but whose members are all, say, teachers or residents in the same unit.

5 Exclude those who are mentally ill or who have severe mental handicap.

6 Confine numbers to eight or less.

7 Use two therapists if possible.

8 Inform each member of the purposes of the group and acquaint each member with every other member's problem(s) to be dealt with in the group.

9 Provide a relaxed setting and a non-threatening atmosphere.

10 Meet regularly – for example, after lunch every day.

11 Monitor and record progress throughout each session.

12 Use open-ended questions; for example, 'Would you like to tell us what you think about school? rather than 'Do you like school?'

13 Enhance feeling of similarity and oneness among the group; the sharing of problems and goals, discovering similarities of background and reasons for joining the group engender a sense of 'team spirit' and group cohesiveness; reinforce this.

14 Decide (in the light of 2 and 3 above) whether to employ strategies (a) to increase adaptive behaviour or (b) to decrease maladaptive behaviour.

15 Select which intervention strategies to implement (see Chapter 8 on behaviour modification) and then apply them to, and within, the group setting.

16 Consistently impress upon members the necessity for therapeutic transfer; that is, focus attention on situations *outside* the group in which a member can apply what he has learned *inside* the group.

17 Where possible, use immediate feedback, encouraging members to respond as honestly and openly as possible to one another.

Application   The earliest reported uses of group modification were for the systematic desensitisation of patients presenting phobic complaints, frigidity and impotence. There were instances of the use of behavioural techniques and assertiveness training groups. Techniques used in one-to-one individual therapies were gradually used in groups, and their applications were directed towards those procedures, already tried and tested, that incorporated a behavioural and learning approach. Group treatment can therefore be effective in (a) decreasing self-defeating, maladaptive behaviours, such as anxiety, phobias, overweight and eating disorders, and smoking; (b) increasing adaptive behaviour, such as acquiring assertiveness, coping skills and decision-making skills. Group behavioural techniques are equally applicable to children, adults and heterogeneous or homogeneous groups. They offer a challenging approach to the alleviation of behavioural problems and the potential for meeting the essential needs of large groups of people.

The primary limitation of group modification arises from the scarcity of seasoned and competent operators, who can both 'manage' a group and apply sound psychological knowledge of the 'ABC' linkages. Although the practice can be learned by non-psychologists, availability of a psychological adviser is recommended. Also, such group practice raises (though no more than most other) potential ethical issues concerning the use of group pressure to change an individual's behaviour.

The advantages, however, are enormous. The group provides an efficient and real-life context for behaviour change; the group itself acts as a major source of reinforcement and therefore shaping of individual behaviour. The group behaviour modification setting can be used as a 'laboratory' in which members can be encouraged to engage in new forms of behaviour without fear of rejection. The setting provides considerable opportunities for modelling prosocial and adaptive behaviours. Each participant can be given the opportunity to perform leadership or teaching roles for other group members. What each learns can thus be publicly passed on to others, to mutual benefit. Group processes and treatment outcomes are susceptible to rigorous monitoring, as with other behavioural procedures. There is considerable evidence of its effectiveness with a wide range of disordered children, particularly with difficult adolescents in residential settings. Given its positive orientation and public accountability, it satisfies rigorous ethical demands and is more likely than most other techniques to encourage the development of a *discipline* of treatment in groups.

Group counselling

Group counselling is the application of counselling relationships and activities, as outlined in Chapter 10, to groups. For example, a group of disordered adolescents are brought together for counselling in an attempt to normalise their behaviour with each other.

We have already indicated that the practice of individual counselling is much older and more universal than suggested by the specialist literature. The same comment applies to group counselling, although this practice can be more accurately dated to the inter-war years, with refugee children and later with the delinquent and psychiatrically disturbed. Group counselling has rarely been used as the primary or exclusive treatment medium, but rather more frequently as an adjunct to other individual treatment – for example, augmenting chemotherapy or individual behaviour modification with schizophrenic adolescents.

A distinction is usually made between therapeutic/interactional and teaching/educational group counselling. The major differences lie in the smaller size and greater emphasis on interaction, interpretation, insight, analysis and exploration of alternative adaptive ploys in therapeutic counselling groups.

How does it work? The practice of group counselling arises from the convergence of group dynamics and the therapeutic potential of counselling. Both of these aspects have been separately set out in this and the previous chapter.

Adolescent problems often arise out of conflict with others – notably parents, teachers and other authority figures. These conflicts are, in turn, associated with the frustration of adolescent 'needs' during a uniquely turbulent period. Group counselling provides an accepting and safe venue for the exploration of these needs and adaptive ways of dealing with them. More specifically, group counselling provides a venue for:

(a) discovering personal identity and socially acceptable goals;
(b) increased understanding of self as a result of other members' feedback and one's own attempt at self-projection;
(c) increased information input about other people, the environment, problems of living and the choices that are available;
(d) acquiring better skills for assimilating and evaluating information about oneself and significant others;
(e) added competence and confidence in facing and dealing with problems;
(f) enhanced sensitivity to other people, their moods and problems and ways of dealing with them;
(g) much improved communication skills, in hearing a variety of expressions and having to express changing beliefs, feelings and intentions;
(h) increased opportunity for acquiring social skills of basic interaction, conversation, group membership, co-operativeness, sensitivity and fellow-feeling;
(i) learning to resist group pressure and acquiring the capacity for independent behaviour;
(j) learning to recognise boundaries for own behaviour and those of others;
(k) practising the shifting ground-rules of relationships in groups.

Group counselling provides a unique opportunity for exploration of the above issues, acquisition of the relevant skills and general social maturation. The power of group dynamics, combined with the diversity of behaviours, even in a homogeneous group, are the reasons for its impact. The above points are particularly pertinent to the interactional or therapeutic use of counselling groups.

Practice

1   Work out what sort of group you want to run and for what purpose.
2   Select your group members on the basis of some shared problem; if at all possible, enable the youngsters to choose or want to join the group rather than being coerced.
3   Decide on group size and composition, if possible keeping it to between five and ten relatively homogeneous youngsters.
4   Choose a room which is quiet, pleasant and comfortable; sit in a circle so as to increase intimacy.
5   Introduce the group and describe its purpose (for example, 'to help find better ways of getting a high than by sniffing glue' or 'to see if you can come up with better ways of coping than by taking overdoses'). You may find it helpful to draw attention to the therapeutic *process* of group interaction as well as to its beneficial outcomes.
6   Set down whatever boundaries you believe are necessary, such as 'there will be no swearing' or 'we shall try to be courteous to each other'.
7   Introduce the topic; encourage members to express their beliefs, feelings and behavioural reactions (actual or probable) to the topic.
8   Convey rapport with and understanding of the group either by encouraging youngsters' response or by clarifying the meaning or implications of what has been said.
9   Attend to the way group members relate to each other, both verbally and in non-verbal communication; draw attention to these modes of relating as appropriate either in a reflective way or through confrontation.
10 Encourage members to interact with each other through experimenting with different modes of expressing feeling, confronting, self-disclosing, listening, encouraging and responding to others' challenges.
11 Focus on particular group members (such as a particularly aggressive or quiet youngster) or aspects of group interaction (such as how everyone speaks at the same time and so does not listen to the others), encouraging the group members to respond in alternative ways and explore which response is the better.
12 Emphasise trust, openness and the benevolence of the group at every opportunity, to encourage confidence and a readiness to risk encounter and revelation among group members.
13 Give positive reinforcement to socially desirable and adaptive analyses and suggestions given by members.
14 Encourage members to explore and set out the disadvantages and difficulties of those beliefs, feelings and behaviour patterns you believe to be maladaptive.
15 Use whatever exercises or games (such as role-playing, team-building games and exercises concerned with guessing how a member is feeling) that you consider appropriate.

16 Use flip charts for illustrating points, drawing attention graphically to group dynamics and setting down a list of alternatives, and use videos to give feedback on self-presentation and social skills modelling wherever appropriate.

17 Remain sensitive to resistance and work through it by countering it through encouragement, ignoring it or alternatively focusing on it and getting the group to handle it as a problem, whether it is being presented by an individual or by the whole group. The latter should not be allowed to occur often – if it does, there is something wrong with group purpose, composition or leadership style.

18 Remain aware of and decide how to handle difficult members such as the silent one, the one who is always giving advice, the dependent one, the scapegoat, the anxious one, the aggressive one and the one who monopolises the group's attention.

19 Decide when and how you want to end the group; be sensitive to the anxieties of group members concerning the loss of group support and how those who still have outstanding problems may best be helped.

20 Terminate the group session by recapitulating the gains made and suggesting further means of adaptive development.

Application Group counselling may be used with children as young as 8 right up to late adolescence. Because counselling sessions rely primarily on verbal communication and the exploration of alternatives, reasonable intellectual and verbal competence is a prerequisite of effective sessions. Almost any topic which is the concern of the counsellor or his group members is a fit subject for counselling because of the group's potential in changing the beliefs, feelings and behavioural recipes of its members. These include such problems as drug misuse, truancy, family conflict, social discomfort, aggressiveness and social irresponsibility. It can be used both on its own and as an adjunct to other treatments.

The main limitation of group counselling is that, of its nature, it can deal with only relatively mild problems of adjustment rather than acute ones which demand immediate control. This is because counselling is a slow-acting, cumulative process, even when it is effective. In many ways also, group counselling is more difficult than that undertaken with individuals. The counsellor has to attend to many more interactions and respond to more focused attention and possible hostility from the group. Effective group counsellors are not plentiful.

Just as groups can be beneficent, so they may inflict harm on their members by intensive group pressure. They can also easily get out of hand, particularly with difficult adolescents who are sensitive to anything they perceive as criticism and are likely to respond to it in a hostile manner. Additionally, there is unfortunately little empirically strong evidence to support group counselling as an effective treatment.

On the other hand, this is a most popular and widely practised medium of treatment, particularly for groups of disordered adolescents. The reasons are not hard to find. Over and above the unmatched power of a group counselling set-up for dealing with certain fundamental issues set out earlier, it is an efficient and cheap therapeutic technique. Although achieving excellence and effectiveness in group counselling is difficult to come by, the skills for a satisfactory level of operation are not hard to acquire. This is particularly true for people who have 'natural' authority, can project care and trust and are not afraid of children's groups. The absence of major empirical evidence of effectiveness is not peculiar to group counselling, and the potential damage to individual members can be guarded against by careful leadership. It is therefore likely to retain its popularity.

Positive peer culture

Positive peer culture (PPC) is a technique of group treatment that seeks to transform negative characteristics of individual adolescents into a positive, caring attitude to others and thence to themselves. So, for example, a group of youngsters shun the attempts of one of them to get the others to run away with him. Instead they point out the self-defeating nature of his act and declare how they would help him face his problem in a more positive way.

From among all group therapies, this is the only one to have emerged specifically from work with delinquent youngsters in residential facilities. Although the practice has been subsequently extended to a number of others such as ordinary schools, the emphasis on delinquent behaviour and residential settings remains. Far from regarding this as a limitation, we would regard it as one of this technique's strongest claims to attention, since so many other methods explicitly rule out the often deeply ingrained problems of delinquents from their purview. It is commonly seen that, in the face of the concerted and serious problems of adolescents, adults adopt responses which are at best ineffective and at worst counterproductive, because they are variants of being punitive at one extreme and giving up at the other. The crux of PPC, on the other hand, is that antisocial and other negative behaviour patterns are forms of acquiring an identity with a supportive peer culture. It contends that it is possible to turn this negative force into a positive one which gains its rewards from caring and being cared for. These, in turn, lead to changing for the better and thereby being accepted by both peers and adults.

Most troublesome youngsters have had adverse experiences to which they have had to adjust in order to survive. In the course of such adjustment they have acquired the strength that allows them to withstand considerable pressure to change for the better from a variety of authority figures. They can usually do this because they are supported by a negative subculture of 'lieutenants'. If this force can be rechannelled, the troublesome youngster can become an expert in seeing through and helping change the maladaptive 'fronting' of other youngsters.

How does it work?   PPC is the articulation of a form of practice. What theoretical basis it has is therefore 'practice' theory, rather than the practice deriving from theory, as for example with behaviour modification. Indeed, there is no special theoretical basis to PPC which is not shared by all group therapies which emphasise the power of the group and skilled directive leadership. The latter is regarded as particularly important in PPC, associated with the names of Vorrath and Brendtro.

In comparison with some other group therapies, this technique emphasises *trust* and openness rather than invasion of privacy and exposure; a climate of *change* rather than one of security; *here and now* rather than the past; and problems as *opportunities* for change rather than troublesome impediments. Every opportunity is taken to highlight *helping* and caring for others as strengths. When youngsters express antisocial and negative sentiments, these are relabelled by the leader, who also presents as an *incompatible but prosocial* and positive model for the youngsters to emulate.

The authors of the technique are reticent in setting out the theoretical bases of PPC. However, both the available literature and the practice show the group meeting as providing an opportunity for laying open problems; sharing and creating trust; analysing 'cause and effect' or the context of problems and why they are sustained; providing negative and positive feedback by a powerful group, which differentially shapes beliefs, feelings and behaviour patterns. The group will go through four stages of development:

1   'Casing' – when young people try to gain information about each other but avoid giving away anything themselves.
2   'Limit testing' – as youngsters begin to reveal themselves, so considerable tension is generated; cliques are formed, and much negative feeling is expressed.
3   'Polarisation of values' – as youngsters begin to discover alternatives to their negative values and behaviour patterns, so they get to the point where they must decide whether to change or not; their anxiety may be displaced on to scapegoats or the leader, but the cliques begin to crumble away and be replaced by the first glimmerings of positive change.
4   'Positive peer culture' – this is the final stage, when youngsters have developed a cohesive group without factions; they begin to demand and receive positive responses to their own and others' problems.

The repetition of these experiences, and their differential reinforcement in a variety of real-life settings, allows for the generalisation of the change – which, with luck should be maintained in the normal environment.

Practice

1   Choose your group, ideally of nine youngsters; seek homogeneity in the age, sex, maturity, sophistication and aggressive potential of the members, but diversity in their personalities and problem profiles.

2   Decide on the venue and seating plan – space where distractions are minimised is recommended. You, the leader, should sit behind a desk to distance yourself from the youngsters and emphasise your leading role; the youngsters should sit in a horseshoe around you.

3   Make sure that the group are seated before you arrive.

4   Introduce the basic idea and structure of the PPC meetings, how long the meetings are likely to take and what is expected of the members.

5   Start the meeting proper by going round the group and asking each member to state what difficulty he has experienced or presented in a concise fashion (about 15 minutes); remember, however, this is the youngsters' meeting – they should take the initiative; your job is to guide their interaction at the start until they have gained the necessary skills.

6   Proceed to 'award the meeting' to the youngster who has asked for the special opportunity to discuss his or her problems; if more than one asks for it, decide on the basis of the urgency of the youngster's problem or other merits of the case.

7   Ensure the meeting progresses on to the 'problem-solving' phase, when the youngster's problems are analysed and alternative responses highlighted; don't play the therapist; attempt unobtrusively to get the group to sort out its own problems rather than relying on the leader. This takes a lot of practice on both the leader's and the group's part.

8   Be on the look-out for 'rigged' meetings, where there is unequal participation by group members.

9   Be alert to group members minimising, overstating or denying their problems or projecting their problems on to others; remain aware of non-verbal cues in the group, such as the location and proximity of members, eye contact and facial expressions.

10   Watch out for negative leaders and those who disturb the positive atmosphere; be ready to isolate and deal with them in the group by isolating them from their 'lieutenants'; remember this is meant to be a 'positive' group, so dealing with these negative influences must be done in a positive way.

11   Foster the building of a positive, cohesive group by making creative use of stress, such as by exaggerating or dramatising a youngster's problems, bringing in others such as parents, close friends or victims.

12   Proceed to give 'the summary' of the meeting (10 minutes) in a serious but relaxed manner, drawing attention positively to the significant features of the meeting; use the opportunity creatively by raising or

lowering group anxiety in relation to their problem conditions; whenever possible, ask a group member to summarise the meeting.
13 Close the meeting.

Application PPC can be used with children from age 10 upwards. Being a verbal medium, a degree of verbal ability is necessary. It can be used with a wide range of personal and social difficulties but is contra-indicated where any of the youngsters are suffering from serious physical or psychiatric problems.

The technique has few serious disadvantages. It requires a strong leader, capable of handling potentially riotous group sessions but with sufficient sensitivity to redeploy negative responses for positive outcomes. The group itself can be seriously threatening to its members. Unless carefully handled, confrontations within the group can spill to the outside and result in damage to the members. Its theoretical basis is poorly developed, and the empirical evidence of effectiveness is not very strong. It is also of potential use only with those problems which do not require immediate curbing.

These limitations are greatly outweighed by the strengths of the technique. As already indicated, this is almost the only technique specifically developed for delinquent youngsters in residential settings, who defeat almost every other attempt at turning their considerable energies to positive interpersonal use. Its theoretical and empirical paucity is not much worse than for many other techniques. The practice carries considerable face validity and provides a coherent plan of action for one of the most difficult types of adolescent. The power of PPC would be enhanced if it were allied with other contrived and naturally occurring reinforcements which would be available in a natural setting. Its advantages are enhanced by the fact that it can be carried out anywhere, does not require any equipment and is very efficient in terms of therapist input. It is blissfully free from jargon and attempts at mystification. Though far from 'pure', the technique effectively addresses a range of issues which are not properly tackled by other therapies, and deserves much wider practice.

Psychodrama

Psychodrama is a technique whereby the dramatic enactment of personal difficulties is intended to release conflicts and provide feedback which will result in amelioration of the problem. So, for example, a girl acts out the conflict with her father and is given the opportunity of witnessing how conflicts escalate through her behaviour.

The use of psychodrama dates from the post-war years. It became particularly popular in the 1950s in psychiatric facilities but was later incorporated in normal education as a means of personal and social development. It is an extension of normal life experiences, particularly during childhood, when the social repertoire is considerably extended by fantasy play and soliloquy.

Unlike other group therapies, this technique relies primarily on action, rather than talking, though the main insights are still mediated by the therapist's interpretations.

How does it work?   The chief underlying premise of psychodrama is that people's conflicts and difficulties arise in real-life settings. These settings generate too much anxiety and are subject to too many variables to allow effective treatment. It is therefore necessary to create 'therapeutic cultures in miniature' where, through drama, personal difficulties can be acted out and alternative adaptive approaches developed.

With this technique, the group and its dynamic are not used as a major medium of change but rather as a context in which real-life dramas can be acted out. The group members act both as extensions of the main actor (as 'ego auxiliaries') and as the audience. The therapist acts as the 'director', casting the subject as the 'protagonist', acting through past or current conflicts and providing feedback which directs the subject towards more adaptive responses. The practice eventually deals with all group members, who benefit not just from the acting out of their own difficulties but also from participating in the resolution of others' problems.

Practice

1   Choose a stage, preferably a real one.
2   Decide on the size and composition of your group; ensure that your group are sufficiently interested and manageable not to disrupt the proceedings while you are 'directing' the drama.
3   'Warm up' the protagonist and the other group members by talking about the purpose of the exercise, what they are expected to do and how, and what benefits will accrue to them from the process.
4   'Set the scene' and start the enactment of the drama; simplify or complicate, as necessary, to bring out what you see as the crucial problem; bring in other group members to act other significant parts as appropriate.
5   Encourage the audience to comment on what is going on and relate their own relevant experiences.
6   Use whatever techniques are relevant to deepen and extend the drama; these include such ploys as 'role reversal' (between the protagonist and another person), 'mirroring' (when the protagonist remains in the audience and his behaviour is imitated on the stage), 'soliloquy' (where inner thoughts and feelings are expressed aloud) and the 'double technique' (when an auxiliary is placed beside the antagonist 'as himself' to help present a fuller and more accurate picture of the self).

7 Interpret and work through the material generated by the drama; emphasise the positive gains in insight and alternative responses.
8 Conclude the session.

Application Psychodrama is used primarily with youngsters who present and experience interpersonal difficulties. It has been used with children from primary-school age to late adolescence, but rarely as a primary or exclusive treatment of choice. Homogeneity of the group in terms of age, intelligence and cultural background is advisable as an aid to group cohesion.

This technique is limited in the range of problems to which it can be applied. It is even more limited in terms of the intensity of problems with which it can be useful. It cannot deal with severe problems which are in need of urgent response nor with those of acting-out and aggressive youngsters who demand a more structured approach.

The demands on time, equipment and expert manpower are great. The director must be capable of setting up dramatic episodes which economically and accurately portray the relevant problem. This requires not only dramatic ability but also cultural and therapeutic insight. Such people are not abundantly found in therapeutic facilities for young people. Finally, the theoretical basis of psychodrama is thin and most suspect, and there is scant evidence of its therapeutic benefits with young people.

On the other hand, carefully used, it is a useful adjunct to other therapeutic attempts. This is particularly so with less verbal children who are nevertheless intelligent enough to be able to tune into the significance of the dramatic experience and the therapists' insights. On the whole, the effort entailed in setting up successful psychodrama experiences can be more usefully directed through other therapies.

Role-playing

Role-playing is one of the commonest and most pervasive human activities, seen even in primitive cultures and among very young children. Its professional use in treatment dates from the early years of this century and can be detected in almost every form of treatment other than service delivery and physical ones.

How does it work? Role-play involves acting out a situation without a stage or the pretence that anything but a role is being played. It provides an opportunity for conveying feelings and information otherwise difficult to communicate; disclosing feelings that are difficult to admit directly; rehearsing new roles or situations; and getting first-hand experience of other people's reactions. It enhances involvement and enables the translation of an idea or a feeling into more tangible reality. Thus, it increases understanding of both oneself and others. Its theoretical basis is wide, drawing on social learning as well as dynamic concepts.

Practice

1   Introduce role-play naturally in a context that warrants it rather than as a treatment method in its own right. It is particularly useful when rehearsal and practice are indicated, when the youngster is unable to express something in words, when an important relationship or response can be clarified only through action and when acting is 'safer' than saying.

2   Choose a group small enough so that every member can participate as a player rather than audience; ask the youngster to describe the people involved and how they feel; encourage others to ask questions so that the fullest picture of the problem may emerge.

3   Reinforce positively the insightful comments made by the players so as to increase their therapeutic power.

4   Ask the youngsters to volunteer for different roles; fill the ones that are left unfilled.

5   Allow the use of 'aliases', *alter egos*, puppets or dolls in role-playing to allow otherwise inarticulate or unforthcoming youngsters to express themselves.

6   Check that the players understand their roles; give them time to prepare how they want to present themselves (as opposed to improvising) if necessary.

7   Provide opportunity for interrupting play to give additional information or to allow a member to drop out.

8   Allow the playing to run until a 'natural' break or when the scene of particular interest has been acted.

9   Open up a discussion with the players about what happened, why, how each person performed and what that highlighted in terms of the problem and adaptive ways of dealing with it; ask each actor to speak about his own feelings and those of others in the role-play; ask how these differed from their perceptions before they started.

10   Rehearse the more common (problem) roles and relationships, even if not specifically brought up by the youngsters; these include mother–son, father–son, siblings, boy–girl, youngster–authority figure, youngster in school, job and other social situations.

Application   Role-playing has been extensively used with children from the age of 7 to late adolescence. It is itself an element of many other treatments and has been applied to problems such as drug abuse, school difficulties, family interactions, a wide range of social skills deficits, antisocial problems and clinical psychological difficulties.

Although role-playing cannot usefully be substituted for service delivery and physical treatments, it has hardly any limitations. It requires no material resources. While training enhances the expertise, most ordinary people can both role-play and encourage others to do so. The analytical and interpretative elements, though welcome and worthwhile, are not as powerful as a role which has been well acted through and provoked 'real' responses from others.

The strengths of role-playing derive from its unequalled power to give insight into and experience of alternative realities, not just of other situations and people's feelings but also one's own. Because of this, role-playing has extensive usage, encouraged by the ready availability of almost everyone as a 'natural' practitioner. There is considerable evidence of its efficacy as a medium of treatment, with reasonable face validity. It is a technique no child therapist can ignore.

Further reading

Barker, P. (1981) *Basic Family Therapy*. London: Granada.

Bentovim, A., Gorell Barnes, G., and Cooklin, A. (eds) (1982) *Family Therapy – Complementary Frameworks of Theory and Practice*. London: Academic Press.

Blumberg, A. and Golombiewski, B. (1976) *Learning and Change in Groups*. Harmondsworth: Penguin.

Brown, B. and Christie, M. (1981) *Social Learning Practice in Residential Child Care*. Oxford: Pergamon.

De Shazer, S. (1982) *Patterns of Brief Family Therapy: An Ecosystemic Approach*. New York: Guilford Press.

Douglas, T. (1976) *Groupwork Practice*. London: Tavistock.

Douglas, T. (1986) *Group Living: The Application of Group Dynamics in Residential Settings*. London: Tavistock.

Feldman, R.A. and Wodarski, J.S. (1975) *Contemporary Approaches to Group Treatment*. San Francisco: Jossey Bass.

Garvin, C. (1987) *Contemporary Groupwork*, 2nd edn. Englewood Cliffs, NJ: Prentice-Hall.

Glasser, P., Sarri, R. and Vinter, R. (1974) *Individual Change through Small Groups*. New York: Free Press.

Greenberg, I. (ed.) (1975) *Psychodrama: Theory and Therapy*. London: Souvenir Press.

Haley, J. (1976) *Problem-Solving Therapy*. New York: Harper & Row.

Haley, J. (1980) *Leaving Home – the Therapy of Disturbed Young People*. New York: McGraw-Hill.

Harris, G. (ed.) (1977) *The Group Treatment of Human Problems: A Social Learning Approach*. New York: Grune & Stratton.

Jennings, S. (1973) *Remedial Drama*. London: Pitman.

Kovel, J. (1978) *A Complete Guide to Therapy*. Harmondsworth: Penguin.

Madanes, C. (1981) *Strategic Family Therapy*. San Francisco: Jossey Bass.

Milroy, E. (1982) *Role-Play: A Practical Guide*. Aberdeen: Aberdeen University Press.

Minuchin, S. (1974) *Families and Family Therapy*. London: Tavistock.

Minuchin, S. and Fishman, H.C. (1981) *Family Therapy Techniques*. Cambridge, MA: Harvard University Press.

Moreno, J.L. (1953) *Who Shall Survive?* New York: Beacon House.

Moreno, J.L. (1959) 'Psychodrama', in S. Arieti (ed.), *American Handbook of Psychiatry*, Vol. 2. New York: Basic Books.

Nelson-Jones, R. (1982) *The Theory and Practice of Counselling Psychology*. London: Holt, Rinehart & Winston.

Ohlsen, M. (1970) *Group Counselling*. New York: Holt, Rinehart & Winston.

Patterson, G.R. and Gullion, M.E. (1971) *Living with Children*. Champaign, IL: Research Press.

Rose, S. (1972) *Treating Children in Groups*. San Francisco: Jossey Bass.

Schaefer, C.E., Briesmeister, J.M. and Fitton, M.E. (1984) *Family Therapy Techniques for Problem Behaviors of Children and Teenagers*. San Francisco: Jossey Bass.

Slavson, S.R. and Schiffer, M. (1975) *Group Psychotherapies for Children*. New York: International University Press.

Smith, P.B. (1980) *Group Processes and Personal Change*. London: Harper & Row.

Sugar, M. (ed.) (1975) *The Adolescent in Group and Family Therapy*. New York: Brunner/ Mazel.

Sulzer-Azaroff, B. and Mayer, G.R. (1977) *Applying Behavior Analysis Procedures with Children and Youth*. New York: Holt, Rinehart & Winston.

Taylor, J.L. and Walford, R. (1972) *Simulation in the Classroom*. Harmondsworth: Penguin.

Treacher, A. and Carpenter, J. (eds) (1984) *Using Family Therapy*. Oxford: Blackwell.

van Ments, M. (1983) *The Effective Use of Role Play: A Handbook for Teachers and Trainers*. London: Kogan Page.

Vorrath, H.H. and Brendtro, L.K. (1985) *Positive Peer Culture*, 2nd edn. New York: Aldine.

12

Environmental Therapies

We started Part II with a highly individualised method of alleviating youngsters' problems through the provision of goods and services. We end it with a method of treatment which is at the opposite extreme. In environmental therapies the individual child is much less important than the group of which he is a member and whose development is fostered by the activities and interventions of those adults who conduct it. The basic idea of such therapies lies in the recognition that no human being ever acts in a vacuum. His behaviour proceeds from his past experience and is a reaction to his perception of the present environment. The environment is thus the context in which all behaviour takes place. It shapes behaviour by both impeding certain acts and stimulating or facilitating others. Because of this, it is evident that a good way of shaping problem behaviour is by attacking its environmental determinants rather than individual behavioural characteristics. After all, no child is problematic wholly irrespective of the circumstances which surround him.

Theoretical basis

Environmental therapies are rooted in the recognition in the early parts of the twentieth century that groups have major potential for changing people who are experiencing difficulties of adjustment. This recognition, associated with the development of Gestalt psychology, took on greater force during the Second World War with its multi-faceted psychological and physical casualties. The early ideas were further extended by the conception of the 'individual within his community' encapsulated in group analysis and some famous early examples of 'therapeutic communities'. The core ideas of the therapeutic community can be summed up in Righton's (1975) words as 'a deliberate use of everyday living experiences, shared by a team of professional workers and on a variety of client groups in order to achieve, jointly, a complete or partial solution of the problems confronted by the members of the client group'.

In such an environment the traditional distinctions between treatment agents and client groups are recognised and dealt with in interpretative and 'transference-based therapy' (see also psychoanalytic therapy in Chapter 10). This is intended to lead to the sharing of information and experiences which will release the stresses to which the problem behaviour is a response. By gradually enabling the client to perceive the therapeutic potential of environmental and group forces, he is given the opportunity to acquire means of coping with stress.

The underlying causal hypothesis is that most deviancy is a 'manifestation of environmental stress'. Despite substantial writing on what we have broadly called 'environmental therapies' it is very difficult to distinguish an explicit unifying rationale even in those more narrowly limited areas such as 'therapeutic communities' where similarities are said to outstrip the differences. Indeed, even a searching recent appraisal of the field (by Hinshelwood and Manning) concludes that much of the writing in this area is theoretically incoherent. It is possible, however, to discern from the literature that the most important element of therapy is the *influence of the peer group* on the determination of individual behaviour, *release of feelings*, the *development of trust, reduction of defensiveness* and ability to see the *'unconscious processes'* rather than just overt behaviour or aspects of the environment. In this sense, environmental therapies can be profitably seen as an integration of some ideas and practices of behaviour therapy (through the control of associations and reinforcements), psychotherapy (in the development of insight and the ability to interpret manifest behaviour) and group therapies (in the utilisation of group processes to shape adaptive behaviour). They all recognise the significant influence of the milieu in shaping behaviours.

The difference between the various techniques (with the exception of security) lies in degrees of emphasis on individual components rather than theoretically distinct viewpoints.

Security, as an environmental treatment, is qualitatively different from the rest despite the fact that it uses most explicitly the qualities of an environment to help towards the alleviation of particular forms of behaviour. It is concerned with dramatically reducing the amount and quality of a youngster's mobility as a means of ensuring that he does not have the opportunity to engage in unacceptable behaviours. The use of security finds its justification in jurisprudence *incapacitation* and commonsense psychology (restricting mobility and access to undesirable opportunities) rather than in any elaborate theory, as is the case with other environmental treatments. Its use is pragmatically determined. Even in the present sense, however, 'security' has a psycho-dynamic aspect. The problem child behaves as if he were devoid of internal controls. Infantile, immature, self-destructive, exaggerated, egocentric and often antisocial behaviour is directed at provoking external control. Relief often follows when adults make a firm decision and impose limits on both the child's mobility and his uncontrolled behaviour.

Status

The strengths of environmental treatments lie in their explicit recognition that environmental opportunity and stimulation are often at least one-half of the causation of each act, whether maladaptive or otherwise. More particularly, the attempt to orientate a whole environment towards maximising the therapeutic potential which is inherent in everyday occurrences, such as sharing work and feeding, utilises elements which would otherwise be wasted even if they did not positively destroy other therapeutic efforts. The recognition of environmental influences is in any case a prime prerequisite of *any* therapy before it can take place. The emphasis on the totality of the environment is likely to be to the greater advantage of all client groups and result in a setting which is potentially beneficent and interesting rather than routine and, to that extent, not worthy of concern.

The limitations of these therapies lie in their very virtues. They are concerned with organising whole environments, and this may be both uneconomic and impractical. The literature is replete with instances of the work that has to be put in to overcome the resistance and impediments to the development of a therapeutic environment. The treatment is not focused on particular problems, and its broad sweep is likely to be less efficient and effective in ameliorating conditions than focal treatments. In this respect therapeutic environments are no better than general broad-spectrum medicines of whose indiscriminate use they are so critical.

The emphasis of the therapeutic medium is on the whole group, which can (and does) get out of hand and, in turn, become destructive to more vulnerable group members. Conducting such treatments properly so that they remain 'therapeutic' therefore demands the highest level of skilled experience, which is not available in abundance. They are not efficient in dealing with critical behaviours which demand individual attention and which are likely to spill over unless contained. Their use has been primarily confined to adult psychiatric settings. There are, however, a number of instances of their use in penal establishments and facilities for maladjusted and antisocial youngsters. They demand much more intensive staff training, change, commitment and support than most personal or organisational resources are capable of providing.

Environmental treatments are not readily amenable to rigorous research. Despite some attempts they also fail in the last resort to satisfy the requirements of accountability in relation to the treatment of children, who do not often enter such programmes with consent based on full knowledge. In general they seem to be more frequently usable with the older, more articulate people who are not profoundly damaged and whose difficulties arise from poor adaptation to particular circumstances.

Overall, this whole method, and the cluster of techniques associated with it, is more impressive by the evocativeness of its slogan-like central concepts and general benevolent intent than by the specificity, efficiency or tolerable ethical costs with which it can be put into practice. Its range of applicability is, in theory and at one extreme, universal. Its use in practice, however, must be considered to be very limited, particularly in relation to children, who must be protected against unfalsifiable, totalitarian claims of beneficence.

Therapeutic communities/therapeutic milieux

Despite some marginal distinctions in the literature between therapeutic communities and therapeutic milieux, the similarities, where they exist and are articulated, clearly outweigh the differences. In view of this, the two are treated together in this section. The terms denote an environment in which the intent underlying all interactions of staff and children is therapeutic; where the central concern is with patient/client integrity and choice; and where personal expressions are allowed even at the risk of damage to the child or his group.

The core ideas comprise the following: *permissiveness* – that is, toleration of deviant behaviour which is openly discussed with a view to the removal of defences; *reality confrontation* – concerned with reflecting the individual's conduct back to him in the hope that he will accept its reality; *communalism* – concerned with sharing activities, tasks and roles and the removal of defensive and impeding organisational barriers; and *democracy* – the predominance of group, majority views rather than of those emanating from 'authority'.

How does it work?   The theoretical basis of the therapy lies in the intensive interactions of group members and the shaping forces of the environment within which they operate, so that all of them are directed at therapeutic outcome. Thus, attention is paid to features of the physical space, availability of reinforcements and the way the physical space determines human interactions – for example, in terms of seating or access to quantity and quality of food. The second core element is the use of peer group dynamics (set out in earlier sections) to shape behaviour.

Practice   The creation and operation of a therapeutic environment/milieu demands comprehensive development of the non-human aspects of the physical environment such as the layout of space, the interrelationships and interaction of individual spaces with the people who inhabit them and the availability of a range of reinforcing elements such as food and play opportunities. Once this has been achieved, attention should then be paid to setting up and conducting groups whose operation must be carefully managed lest they wreak even greater destruction than the benefits which they impart to their members.

Throughout, attention is paid to the twin elements of *environmental determinants* and *group interactions*. There are numerous different ways of running groups in therapeutic communities. Their flavour and emphasis shift, in any case, with changes in membership, prevailing group atmospheres and perceptions of the 'agenda'. There are therefore no standard 'textbook' guidelines for conducting such communities. There are as many varieties of emphasis as people who run them, as can be seen from published literature. The core and generally accepted medium of treatment is the holding of 'therapeutic meetings', which include all the workers and clients/patients, irrespective of numbers.

Despite diversity of practice, general guidelines for the conduct of the crucial therapeutic meetings can be recommended:

1 Decide on what you want from the meeting; all the other participants will have their own 'agenda' or purposes for participation.

2 Be alert to the shifts and developments that may emerge at the meeting; if there have been 'events' (such as somebody's wrist-cutting or failure to do their allotted share of work) which are likely to be brought out, make sure you have done some thinking/planning about the probable outcomes.

3 Ensure that the physical environment is as conducive to the preferred outcome as you can make it; in this respect the timing (before or after a meal), seating arrangements (level and who sits next to whom) and presence of vulnerable items in the event of a physical blow-up are obvious examples.

4 Introduce the meeting or allow it to start by sharing information or presenting an explicit agenda; there are bound to be implicit agenda items, such as who or what should become the focus of therapeutic interpretation and group attention.

5 Decide on how to lead into the problems that are to be identified and work through the defences that surround them.

6 Ensure that the group members remain attentive and continue to participate in the meeting and its outcome.

7 If more than one problem comes out, help sort out the priorities and how they are to be tackled; particular attention must be paid to converting the usually destructive and accusatory interaction of the group members into mutual help and development.

8 Beware both of the victimisation of individual members and of the tendency of some to sink into apathy and withdrawal.

9 Attend particularly to the balance between the necessary 'heat' of open confrontation and the 'cool' which is required for continuing with a meeting and ending it on a positive, optimistic note.

Application Therapeutic communities and milieux aim at creating an environment which, through the intensive interaction of their members, leads to a resolution of their problems. They demand some degree of verbal participation and are therefore unsuitable for very young children or the profoundly mentally handicapped or disturbed. They have been used for the mildly mentally handicapped and those suffering from schizophrenia, personality disorders, neuroses and drug-related problems. The emphasis on socio-psychiatric and dynamic interpretations seems to exclude physical and cognitive problems.

Limitations arise from the narrow range of problems to which the treatment can be usefully directed; the enormous demands on skilled manpower; high levels of stress generated for both the clients and the staff; and the relative opacity of focus and uncertainty of outcome. There is also considerable variability of practice even within the same facilities, depending on which individual or group is dominant. This suggests that the therapeutic community is more an ideology of treatment than a coherent or rigorous technique. We would consider intervention in the lives of problem children too ethically fraught to warrant a generalised intervention which, of its nature, cannot be (and through research has not been) shown to be beneficial.

The strength of the therapeutic community ideas derives from emphasis on and drawing attention to the significant influence of environment and group in shaping ideas, feelings and behaviour. The core ideas provide a powerful structure for running an environment which places fundamental value on people as human beings rather than as objects of treatment. By its emphasis on human aspects of treatment, it acts as a necessary antidote to the potentially mechanistic tendencies of certain other forms of treatment. There are sufficient distinguished practitioners of high integrity operating under this banner to ensure that it will not be ignored.

Planned environment therapy (PET)

Planned environment therapy is concerned with the purposive use of everyday experiences, shared by the therapists and particular client groups, to solve the problems experienced by group members. So, for example, the experience of shared living is used by the therapists to expose and ameliorate conflicts among problem adolescents.

How does it work?   The theoretical basis of PET is not distinguishable from that of therapeutic communities set out earlier. None of the writers sets out features which distinguish it from a whole host of other attempts broadly concerned with using an environment therapeutically. They make no distinction whatever between therapeutic communities and PET, and some regard it as 'attitude of mind' and 'not a particular type of activity, but a point of view'.

Practice   As before, despite the large body of writings broadly covering this area, it is not possible to discern a set of operational principles which can be authoritatively described as providing adequate guidelines to practice. In so far as they can be discerned, statements about the management and care of children are not distinctively PET related. Interpretations of problems are primarily dynamic rather than behavioural. Thus, treatment is more often concerned with pulling down general maladaptive 'defences' than with taking specific ameliorative measures. The critical elements can therefore be seen as thoroughgoing therapeutic *intent*, *skills at group management* and ability to provide *dynamic interpretatons* of behaviour. Since PET provides no coherent or special variants of these, they can be better gleaned from earlier chapters on other techniques.

Application   As far as can be ascertained, this technique is suitable for those youngsters whose deviant behaviour is not critical, serious or in need of urgent curbing and control. Older, verbally more adept adolescents are said to be better suited to this treatment regime. Conversely, however, such adolescents have better-established patterns of problem behaviour which are less readily susceptible to such broad-spectrum treatment. Weaknesses and strengths are akin to those of therapeutic communities.

Security

'Security' is a modern term denoting the restriction of mobility through placement in an environment from which the person cannot readily depart. To this extent it is distinguishable from other forms of security which achieve the same result by the use of either debilitating medication or a 'human wall'. It is used as an aid to the treatment of those children who are deemed to present an unacceptable risk to themselves or others if treated under open conditions. So, for example, a suicidal child is placed in security as a means of providing him with intensive supervision and preventing his suicide.

How does it work?   Security is achieved simply by placing an impediment in the form of walls, unbreakable windows and locked doors through which a child cannot readily pass. This is a physical fact which cannot make any pretension on its own to therapeutic power, other than in its ability to prevent a recurrence of a serious act such as murder, rape or self-injury. However, secure environments for children should ideally be operated by people with a wide range of therapeutic qualities and skills. The intensive, continuing interaction of the child and the staff creates an environment in which problems can be exposed and worked through in a beneficent and therapeutic manner. This interaction powerfully augments the benefit that the child gains from not being able to continue committing acts which place him and others at unacceptable risk.

The therapeutic action of a secure environment is potentially twofold: incapacitation and reduction of opportunity for continuing to experience or present problems and, through this, *gradual unlearning*; optimal opportunity for *regulating positive and negative experiences* and therefore maximising appropriate learning. Although some amelioration of problems may take place for the first reason, this must be augmented by an active programme of treatment, using a variety of methods. In general terms, security may be a necessary prerequisite of treatment but rarely achieves treatment objectives by itself.

Practice   The provision of a secure environment is made within the penal, health and social services. In each of these, both building and human are described and *prescribed* to high levels of detail in relevant circulars and other government documents. In the case of both the penal and social services in the United Kingdom, the use of secure accommodation is closely regulated through judicial authority. At present, placement in facilities in the health service under mental health regulations does not have to carry the same judicial authority, but is rather dependent on psychiatric authority and general public acceptance as set down in the relevant legislation.

Application   Security may be deemed necessary for those children who either have committed grave crimes or have a history of absconding, are likely to abscond and would place themselves and/or others at risk if they were to abscond again. With appropriate authority, there is no minimum age, although it should be possible to reduce risks of the above kind to an acceptable level with children younger than 10 years without the use of security.

Disadvantages of security include the great financial cost of creating and maintaining a decent environment for children and their care-givers. The hothouse atmosphere which results from the inescapable confrontations of the child with his own problems and those of others can generate high levels of anxiety and anguish which, unless properly channelled, can be damaging. There is also an understandable tendency on the part of the youngsters, their parents and the general public to see therapeutic restriction on the child's mobility in the same light as penal incarceration. Furthermore, the inevitable conflicts and behavioural problems may bring into play questionable methods of management which may further destroy or undermine the child's self-respect and emerging sense of responsibility. Last, but not least, locking up children is the extreme permissible sanction against intolerably troubled and troublesome children. As such it raises fundamental ethical issues which demand resolution in each individual case.

PART III

THE MASTER CODE

Part III, which we have called 'The Master Code', is intended as a reference chart for treatment planning and practice. It is arranged according to the six broad problem areas or classification outlined in Chapter 2 (see pages 25–6). These are:

01 Physical problems
02 Intellectual/educational problems
03 Home and family problems
04 Social skills problems
05 Antisocial behaviour
06 Personal problems

Within each *problem area*, particular *attributes* are listed, and each attribute is subdivided into individual *behaviours*. As well as the six main problem areas (01 to 06), atrributes and behaviours are also numbered in a sequence starting 01. Thus, 01.**01**.01 indicates the problem area 'physical problems', the attribute 'brain damage' and the behaviour 'impairment of memory'. In each case, the first pair of numbers shows the problem area, the middle two bold numbers the attribute and the third pair of numbers (where necessary) the behaviour.

Within each particular problem behaviour, the chart sets out treatment *aims*, *methods* and *techniques*. The techniques listed may then be found in the Contents list at the start of the book and the relevant pages consulted for detailed discussion in Part II.

The abbreviation BM means 'behaviour modification'; PET means 'planned environment therapy'; PPC means 'positive peer culture'.

01 PHYSICAL PROBLEMS

Behaviour	Aim	Method	Techniques

01.01 Brain damage

Behaviour	Aim	Method	Techniques
01 Impairment of memory	Improve memory	Behaviour modification	Chaining Cognitive BM Differential reinforcement Operant conditioning Positive reinforcement Prompting
		Cognitive	Feedback Remedial
02 Poor motor co-ordination	Improve co-ordination	Physical	Biofeedback Medication Physical exercise Physiotherapy
		Behaviour modification	Chaining Modelling Positive reinforcement Shaping
03 Overactivity	Reduce level of activity	Physical Behaviour modification	Medication Aversive conditioning Differential reinforcement Extinction Operant conditioning Time out Token economy
		Cognitive	Feedback
04 Impulsivity	Reduce impulsivity	Physical Behaviour modification	Medication Aversive conditioning Differential reinforcement Extinction Flooding Time out Token economy
		Group therapy	Group modification Role-play
		Environmental therapy	Therapeutic community

Behaviour	Aim	Method	Techniques
05 Emotional instability (see also 06.**08**)	Stabilise	Physical Behaviour modification Group therapy Environmental therapy	Medication Self-management Shaping Time out Token economy Psychodrama Role-play Therapeutic community

01.**02 Motor disorders**

Behaviour	Aim	Method	Techniques
01 Tics, twitches	Eliminate/ reduce	Physical Behaviour modification Cognitive	Biofeedback Medication Aversive conditioning Extinction Negative practice Relaxation therapy Feedback
02 Bizarre postures	As above	As above	
03 Poor gross co-ordination	Improve co-ordination	Physical Behaviour modification	Biofeedback Medication Physiotherapy practice Positive reinforcement Shaping
04 Poor fine co-ordination	As above	As above	

01.**03 Epilepsy**

Behaviour	Aim	Method	Techniques
01 *Grand mal* seizures	Eliminate	Physical Behaviour modification	Biofeedback Medication
02 *Petit mal*	As above	As above	
03 Minor fits	As above	As above	

01.**04 Psychoses**

Behaviour	Aim	Method	Techniques
01 Impairment of cognitive functioning	Improve cognitive functioning	Physical Behaviour modification Cognitive	Medication Operant conditioning Positive reinforcement Shaping Token economy Social skills

Behaviour	Aim	Method	Techniques
02 Language disorder	Normalise	As above + Group therapy	Group modification Role-play
03 Delusions	Eliminate	As above + Cognitive	Feedback
04 Halluci-nations	As above	As above	
05 Disorder of affect (see also 06.**08**)	Normalise affect	As above	
06 Social withdrawal	Improve social contact	As above	
07 Attention interference	Improve attention	As above	
08 Loss of pleasure	Improve capacity for pleasure	As above	
09 Lack of insight	Improve insight	As above	
10 Loss of personal identity (see also 06.**14**)	Improve sense of identity	As above	
11 Ideas of reference	Eliminate	As above	
12 Thought disorder	As above	As above	
13 Ritualistic	Reduce/ eliminate	As above	

01.**05 Physical condition**

01 Abnormal physical size	Reduce impact	Physical Cognitive Talking therapy	Medication Surgical Social skills Counselling

Behaviour	Aim	Method	Techniques
02 Poor physical condition	Improve condition	Physical	Exercise Medication
03 Failure to thrive	Normalise	Service delivery	Seek specialist advice
		Physical	Exercise Medication
04 Poor personal hygiene	Establish good habits	Behaviour modification	Chaining Contracting Differential reinforcement Modelling Prompting Shaping Token economy
05 Infections related to hygiene	Eliminate	Physical	Medication
06 Frequent minor ailments	Reduce	Service delivery	Seek specialist advice
		Physical	Medication
07 Accident proneness	Reduce	Behaviour modification	Cognitive BM Prompting Token economy
08 Emaciation	Improve condition	As 01.05.02 and 01.05.03	
09 Obesity	Reduce	Physical	Medication
		Behaviour modification	Aversive conditioning Cognitive BM Contracting Covert conditioning
		Cognitive Group therapy	Feedback Group counselling Group modification PPC
10 Tattoos	Eliminate	Physical	Medication Surgical

01.06 Eyesight

01 Defective vision	Improve	Service delivery	Seek specialist advice
02 Colour deficiency	Compensate	As above	
03 Squint	Eliminate	As above	

Behaviour	Aim	Method	Techniques

01.07 Hearing

Behaviour	Aim	Method	Techniques
01 Permanent hearing loss	Enable coping	Service delivery	Seek specialist advice
02 Temporary hearing loss	As above	As above	

01.08 Speech

Behaviour	Aim	Method	Techniques
01 Stammer	Eliminate	Physical Behaviour modification	Biofeedback
			Assertiveness training
			Aversive conditioning
			Chaining
			Cognitive BM
			Differential reinforcement
			Modelling
			Positive/negative reinforcement
			Prompting
			Relaxation
			Shaping
			Token economy
		Cognitive	Feedback
			Social skills
			Speech therapy
		Group therapy	Psychodrama
			Role-play
02 Lisp	Eliminate	As above	
03 Other articulatory defect(s)	As above	As above	
04 Aphasia	Normalise speech	Physical Behaviour modification	Biofeedback
			Assertiveness training
			Chaining
			Cognitive BM
			Modelling
			Prompting
			Shaping
			Token economy
		Cognitive	Feedback
			Social skills
			Speech therapy
		Group therapy	Group modification
			Psychodrama
			Role-play

Behaviour	Aim	Method	Techniques
05 Speech delay (development)	Accelerate speech	Service delivery	Seek specialist advice
		Physical	Biofeedback
		Cognitive	Feedback
06 Elective mutism	Produce speech	Physical	Biofeedback
		Behaviour modification	Assertiveness training
			Cognitive BM
(see also 06.**10**)			Contracting
			Differential reinforcement
			Modelling
			Prompting
			Shaping
			Token economy
		Cognitive	Feedback
			Social skills
		Talking therapy	Counselling
			Psychotherapy
		Group therapy	Family therapy
			Group counselling
			Group modification
			Psychodrama
			Role-play
		Environmental therapy	Therapeutic community

01.**09 Elimination disorders**

Behaviour	Aim	Method	Techniques
01 Nocturnal enuresis	Eliminate	Service delivery	Seek specialist advice
		Physical	Biofeedback
			Chemotherapy
		Behaviour modification	Aversive conditioning
			Contracting
			Differential reinforcement
			Prompting
			Shaping
			Token economy
02 Diurnal enuresis	As above	As above	
03 Nocturnal encopresis	As above	As above	
04 Diurnal encopresis	As above	As above	
05 Retention of faeces	As above	As above	

Behaviour	Aim	Method	Techniques

01.10 Menstrual disorders

Behaviour	Aim	Method	Techniques
01 Menstrual discomfort	Reduce	Service delivery	Seek specialist advice
		Physical	Biofeedback Chemotherapy
		Behaviour modification	Aversive conditioning Contracting Differential reinforcement Prompting Shaping Token economy
02 Cessation of periods	Normalise	As above	
03 Irregular periods	Regularise	As above	
04 Pre-menstrual tension	Reduce/ eliminate	As above	

01.11 Psychosomatic disorders

Behaviour	Aim	Method	Techniques
01 Asthma	Reduce/ eliminate	Physical	Biofeedback Chemotherapy Physical exercise Psychotherapy
		Behaviour modification	Cognitive BM Relaxation
		Talking therapy	Counselling
		Group therapy	Group counselling Group modification
02 Over-breathing	Eliminate	As above + Service delivery	Seek specialist advice
03 Alopecia	Eliminate/ improve appearance	As above	
04 Eczema	Reduce/ eliminate	Service delivery	Seek specialist advice
		Physical	Chemotherapy

(see also
06.10)

Behaviour	Aim	Method	Techniques
05 Loss/ disorder of sensory functions	Normalise	Physical	Biofeedback Chemotherapy Physiotherapy Physical exercise
		Behaviour modification	Cognitive BM Differential reinforcement Paradoxical intention
		Cognitive Talking therapy	Social skills Counselling Psychotherapy
		Group therapy	Group counselling Psychodrama
06 Loss/ disorder of motor functions	Normalise	As above	
07 Loss of voice	Restore	As above +	
		Service delivery	Seek specialist advice

01.12 Eating disorders

Behaviour	Aim	Method	Techniques
01 Anorexia nervosa	Normalise eating	Physical BM	Chemotherapy Assertiveness training Cognitive BM Contracting Differential reinforcement Modelling Operant conditioning Positive reinforcement Prompting Self-management/control Token economy
		Cognitive Talking therapy Group therapy	Feedback Counselling Psychotherapy Family therapy Group counselling Group modification PPC
		Environmental therapy	Therapeutic community
02 Under-eating	Normalise eating	As above	

Behaviour	Aim	Method	Techniques
03 Overeating	As above	As above	
04 Food fads	As above	As above +	
		Behaviour modification	Differential reinforcement
05 Self-induced vomiting	Eliminate	Physical Behaviour modification	Chemotherapy Aversive conditioning Contracting Covert conditioning Extinction Positive reinforcement Self-management Time out
		Cognitive	Feedback Social skills
		Group therapy	Group modification
06 Eating non-foods	Eliminate	Physical Behaviour modification	Chemotherapy Aversive conditioning Contracting Differential reinforcement Time out Token economy
		Cognitive	Social skills
		Group therapy	Group modification

01.13 Drug use

01 Medical drug abuse	Eliminate	Behaviour modification	Aversive conditioning Cognitive BM Contracting Covert conditioning Self-management/control Token economy
		Cognitive	Feedback Social skills
		Talking therapy	Counselling Psychotherapy
		Group therapy	Family therapy Group counselling Group modification PPC
		Environmental therapy	Security Therapeutic community

Behaviour	Aim	Method	Techniques
02 Non-medical drug abuse	Eliminate	As above +	
		Physical	Chemotherapy
03 Abuse of alcohol	Eliminate	Physical	Chemotherapy
		Behaviour modification	Aversive conditioning
			Chaining
			Cognitive BM
			Contracting
			Covert conditioning
			Extinction
		Cognitive	Social skills
		Talking therapy	Counselling
		Group therapy	Family therapy
			Group counselling
			Group modification
			PPC
		Environmental therapy	Security
			Therapeutic community
04 Excessive smoking	Eliminate	As above	
05 Solvent abuse	Eliminate	As above	

01.14 Sleep disorders

Behaviour	Aim	Method	Techniques
01 Insomnia	Eliminate	Physical	Biofeedback
			Chemotherapy
			Physical exercise
		Behaviour modification	Relaxation
02 Excessive sleeping	Reduce	Physical	Chemotherapy
		Behaviour modification	Aversive conditioning
			Contracting
			Prompting
			Token economy
		Group therapy	Group modification
03 Recurrent unusual drowsiness	As above	As above	
04 Night terror(s)	Eliminate	Physical	Chemotherapy
			Physical exercise
		Behaviour modification	Relaxation
		Talking therapy	Counselling
			Psychotherapy

Behaviour	Aim	Method	Techniques
05 Sleep-walking	As above	Physical	Chemotherapy
		Behaviour modification	Aversive conditioning
		Talking therapy	Counselling
			Psychotherapy
		Environmental therapy	Security

01.**15 Other medical conditions**

Behaviour	Aim	Method	Techniques
01 Alimentary	Eliminate/alleviate	Service delivery	Seek specialist advice
02 Allergies	As above	As above	
03 Cardio-vascular	As above	As above	
04 CNS	As above	As above	
05 Dental	As above	As above	
06 ENT	As above	As above	
07 Genito-urinary	As above	As above	
08 Infections and infestations	As above	As above	
09 Metabolism	As above	As above	
10 Muscular/skeletal	As above	As above	
11 Nervous	As above	As above	
12 Nutrition	As above	As above	
13 Respiratory	As above	As above	
14 Skin	As above	As above	
15 Surgical/orthopaedic	As above	As above	

02 INTELLECTUAL/EDUCATIONAL PROBLEMS

02.**01 Social adaptation**

Behaviour	Aim	Method	Techniques
01 Inadequate practical knowledge	Increase knowledge	Behaviour modification	Differential reinforcement
			Modelling
			Operant conditioning
			Positive reinforcement

Behaviour	Aim	Method	Techniques
		Cognitive	Prompting Self-management Feedback Remedial
02 Limited self-help skills	Increase	As above	
03 Limited survival skills	Increase skills	As above	
04 Inadequate pertinent personal information	Increase	As above	
05 Over-dependent on others' guidance and help	Reduce dependence	Behaviour modification	Assertiveness training Contract Modelling Operant conditioning Positive/negative reinforcement Prompting Shaping Token economy
		Cognitive	Feedback Remedial Social skills
		Group therapy	Group modification
		Environmental therapy	Therapeutic community

02.02 Intelligence

Behaviour	Aim	Method	Techniques
01 Limited intelligence	Improve functioning	Service delivery	Seek specialist advice
		Behaviour modification	Chaining Contracting Covert conditioning Modelling Operant conditioning Prompting Shaping Token economy
		Cognitive	Remedial education Social skills
		Group therapy	Group modification

Behaviour	Aim	Method	Techniques
02 Functioning well below potential	As above	Cognitive	As above + Feedback
03 Verbal skills deficit	As above	Service delivery	As above + Seek specialist advice
04 Practical skills deficit	As above		As above

02.03 Distractibility

01 Easily distracted from tasks	Reduce distract-ibility	Behaviour modification	Aversive conditioning Contracting Differential reinforcement Positive reinforcement Prompting Token economy
		Cognitive	Feedback
		Group therapy	Group modification
02 Poor span of attention	Increase attention span		As above

02.04 Memory

01 Short-term memory deficit	Improve memory	Behaviour modification	Chaining Contracting Positive/negative reinforcement
(see also 01.04)		Cognitive	Token economy Feedback Remedial
02 Long-term memory deficit	As above		As above
03 Specific memory disorder	As above		As above

02.05 Oral communication

01 Poor vocabulary	Increase	Service delivery	Seek specialist advice
		Behaviour modification	Chaining Contracting Modelling

Behaviour	Aim	Method	Techniques
		Cognitive	Operant conditioning
			Prompting
			Shaping
			Token economy
			Feedback
			Remedial
			Social skills
		Group therapy	Group modification
			Role-play
02 Poor grammar	Improve	As above	
03 Odd speech habits	Eliminate	As above +	
		Behaviour modification	Aversive conditioning
(see also 01.**08**)			

02.**06** Reading

Behaviour	Aim	Method	Techniques
01 Cannot read	Develop reading skills	Service delivery	Seek specialist advice
		Behaviour modification	Chaining
			Contracting
			Differential reinforcement
			Operant conditioning
			Positive reinforcement
			Prompting
			Shaping
		Cognitive	Remedial
02 Retarded in reading	Improve	As above	
03 Poor comprehension of written materal	Improve	As above	
04 Inadequate vocabulary	Improve	As above	
05 Poor word-building skills	Improve	As above	

02.**07** Spelling

Behaviour	Aim	Method	Techniques
01 Retarded	Improve	Service delivery	Seek specialist advice

Behaviour	Aim	Method	Techniques
		Behaviour modification	Chaining
			Contracting
			Differential reinforcement
			Modelling
			Operant conditioning
			Positive reinforcement
			Prompting
			Shaping
		Cognitive	Remedial
02 Retarded phonic skills	Improve	As above	
03 Reverses letter(s)/ word(s)	Eliminate	As above	

02.**08 Written communication**

Behaviour	Aim	Method	Techniques
01 Illegible handwriting	Improve	Service delivery	Seek specialist advice
		Behaviour modification	Chaining
			Contracting
			Differential reinforcement
			Modelling
			Operant conditioning
			Positive reinforcement
			Prompting
			Shaping
		Cognitive	Remedial
02 Poor written expression	Improve	As above	
03 Poor punctuation	Improve	As above	
04 Distorted grammar	Normalise	As above	

02.**09 Numeracy**

Behaviour	Aim	Method	Techniques
01 Retarded	Improve	Service delivery	Seek specialist advice
		Behaviour modification	Chaining
			Contracting
			Differential reinforcement
			Modelling
			Operant conditioning

Behaviour	Aim	Method	Techniques
			Positive reinforcement
			Prompting
			Shaping
		Cognitive	Remedial

02.10 Negative attitude to schooling

Behaviour	Aim	Method	Techniques
01 Uninterested	Develop interest	Behaviour modification	Contracting
			Positive reinforcement
			Token economy
		Cognitive	Feedback
		Group therapy	Group modification
02 Poor achievement motivation	Increase motivation	Behaviour modification	Assertiveness training
			Cognitive BM
			Contracting
			Differential reinforcement
			Modelling
			Positive reinforcement
			Token economy
		Cognitive	Feedback
		Talking therapy	Counselling
		Group therapy	Group counselling
			Group modification
			PPC
03 Avoids school	Establish attendance	Service delivery	Seek specialist help
		Behaviour modification	Contracting
			Differential reinforcement
			Modelling
			Positive/negative reinforcement
			Prompting
			Token economy
		Group therapy	Group modification
			PPC
04 Hostile to schooling (see also 05.05 and 05.06)	Eliminate	Behaviour modification	Assertiveness training
			Aversive conditioning
			Contracting
			Differential reinforcement
			Modelling
			Operant conditioning
			Positive reinforcement
			Prompting
			Self-management
			Shaping

Behaviour	Aim	Method	Techniques
		Cognitive Group therapy	Time out Token economy Social skills Group modification PPC

03 HOME AND FAMILY PROBLEMS

03.01 No home base

Behaviour	Aim	Method	Techniques
01 No parents or whereabouts unknown	Provide substitute	Service delivery	Seek specialist advice
02 No relative willing to accommodate	Provide home base	As above	
03 Parents homeless/ scheduled accommodation	Provide accommo-dation	As above	
04 Parents unwilling/ unable to accommodate	Provide substitute	As above	

03.02 Locality

Behaviour	Aim	Method	Techniques
01 Slum clearance	Provide alternative accommo-dation	Service delivery	Seek specialist advice
02 Poor amenities	Provide alternative	As above	
03 Delinquent area	As above	As above	
04 Culture contrary to family's	Eliminate	Service delivery Behaviour modification Cognitive Talking therapy	Seek specialist advice Assertiveness training Social skills Counselling

Behaviour	Aim	Method	Techniques

03.**03 Material deprivation**

Behaviour	Aim	Method	Techniques
01 Inadequate /dirty house	Improve	Service delivery	Seek specialist advice
02 Over-crowded	Provide adequate housing		As above
03 Inadequate toilet and washing facilities	Improve		As above
04 Water/gas/ electricity cut off	Restore service		As above
05 Insufficient food/ clothing	Provide adequate resources		As above
06 Lack of personal possessions	Provide possessions		As above

03.**04 Status in neighbourhood**

Behaviour	Aim	Method	Techniques
01 Stigmatised	Remove/ reduce impact	Service delivery	Seek specialist advice
		Behaviour modification	Cognitive BM
		Cognitive	Social skills
		Talking therapy	Counselling
		Group therapy	Family therapy
02 Ostracised	Remove/ reduce impact		As above
03 Victimised	As above		As above
04 Serious conflict with community	Eliminate/ reduce	Service delivery	Seek specialist advice
		Behaviour modification	Assertiveness training
			Cognitive BM
			Contracting
			Differential reinforcement
			Modelling
			Shaping

Behaviour	Aim	Method	Techniques
		Cognitive Talking therapy Group therapy	Social skills Counselling Family therapy Group counselling (in the community)

03.05 Child's status

Behaviour	Aim	Method	Techniques
01 Illegitimate	Reduce impact	Behaviour modification Talking therapy	Cognitive BM Desensitisation Counselling
02 Adopted	Enable coping	Service delivery Behaviour modification Talking therapy	Seek specialist advice Cognitive BM Desensitisation Counselling
03 Fostered	Enable coping	As above	
04 Does not know parents	Facilitate contact, if appropriate	As above	

03.06 Parents apart

Behaviour	Aim	Method	Techniques
01 One parent dead	Reduce impact	Service delivery Talking therapy	Seek specialist advice Counselling Psychotherapy
02 Single-parent family	As above	As above	
03 Divorced	As above	As above	
04 Separated	As above	As above	
05 Living apart	As above	As above	
06 Child unsure which parent to live with	Reduce impact/ enable child to decide	As above	

03.07 Family instability

Behaviour	Aim	Method	Techniques
01 Parental separations	Reduce impact	Service delivery Talking therapy Group therapy	Seek specialist advice Counselling Family therapy

Behaviour	Aim	Method	Techniques
02 Short-term cohabitation	Reduce impact	Talking therapy Group therapy	Counselling Family therapy
03 Promiscuous parents	Reduce impact	Talking therapy Group therapy	Counselling Family therapy
04 Other disturbing person in home	Reduce impact	Service delivery Talking therapy Group therapy	Seek specialist advice Counselling Family therapy

03.**08 Adverse parental factors**

Behaviour	Aim	Method	Techniques
01 Physical ailment/ defect	Alleviate/ reduce impact	Service delivery Physical Talking therapy	Seek specialist advice Chemotherapy Counselling
02 Mental disorder	As above	Service delivery Behaviour modification Talking therapy Group therapy	Seek specialist advice Cognitive BM Counselling Family therapy
03 Alcoholic /heavy drinker	Reduce impact	Service delivery Behaviour modification Talking therapy	Seek specialist advice Cognitive BM Counselling
04 Gambler	Reduce impact	As above	
05 Offender	Reduce impact	As above	
06 Violent/ cruel	Reduce impact/ alleviate	Service delivery Behaviour modification Cognitive Talking therapy Group therapy	Seek specialist advice Assertiveness training Cognitive BM Social skills Counselling Family therapy
07 Rigid/ authoritarian	Reduce impact	Behaviour modification Talking therapy Group therapy	Cognitive BM Counselling Family therapy
08 Anti- authority	Reduce impact	As above	
09 (Un) employment	Reduce impact	Talking therapy	Counselling

Behaviour	Aim	Method	Techniques
10 Prostitution	Reduce impact	As above	
11 Attempted suicide	Reduce impact	Service delivery	Seek specialist advice
		Behaviour modification	Cognitive BM
		Talking therapy	Counselling
		Group therapy	Family therapy

03.09 Parental inadequacy

Behaviour	Aim	Method	Techniques
01 Physical	Reduce impact/ alleviate	Service delivery	Seek specialist advice and services
		Behaviour modification	Cognitive BM
		Talking therapy	Counselling
02 Intellectual	Reduce impact	As above	
03 Coping with outsiders	Improve	Behaviour modification	Assertiveness training
			Cognitive BM
			Modelling
		Cognitive	Social skills
		Talking therapy	Counselling
		Group therapy	Role-play
04 Coping with each other	As above	As above +	
		Group therapy	Family therapy
05 Coping with house-keeping	As above	Service delivery	Seek specialist advice
		Talking therapy	Counselling
06 Coping with children	As above	Service delivery	Seek specialist advice

03.10 Family conflict

Behaviour	Aim	Method	Techniques
01 Marital disharmony	Reduce impact	Service delivery	Seek specialist advice
		Behaviour modification	Cognitive BM
		Talking therapy	Counselling
		Group therapy	Family therapy
02 Verbal abuse	Reduce impact/ alleviate	Service delivery	Seek specialist advice
		Behaviour modification	Assertiveness training
			Cognitive BM
		Talking therapy	Counselling
		Group therapy	Family therapy

Behaviour	Aim	Method	Techniques
03 Physical aggression (see also 03.**15**)	As above	As above	
04 Parental conflict with children	As above	Service delivery Behaviour modification	Seek specialist advice Contracting Modelling Shaping Token economy
		Cognitive Talking therapy Group therapy	Social skills Counselling Family therapy
05 Children's conflict with each other	Reduce	As above	

03.**11 Family involvement**

Behaviour	Aim	Method	Techniques
01 Parental over-protection	Reduce	Service delivery Behaviour modification Cognitive Talking therapy Group therapy	Seek specialist advice Assertiveness training Cognitive BM Social skills Counselling Family therapy Role-play
02 Parent–child indifference	Increase mutual interest	Service delivery Behaviour modification Cognitive Talking therapy Group therapy	Seek specialist advice Cognitive BM Social skills Counselling Family therapy Role-play
03 Parent–child rejection	Alleviate/ reduce impact	Service delivery Cognitive Talking therapy Group therapy	Seek specialist advice Social skills Counselling Psychotherapy Family therapy
04 Sibling–child indifference/ rejection	As above	As above	

Behaviour	Aim	Method	Techniques

03.12 Affectional bonds

Behaviour	Aim	Method	Techniques
01 Parent–child over-dependence	Reduce	Service delivery Behaviour modification Cognitive Talking therapy Group therapy	Seek specialist advice Assertiveness training Modelling Feedback Social skills Counselling Psychotherapy Family therapy Psychodrama Role-play
02 Parent(s) intolerant	Reduce impact	Service delivery Behaviour modification Cognitive Talking therapy Group therapy	Seek specialist advice Contracting Social skills Counselling Family therapy
03 Parent–child hostility	Alleviate hostility	Service delivery Cognitive Talking therapy Group therapy	Seek specialist advice Social skills Counselling Psychotherapy Family therapy

03.13 Parental guidance

Behaviour	Aim	Method	Techniques
01 Denies the need	Develop recognition	Service delivery Talking therapy Group therapy	Seek specialist advice Counselling Family therapy
02 Inadequate	Improve	As above	
03 Inconsistent	Reduce inconsistency	As above	
04 Deviant	Reduce impact	Service delivery Behaviour modification Talking therapy Group therapy	Seek specialist advice Assertiveness training Cognitive BM Counselling Group counselling

03.14 Parental control

Behaviour	Aim	Method	Techniques
01 Inadequate	Improve	Service delivery Behaviour modification	Seek specialist advice Contracting Modelling Operant conditioning Positive reinforcement

Behaviour	Aim	Method	Techniques
		Cognitive	Prompting
			Shaping
			Token economy
			Feedback
		Talking therapy	Counselling
		Group therapy	Family therapy
02 Inconsistent	Reduce inconsistency	As above	
03 Harsh	Reduce	As above +	
		Behaviour modification	Aversive conditioning
04 Through bribery	Eliminate	As above	
05 Through collusion against other parent	Reduce	As above	
06 Through collusion against outside authority	As above	As above	

03.15 Child abuse

Behaviour	Aim	Method	Techniques
01 Pawn between parents	Reduce impact	Service delivery	Seek specialist advice
		Behaviour modification	Assertiveness training
		Talking therapy	Counselling
		Group therapy	Family therapy
02 Emotional blackmail	Eliminate	As above	
03 Scape-goating	As above	As above	
04 Physical	As above	As above	
05 Sexual	As above	As above	

03.16 Adverse sibling factors

Behaviour	Aim	Method	Techniques
01 Physical defect	Reduce impact	Behaviour modification	Desensitisation
		Talking therapy	Counselling

(see also
01.**05**)

Behaviour	Aim	Method	Techniques
02 Mental disorder	As above	As above	
03 Alcoholic/ heavy drinker	As above	As above	
04 Prostitution	As above	As above	
05 In care	As above	As above	
06 Offender	As above	As above	
07 In penal establishment	As above	As above	
08 In other residential establishment	As above	As above	

03.17 Deviant identification

Behaviour	Aim	Method	Techniques
01 With parent(s)	Establish non-deviant identification Reduce impact	Service delivery Cognitive Talking therapy Group therapy	Seek specialist advice Feedback Social skills Counselling Family therapy Role-play
02 With siblings	As above	Cognitive Talking therapy Group therapy	Feedback Social skills Counselling Family therapy Role-play

03.18 Child's attitude to home

Behaviour	Aim	Method	Techniques
01 Runs away from home	Eliminate	Service delivery Behaviour modification Talking therapy Group therapy Environmental therapy	Parent training Seek specialist advice Contingency contracting Positive reinforcement Token economy Counselling Family therapy Role-play PET Security Therapeutic community
02 Wanders away from home	Eliminate	As above	

Behaviour	Aim	Method	Techniques
03 Steals from home	Eliminate	Service delivery	Seek specialist advice
		Behaviour modification	Aversive conditioning
			Cognitive BM
			Contingency contracting
			Time out
		Cognitive	Feedback
		Talking therapy	Counselling
		Group therapy	Family therapy
04 Stays out late	Eliminate	Service delivery	Seek specialist advice
		Behaviour modification	Cognitive BM
			Contingency contracting
			Differential reinforcement
			Positive reinforcement
			Token economy
		Talking therapy	Counselling
		Group therapy	Family therapy
05 Destructive/ violent	Eliminate	Service delivery	Seek specialist advice
		Physical	Chemotherapy
		Behaviour modification	Assertiveness training
			Cognitive BM
			Contracting
			Relaxation
			Time out
			Token economy
		Cognitive	Feedback
			Social skills
		Talking therapy	Counselling
			Psychotherapy
		Group therapy	Family therapy
			Psychodrama
			Role-play
		Environmental therapy	Security
			Therapeutic community

04 SOCIAL SKILLS PROBLEMS

04.01 Self-presentation

01 Dirty, odorous	Improve presentation	Service delivery	Seek specialist advice
		Behaviour modification	Cognitive BM
			Contracting
			Differential reinforcement
			Modelling

Behaviour	Aim	Method	Techniques
		Cognitive	Positive reinforcement
			Shaping
			Token economy
			Feedback
			Social skills
		Talking therapy	Counselling
		Group therapy	PPC
02 Inappropriate body movement or posture	Improve posture	Behaviour modification	Differential reinforcement
			Modelling
			Operant conditioning
			Positive reinforcement
			Prompting
			Token economy
		Cognitive	Feedback
			Social skills
		Talking therapy	Counselling
		Group therapy	Group modification
			PPC
03 Facial grimaces	Eliminate	Behaviour modification	Aversive conditioning
			Modelling
			Negative practice
			Positive reinforcement
			Relaxation
		Cognitive	Feedback
			Social skills
04 Odd speech rate/ volume	Normalise speech	Behaviour modification	Extinction
			Modelling
			Negative practice
			Positive reinforcement
			Prompting
			Token economy
		Cognitive	Social skills
			Speech therapy
		Group therapy	Role-play
05 Poor manners	Teach etiquette	Behaviour modification	Chaining
			Contracting
			Modelling
			Operant conditioning
			Positive reinforcement
			Prompting
			Shaping
			Time out
			Token economy
		Cognitive	Social skills
		Group therapy	PPC

Behaviour	Aim	Method	Techniques

04.02 Basic interaction difficulties

Behaviour	Aim	Method	Techniques
01 Inappropriate eye contact	Normalise eye contact	Behaviour modification	Assertiveness training Differential reinforcement Operant conditioning Positive reinforcement
		Cognitive Talking therapy	Social skills Counselling
02 Inappropriate facial expression	Normalise expression	Behaviour modification	Assertiveness training Differential reinforcement Modelling Operant conditioning Positive reinforcement
		Cognitive Talking therapy	Social skills Counselling
03 Inappropriate use of gestures	Normalise use	As above	
04 Stands too close/ too far	Normalise distancing	As above	
05 Touches people inappropriately	Normalise contact	As above	
06 Inept attempts to make friends	Establish appropriate skills	Behaviour modification	Aversive conditioning Contingency contracting Differential reinforcement Extinction Modelling Operant conditioning Prompting Time out Token economy
		Cognitive	Feedback Social skills
		Group therapy	Group modification PPC Role-play

04.03 Conversation

Behaviour	Aim	Method	Techniques
01 Does not initiate \	Establish conversation skills	Behaviour modification	Assertiveness training Cognitive BM Contingency contracting Differential reinforcement

Behaviour	Aim	Method	Techniques
			Modelling
			Operant conditioning
			Positive reinforcement
			Prompting
			Token economy
		Cognitive	Social skills
		Talking therapy	Counselling
		Group therapy	Role-play
02 Does not respond	Establish responding skills	As above	
03 Makes noises while others speak	Eliminate	Behaviour modification	Cognitive BM
			Contingency contracting
			Extinction
			Negative practice
			Time out
			Token economy
		Cognitive	Feedback
			Social skills
04 Interrupts	Eliminate	As above	
05 Persistent/ excessive questioning	Reduce	Behaviour modification	Aversive conditioning
			Cognitive BM
			Contingency contracting
			Extinction
			Flooding
			Negative practice
			Time out
			Token economy
		Cognitive	Feedback
			Social skills
06 Constantly complains/ whines	Reduce	Behaviour modification	Contingency contracting
			Extinction
			Negative practice
			Operant conditioning
			Time out
			Token economy
		Cognitive	Feedback
			Social skills

04.04 Social discomfort

Behaviour	Aim	Method	Techniques
01 Shy, uneasy	Reduce unease	Behaviour modification	Assertiveness training
			Cognitive BM

Behaviour	Aim	Method	Techniques
			Desensitisation
			Modelling
			Prompting
			Relaxation
			Token economy
		Cognitive	Feedback
			Social skills
		Group therapy	Group modification
			Role-play
			PPC
02 Easily embarrassed	Reduce unease	Behaviour modification	Assertiveness training
			Cognitive BM
			Desensitisation
			Modelling
			Prompting
			Relaxation
			Token economy
03 Avoids social contact	Establish appropriate contact	As above +	
		Behaviour modification	Differential reinforcement
04 Shows anxiety in interaction	Reduce anxiety	Physical	Medication
			Biofeedback
		Behaviour modification	Assertiveness training
			Cognitive BM
			Desensitisation
			Flooding
			Modelling
			Relaxation
			Token economy
		Cognitive	Feedback
			Social skills
		Talking therapy	Psychotherapy
		Group therapy	Group modification
			PPC
			Psychodrama
			Role-play

04.05 Unpopularity

Behaviour	Aim	Method	Techniques
01 Ignored by others	Increase recognition by others	Behaviour modification	Assertiveness training
			Modelling
			Prompting
			Token economy
		Cognitive	Feedback
			Social skills

Behaviour	Aim	Method	Techniques
		Group therapy	Group modification
			PPC
			Role-play
		Environmental therapy	Therapeutic community
02 Disliked by others	Increase popularity	Behaviour modification	Cognitive BM
			Modelling
			Operant conditioning
			Prompting
			Token economy
		Cognitive	Feedback
			Social skills
		Group therapy	Group modification
			PPC
			Role-play
		Environmental therapy	Therapeutic community
03 Bullied by others	Establish coping	Physical	Exercise
		Behaviour modification	Assertiveness training
		Cognitive	Feedback
			Social skills
		Group therapy	Group modification
			PPC
			Role-play
		Environmental therapy	Therapeutic community
04 Scape-goated	Establish coping	Physical	Exercise
		Behaviour modification	Assertiveness training
			Modelling
			Shaping
		Cognitive	Feedback
			Social skills
		Talking therapy	Counselling
		Group therapy	Group counselling
			Group modification
			PPC
			Role-play
		Environmental therapy	Therapeutic community
05 Taunted by others	As above	As above	

Behaviour	Aim	Method	Techniques
06 Has no friends	Facilitate making friends	Cognitive Group therapy therapy Environmental therapy	Social skills Group modification PPC Therapeutic community

04.06 Attitude to children

Behaviour	Aim	Method	Techniques
01 Indifferent to others' condition/ presence	Develop concern for others	Behaviour modification Group therapy Environmental therapy	Contingency contracting Differential reinforcement Modelling Operant conditioning Token economy Group modification PPC Prompting Therapeutic community
02 Manipu- latory	Reduce	Behaviour modification Cognitive Group therapy Environmental therapy	Aversive conditioning Differential reinforcement Extinction Feedback Group modification PPC Therapeutic community
03 Domineering	Reduce	Behaviour modification Cognitive Group therapy Environmental therapy	Aversive conditioning Contingency contracting Differential reinforcement Feedback Social skills Group modification PPC Role-play Therapeutic community
04 Antagonistic	Reduce	As above	
05 Hostile	Reduce	As above	
06 Intrusive	Reduce	As above	
07 Submissive	Increase assertiveness	Behaviour modification	Assertiveness training Cognitive BM Contingency contracting Differential reinforcement Modelling

Behaviour	Aim	Method	Techniques
		Cognitive	Operant conditioning
			Prompting
			Token economy
			Feedback
			Social skills
		Group therapy	Group modification
			PPC
			Role-play
		Environmental therapy	Therapeutic community
08 Over-dependent	Reduce dependency	Behaviour modification	Assertiveness training
			Cognitive BM
			Contingency contracting
			Differential reinforcement
			Operant conditioning
			Token economy
			Feedback Cognitive
			Social skills
		Environmental therapy	Therapeutic community

04.07 Attitude to adults

Behaviour	Aim	Method	Techniques
01 Indifferent to others' condition/ presence	Develop concern for others	Behaviour modification	Contingency contracting
			Differential reinforcement
			Modelling
			Operant conditioning
			Token economy
		Group therapy	Group modification
			PPC
		Environmental therapy	Therapeutic community
02 Manipu-latory	Reduce	Behaviour modification	Aversive conditioning
			Differential reinforcement
			Extinction
		Cognitive	Feedback
		Group therapy	Group modification
			PPC
		Environmental therapy	Therapeutic community
03 Domineering	Reduce	Behaviour modification	Aversive conditioning
			Contingency contracting
			Differential reinforcement
		Cognitive	Feedback
			Social skills

Behaviour	Aim	Method	Techniques
		Group therapy	Group modification
			PPC
			Role-play
		Environmental therapy	Therapeutic community
04 Antagonistic	Reduce antagonism	As above	
05 Hostile	Reduce hostility	As above	
06 Intrusive	Reduce intrusiveness	As above +	
		Behaviour modification	Extinction
07 Submissive	Increase assertiveness	Behaviour modification	Assertiveness training
			Cognitive BM
			Contingency contracting
			Differential reinforcement
			Modelling
			Operant conditioning
			Prompting
			Token economy
		Cognitive	Feedback
			Social skills
		Group therapy	Group modification
			PPC
			Role-play
		Environmental therapy	Therapeutic community
08 Over-dependent	Reduce dependency	Behaviour modification	Assertiveness training
			Cognitive BM
			Contingency contracting
			Differential reinforcement
			Operant conditioning
			Token economy
		Cognitive	Feedback
			Social skills
		Environmental therapy	Therapeutic community
09 Defiant	Eliminate	Behaviour modification	Aversive conditioning
			Contingency contracting
			Extinction
			Time out
			Token economy

Behaviour	Aim	Method	Techniques
		Cognitive	Feedback
			Social skills
		Group therapy	Group modification
			PPC
		Environmental therapy	Therapeutic community
10 Over-familiar	Reduce familiarity	Behaviour modification	Aversive conditioning
			Differential reinforcement
			Extinction
			Modelling
			Token economy
		Cognitive	Feedback
			Social skills
		Group therapy	Group modification
			PPC
			Role-play

04.08 Sensitivity to others

01 Under-sensitive	Increase sensitivity	Behaviour modification	Cognitive BM
			Contingency contracting
			Modelling
			Operant conditioning
			Prompting
			Token economy
		Cognitive	Feedback
			Social skills
		Talking therapy	Counselling
		Group therapy	Group counselling
			Group modification
			Role-play
		Environmental therapy	Therapeutic community
02 Over-sensitive	Reduce sensitivity	Behaviour modification	Cognitive BM
			Contingency contracting
			Desensitisation
			Modelling
			Operant conditioning
			Prompting
			Token economy
		Cognitive	Feedback
			Social skills
		Talking therapy	Counselling
		Group therapy	Group counselling
			Group modification

Behaviour	Aim	Method	Techniques
		Environmental therapy	Role-play Therapeutic community
03 Mis-interprets signals	Improve social perception	Behaviour modification	Aversive conditioning Cognitive BM Contingency contracting Differential reinforcement Modelling Operant conditioning Prompting Token economy
		Cognitive	Feedback Social skills
		Group therapy	Group modification Role-play
		Environmental therapy	Therapeutic community
04 Actively ignores signals	Improve regard	As above	
05 Socially inflexible	Increase social adapt-ability	Behaviour modification	Cognitive BM Contingency contracting Differential reinforcement Modelling Operant conditioning Prompting Time out Token economy
		Cognitive	Feedback Social skills
		Talking therapy	Counselling
		Group therapy	Group counselling Group modification PPC Role-play
		Environmental therapy	Therapeutic community

04.09 Fellow-feeling (sympathy)

Behaviour	Aim	Method	Techniques
01 Does not offer to	Increase helpfulness	Behaviour modification	Cognitive BM Contingency contracting Differential reinforcement Modelling Operant conditioning Prompting Token economy

Behaviour	Aim	Method	Techniques
		Cognitive	Feedback
			Social skills
		Talking therapy	Counselling
		Group therapy	Group counselling
			Group modification
			PPC
			Role-play
		Environmental therapy	Therapeutic community
02 Shows no interest in/to others	Increase responsiveness	As above	
03 Unpleasant to others	Develop pleasantness	As above	
04 Unsupportive when others are troubled	Develop supportiveness	As above	
05 Does not show appreciation	Develop appreciativeness	As above	
06 Does not share	Develop sharing	As above	
07 Does not concede	Increase persuasibility	As above	
08 Does not co-operate	Increase co-operativeness	As above	

04.10 Situational problems

Behaviour	Aim	Method	Techniques
01 Making and keeping friends	Improve ability to relate	Behaviour modification	Assertiveness training
			Cognitive BM
			Contingency contracting
			Differential reinforcement
			Modelling
			Operant conditioning
			Token economy
		Cognitive	Feedback
			Social skills
		Talking therapy	Counselling
		Group therapy	Group counselling
			Group modification
			PPC
		Environmental therapy	Therapeutic community

Behaviour	Aim	Method	Techniques
02 Getting and keeping a job	Develop employment skills	Service delivery Behaviour modification Cognitive Talking therapy Group therapy	Seek specialist advice Assertiveness training Cognitive BM Social skills Counselling Group modification
03 Does not have/sustain satisfying interests	Establish hobbies	Service delivery Behaviour modification	Seek specialist advice plus provide means to continue Contingency contracting Modelling Positive reinforcement Token economy

05 ANTISOCIAL BEHAVIOUR

05.01 Disruptiveness

Behaviour	Aim	Method	Techniques
01 Stirs up trouble	Eliminate	Physical Behaviour modification Cognitive Group therapy Environmental therapy	Chemotherapy Aversive conditioning Cognitive BM Contingency contracting Differential reinforcement Extinction Operant conditioning Time out Token economy Feedback Group modification PPC Role-play Therapeutic community
02 Makes allegations	Eliminate	Behaviour modification Talking therapy Group therapy Environmental therapy	Aversive conditioning Contingency contracting Extinction Paradoxical intention Time out Token economy Counselling Group counselling Group modification PPC Role-play Therapeutic community

Behaviour	Aim	Method	Techniques
03 Temper tantrums	Eliminate	Physical Behaviour modification	Chemotherapy Aversive conditioning Contingency contracting Differential reinforcement Extinction Time out Token economy
		Group therapy	Group modification PPC Role-play
		Environmental therapy	Therapeutic community
04 Disturbs others	Reduce	Physical Behaviour modification	Chemotherapy Aversive conditioning Cognitive BM Contingency contracting Differential reinforcement Extinction Time out Token economy
		Cognitive	Feedback Social skills
		Talking therapy	Counselling
		Group therapy	Group counselling Group modification PPC Role-play
		Environmental therapy	Therapeutic community

05.02 Truancy

Behaviour	Aim	Method	Techniques
01 Does not attend school	Establish attendance	Behaviour modification	Aversive conditioning Cognitive BM Contingency contracting Prompting Token economy
		Group therapy	Family therapy PPC
		Environmental therapy	Therapeutic community
02 School refusal	Establish attendance	As above	

Behaviour	Aim	Method	Techniques
05.03 Absconding			
01 Runs away	Eliminate	Physical	Chemotherapy
		Behaviour	Aversive conditioning
		modification	Contingency contracting
			Differential reinforcement
			Operant conditioning
			Token economy
		Talking therapy	Counselling
		Group therapy	Family therapy
			Group counselling
			Group modification
			PPC
		Environmental	Security
		therapy	Therapeutic community
02 Plans and executes absconding	Eliminate	As above	
03 Encourages others to abscond	Eliminate	Behaviour	Aversive conditioning
		modification	Contingency contracting
			Differential reinforcement
			Operant conditioning
			Time out
			Token economy
		Cognitive	Feedback
		Talking therapy	Counselling
		Group therapy	Group counselling
			Group modification
			PPC
		Environmental therapy	Therapeutic community
05.04 Self-destructiveness			
01 Takes overdoses or poisons	Eliminate	Service delivery	Seek specialist advice
		Physical	Chemotherapy
		Behaviour	Aversive conditioning
		modification	Cognitive BM
			Contingency contracting
			Token economy
		Talking therapy	Counselling
			Psychotherapy
		Group therapy	Family therapy
			Group counselling
			Group modification

Behaviour	Aim	Method	Techniques
		Environmental therapy	PPC
			Psychodrama
			Security
			Therapeutic community
02 Self-inflicted wounds	Eliminate	Service delivery	Seek specialist advice
		Physical	Medication
		Behaviour modification	Aversive conditioning
			Cognitive BM
			Contingency contracting
			Extinction
			Time out
			Token economy
		Talking therapy	Counselling
			Psychotherapy
		Group therapy	Family therapy
			Group counselling
			Group modification
			PPC
			Psychodrama
		Environmental therapy	Security
			Therapeutic community
03 Attempts to obtain harmful materials	Eliminate	Behaviour modification	Aversive conditioning
			Contingency contracting
			Time out
			Token economy
		Group therapy	Group modification
			PPC
		Environmental therapy	Security
			Therapeutic community
04 Encourages others to hurt self	As above	Behaviour modification	Aversive conditioning
			Cognitive BM
			Contingency contracting
			Time out
			Token economy
		Talking therapy	Counselling
			Psychotherapy
		Group therapy	Family therapy
			Group counselling
			Group modification
			PPC
			Psychodrama
		Environmental therapy	Security
			Therapeutic community
05 Head-banging	As above	Service delivery	Seek specialist advice

Behaviour	Aim	Method	Techniques
		Physical	Chemotherapy
		Behaviour	Aversive conditioning
		modification	Contingency contracting
			Differential reinforcement
			Extinction
			Time out
			Token economy
		Group therapy	Group modification
			PPC
		Environmental	Therapeutic community
		therapy	
06 Serious suicide attempts	As above	Service delivery	Seek specialist advice
		Physical	Chemotherapy
		Behaviour	Cognitive
		modification	Contingency contracting
			Token economy
		Talking therapy	Counselling
			Psychotherapy
		Group therapy	Family therapy
			Group counselling
			Group modification
			PPC
			Psychodrama
		Environmental	Security
		therapy	Therapeutic community

05.05 Verbal aggression

Behaviour	Aim	Method	Techniques
01 Criticises	Eliminate	Behaviour	Aversive conditioning
		modification	Cognitive BM
			Contingency contracting
			Differential reinforcement
			Time out
			Token economy
		Cognitive	Feedback
			Social skills
		Group therapy	Group counselling
			Group modification
			PPC
			Role-play
		Environmental	Therapeutic community
		therapy	
02 Antagonises	As above	As above	

Behaviour	Aim	Method	Techniques
03 Threatens	As above	As above	
04 Swears	As above	As above	
05 Gestures/ snarls	As above	As above	
06 Screams abuse	As above	As above	

05.06 Physical aggression

Behaviour	Aim	Method	Techniques
01 Nips	Eliminate	Physical Behaviour modification	Chemotherapy
			Aversive conditioning
			Cognitive BM
			Contingency contracting
			Differential reinforcement
			Time out
			Token economy
		Group therapy	Group modification
			PPC
			Role-play
		Environmental therapy	Therapeutic community
02 Hits/punches	As above	As above	
03 Kicks	As above	As above	
04 Spits	As above	As above	
05 Bites	As above	As above	
06 Throws objects	As above	As above	
07 Bullies	As above	As above	
08 Head-butts	As above	Physical Behaviour modification	Chemotherapy
			Aversive conditioning
			Cognitive BM
			Contracting
			Differential reinforcement
			Time out
			Token economy
		Cognitive Talking therapy	Social skills
			Counselling
		Group therapy	Group counselling
			Group modification
			PPC
		Environmental therapy	Security
			Therapeutic community

Behaviour	Aim	Method	Techniques
09 Physically assaults	Eliminate	As above	
10 Violent	As above	As above	
11 Injures others deliberately	As above	As above	
12 Homicide	Eliminate	Physical Environmental therapy	Chemotherapy Security

05.07 Uncommon sexual interests

Behaviour	Aim	Method	Techniques
01 Engages in transvestism	Eliminate	Behaviour modification	Assertiveness training Aversive conditioning Cognitive BM Differential reinforcement Modelling Operant conditioning Time out Token economy
		Cognitive Talking therapy	Feedback Counselling Psychotherapy
		Group therapy	Family therapy Group counselling Group modification PPC Role-play
02 Engages in fetishism	As above	As above	
03 Engages in exhibitionism	As above	As above	
04 Engages in homosexuality	As above	As above	
05 Others	As above	As above	

05.08 Sexual misbehaviour

Behaviour	Aim	Method	Techniques
01 Attempts to masturbate others without consent	Eliminate	Physical Behaviour modification	Chemotherapy Aversive conditioning Cognitive BM Contingency contracting Time out Token economy

Behaviour	Aim	Method	Techniques
		Cognitive Talking therapy Group therapy	Feedback Counselling Group counselling Group modification PPC
		Environmental therapy	Therapeutic community
02 Attempts to engage others in inappropriate sexual activity	As above	As above	
03 Talks inappropriately about sex	As above	Behaviour modification	Aversive conditioning Cognitive BM Contingency contracting Extinction Time out Token economy
		Cognitive Talking therapy Group therapy	Feedback Counselling Group counselling Group modification PPC
		Environmental therapy	Therapeutic community
04 Inappropriate sexual contact	As above	As above	
05 Lack of sexual control	Increase control	Physical Behaviour modification	Chemotherapy Aversive conditioning Cognitive BM Contingency contracting Time out Token economy
		Cognitive Talking therapy Group therapy	Feedback Counselling Group counselling Group modification PPC
		Environmental therapy	Security Therapeutic community

Behaviour	Aim	Method	Techniques
06 Soliciting	Eliminate	Behaviour modification	Contingency contracting
		Talking therapy	Counselling
		Group therapy	Group counselling
			Group modification
			PPC
		Environmental therapy	Security
			Therapeutic community

05.09 Sexual offences

Behaviour	Aim	Method	Techniques
01 Indecent exposure	Eliminate	Behaviour modification	Assertiveness training
			Aversive conditioning
			Cognitive BM
			Contracting
			Token economy
		Cognitive	Social skills
		Talking therapy	Counselling
		Group therapy	Group counselling
			Group modification
			PPC
		Environmental therapy	Therapeutic community
02 Sexual assault	As above	As above +	
		Environmental therapy	Security
03 Unlawful sexual intercourse	As above	Service delivery	Seek specialist advice
		Behaviour modification	Aversive conditioning
			Contingency contracting
			Covert conditioning
			Self-management
		Talking therapy	Counselling
		Group therapy	Group counselling
		Environmental therapy	Security
			Therapeutic community
04 Rape	As above	Service delivery	Seek specialist advice
		Behaviour modification	Assertiveness training
			Aversive conditioning
			Cognitive BM
			Contracting
		Talking therapy	Counselling
		Group therapy	Group counselling
			Group modification
			PPC
		Environmental therapy	Security
			Therapeutic community

Behaviour	Aim	Method	Techniques

05.10 Property offences

Behaviour	Aim	Method	Techniques
01 Theft	Eliminate	Service delivery Behaviour modification	Seek specialist advice Aversive conditioning Cognitive BM Contingency contracting Token economy
		Talking therapy Group therapy	Counselling Group counselling Group modification PPC
		Environmental therapy	Security Therapeutic community
02 Burglary	As above	As above	
03 Damages/ destroys property	As above	As above	
04 Robbery	Eliminate	Service delivery Behaviour modification	Seek specialist advice Aversive conditioning Cognitive BM Contingency contracting Token economy
		Talking therapy Group therapy	Counselling Group counselling Group modification PPC
		Environmental therapy	Security Therapeutic community

05.11 Arson

Behaviour	Aim	Method	Techniques
01 Attempts to obtain flammable materials	Eliminate	Service delivery Behaviour modification	Seek specialist advice Aversive conditioning Contingency contracting Time out Token economy
		Talking therapy	Counselling Psychotherapy
		Group therapy	Group counselling Group modification PPC
		Environmental therapy	Therapeutic community
02 Lights/ sets fires	Eliminate	Service delivery Behaviour modification	Seek specialist advice Aversive conditioning Contingency contracting

Behaviour	Aim	Method	Techniques
		Talking therapy	Counselling
			Psychotherapy
		Group therapy	Group counselling
			Group modification
			PPC
		Environmental therapy	Security
			Therapeutic community
03 Assembles/ sets explosives	Eliminate	As above	

05.12 Response to control

Behaviour	Aim	Method	Techniques
01 Defies agents of control	Reduce	Behaviour modification	Aversive conditioning
			Contingency contracting
			Differential reinforcement
			Extinction
			Operant conditioning
			Time out
			Token economy
		Cognitive	Social skills
		Group therapy	Group modification
			PPC
		Environmental therapy	Therapeutic community
02 Tests out limits	Reduce	Behaviour modification	Assertiveness training
			Aversive conditioning
			Contingency contracting
			Extinction
			Modelling
			Operant conditioning
			Time out
			Token economy
		Cognitive	Feedback
			Social skills
		Talking therapy	Counselling
		Group therapy	Group counselling
			Group modification
		Environmental therapy	Therapeutic community
03 Forces confrontation	Eliminate	As above	
04 Unreasonably seeks attention	Reduce	As above	

Behaviour	Aim	Method	Techniques

06 PERSONAL PROBLEMS

06.01 Extraversion

Behaviour	Aim	Method	Techniques
01 Seeks company to excess	Reduce	Physical Behaviour modification	Chemotherapy Aversive conditioning Contingency contracting Covert conditioning Differential reinforcement Extinction Massed practice Operant conditioning Prompting Relaxation Self-management/control Time out Token economy
		Cognitive	Social skills
		Group therapy	Group modification PPC
		Environmental therapy	Therapeutic community
02 Constantly seeks excitement	As above	As above	
03 Talks too much	As above	As above	
04 Tells all to others	As above	As above	

06.02 Introversion

Behaviour	Aim	Method	Techniques
01 Avoids groups	Reduce	Physical Behaviour modification	Chemotherapy Assertiveness training Contingency contracting Differential reinforcement Operant conditioning Prompting Relaxation Self-management Token economy
		Cognitive	Social skills
		Group therapy	Group modification PPC
		Environmental therapy	Therapeutic community

Behaviour	Aim	Method	Techniques
02 Secretive	Reduce	Behaviour modification	Assertiveness training
			Contingency contracting
			Differential reinforcement
			Prompting
			Token economy
		Cognitive	Social skills
		Talking therapy	Counselling
		Group therapy	Group counselling
			Group modification
			PPC
		Environmental therapy	Therapeutic community
03 Loner	Reduce		As above

06.03 Egocentricity

Behaviour	Aim	Method	Techniques
01 Uses others for own ends	Reduce	Behaviour modification	Aversive conditioning
			Cognitive BM
			Contingency contracting
			Differential reinforcement
			Operant conditioning
			Prompting
			Time out
			Token economy
		Cognitive	Social skills
		Talking therapy	Counselling
		Group therapy	Group modification
			PPC
			Role-play
		Environmental therapy	Therapeutic community
02 Preoccupied with own gratification	Reduce		As above
03 Greedy, overdemanding	Reduce		As above
04 Insists on having own way	Reduce	Behaviour modification	Aversive conditioning
			Contingency contracting
			Extinction
			Time out
			Token economy
		Cognitive	Feedback
			Social skills
		Talking therapy	Counselling

Behaviour	Aim	Method	Techniques
		Group therapy	Group counselling Group modification PPC
		Environmental therapy	Therapeutic community

06.04 Immaturity/precocity

Behaviour	Aim	Method	Techniques
01 Engages in behaviour appropriate to younger child	Increase age-related behaviour	Behaviour modification	Aversive conditioning Contingency contracting Differential reinforcement Extinction Modelling Operant conditioning Prompting Time out Token economy
		Cognitive	Social skills
		Group therapy	Group modification PPC
		Environmental therapy	Therapeutic community
02 Engages in behaviour appropriate to older child	Normalise	As above	

06.05 Frustration tolerance

Behaviour	Aim	Method	Techniques
01 Impatient	Increase patience	Physical	Chemotherapy
		Behaviour modification	Aversive conditioning Contingency contracting Differential reinforcement Extinction Modelling Operant conditioning Time out Token economy
		Group therapy	Group modification
02 Cannot tolerate delay of gratification	Increase tolerance	As above	
03 Throws tantrums if thwarted	Eliminate	As above	

Behaviour	Aim	Method	Techniques
04 Lacks tenacity	Develop persistence	Behaviour modification	Assertiveness training Aversive conditioning Contingency contracting Modelling Prompting Shaping Token economy

06.06 Personality disorders

Behaviour	Aim	Method	Techniques
01 Extreme egocentricity	Reduce	See 06.03	
02 Extreme coldness	Increase emotionality	See 06.03	
03 Calculating	Increase spontaneity	Behaviour modification	Aversive conditioning Contingency contracting Differential reinforcement Operant conditioning Time out Token economy
		Cognitive	Social skills
		Group therapy	Group modification PPC
		Environmental therapy	Therapeutic community
04 Does not learn from mistakes	Establish regard for consequences	Behaviour modification	Cognitive BM Contingency contracting Differential reinforcement Modelling Operant conditioning Prompting Token economy
		Cognitive	Social skills
		Group therapy	Group modification PPC
		Environmental therapy	Therapeutic community
05 No remorse or guilt	Increase emotional response	Behaviour modification	Aversive conditioning Contingency contracting Differential reinforcement Operant conditioning Prompting Time out Token economy

Behaviour	Aim	Method	Techniques
		Cognitive	Social skills
		Group therapy	Group modification
			PPC
		Environmental therapy	PET
			Therapeutic community
06 Cheats and lies	Eliminate	Behaviour modification	Aversive conditioning
			Contingency contracting
			Operant conditioning
			Time out
			Token economy
		Cognitive	Social skills
		Group therapy	Group modification
			PPC
		Environmental therapy	Therapeutic community

06.07 Impulsivity

Behaviour	Aim	Method	Techniques
01 Acts without thought	Reduce	Physical	Chemotherapy
		Behaviour modification	Aversive conditioning
			Cognitive BM
			Contingency contracting
			Differential reinforcement
			Operant conditioning
			Prompting
			Self-management
			Shaping
			Time out
			Token economy
		Cognitive	Feedback
		Group therapy	Group modification
			PPC
		Environmental therapy	Therapeutic community
02 Does not control self	Develop		As above
03 Restless	Reduce		As above
04 Easily bored	Develop interests	Physical	Chemotherapy
		Behaviour modification	Cognitive BM
			Contingency contracting
			Differential conditioning
			Modelling
			Operant conditioning
			Prompting

Behaviour	Aim	Method	Techniques
			Shaping
			Time out
			Token economy
		Group therapy	Group modification
05 Poor resistance to temptation	Increase resistance	As above +	
		Behaviour modification	Aversive conditioning

06.08 Emotional instability

Behaviour	Aim	Method	Techniques
01 Cries/ laughs easily	Normalise	Physical	Biofeedback
			Chemotherapy
		Behaviour modification	Assertiveness training
			Aversive conditioning
(see also 06.09)			Contingency contracting
			Covert conditioning
			Differential reinforcement
			Extinction
			Modelling
			Operant conditioning
			Prompting
			Relaxation
			Time out
			Token economy
		Cognitive	Social skills
		Talking therapy	Counselling
			Psychotherapy
		Group therapy	Group modification
			PPC
			Psychodrama
		Environmental therapy	Therapeutic community
02 Gets over-excited	Reduce	Physical	Biofeedback
			Chemotherapy
			Exercise
		Behaviour modification	Assertiveness training
			Aversive conditioning
			Contingency contracting
			Differential reinforcement
			Extinction
			Modelling
			Operant conditioning
			Relaxation
			Time out
			Token economy

Behaviour	Aim	Method	Techniques
		Talking therapy	Counselling
			Psychotherapy
		Group therapy	Group modification
			Psychodrama
		Environmental therapy	Therapeutic community
03 Sulky, petulant	Eliminate	Physical	Chemotherapy
		Behaviour modification	Assertiveness training
			Aversive conditioning
(see also 06.**04** and 06.**05**)			Contingency contracting
			Differential reinforcement
			Extinction
			Modelling
			Operant conditioning
			Relaxation
			Time out
			Token economy
		Cognitive	Social skills
		Talking therapy	Counselling
			Psychotherapy
		Group therapy	Group counselling
			Group modification
			Psychodrama
			Role-play
		Environmental therapy	Therapeutic community
04 Overreacts to stress	Reduce	Service delivery	Seek specialist advice
		Physical	Biofeedback
			Chemotherapy
			Exercise
(see also 06.**10**)		Behaviour modification	Assertiveness training
			Aversive conditioning
			Contingency contracting
			Differential reinforcement
			Operant conditioning
			Relaxation
			Time out
			Token economy
		Cognitive	Social skills
		Talking therapy	Counselling
		Group therapy	Group counselling
			Group modification
			Psychodrama
			Role-play
		Environmental therapy	Therapeutic community

Behaviour	Aim	Method	Techniques
05 Has pronounced mood swings	Reduce	Physical	Chemotherapy
		Behaviour modification	Assertiveness training
			Aversive conditioning
			Differential reinforcement
			Extinction
			Modelling
			Operant conditioning
			Prompting
			Relaxation
			Time out
			Token economy
		Cognitive	Social skills
		Talking therapy	Counselling
			Psychotherapy
		Group therapy	Group modification
			PPC
			Psychodrama
			Role-play
		Environmental therapy	Therapeutic community
06 Fearful (see also 06.**10**)	Eliminate	Physical	Biofeedback
			Chemotherapy
		Behaviour modification	Assertiveness training
			Aversive conditioning
			Contingency contracting
			Desensitisation
			Differential reinforcement
			Extinction
			Flooding
			Operant conditioning
			Relaxation
			Time out
			Token economy
		Cognitive	Social skills
		Talking therapy	Counselling
			Hypnosis
			Psychotherapy
		Group therapy	Group modification
			Psychodrama
			Role-play
		Environmental therapy	Therapeutic community
07 Exaggerated emotional response	Reduce	Physical	Biofeedback
			Chemotherapy
		Behaviour modification	Aversive conditioning
			Contingency contracting
			Covert conditioning

Behaviour	Aim	Method	Techniques
(see also 06.**04** and 06.**10**)			Desensitisation
			Extinction
			Flooding
			Modelling
			Operant conditioning
			Prompting
			Relaxation
			Time out
			Token economy
		Cognitive	Social skills
		Talking therapy	Counselling
			Psychotherapy
		Group therapy	Group modification
			Psychodrama
			Role-play
		Environmental therapy	Therapeutic community
08 Superficial, shallow emotions (see also 04.**09**)	Increase emotional response	Physical Behaviour modification	Biofeedback
			Assertiveness training
			Contingency contracting
			Differential reinforcement
			Modelling
			Operant conditioning
			Prompting
			Time out
			Token economy
		Cognitive	Social skills
		Group therapy	Group modification
			PPC
			Role-play
		Environmental therapy	Therapeutic community
09 Bland does not show emotion (see also 04.**09**)	Establish emotional responsive-ness	Behaviour modification	Assertiveness training
			Contingency contracting
			Differential reinforcement
			Modelling
			Prompting
			Time out
			Token economy
		Cognitive	Social skills
		Group therapy	Group modification
			PPC
			Role-play
		Environmental therapy	Therapeutic community

Behaviour	Aim	Method	Techniques
10 Emotionally cold	Increase emotional responsive-ness	Behaviour modification	Assertiveness training
			Contingency contracting
			Differential reinforcement
			Operant conditioning
(see also 04.**09**)			Prompting
			Time out
			Token economy
		Cognitive	Social skills
		Group therapy	Group modification
			PPC
			Role-play
		Environmental therapy	Therapeutic community

06.**09** Depression

Behaviour	Aim	Method	Techniques
01 Excessively and continually unhappy	Eliminate	Physical	Chemotherapy
		Behaviour modification	Cognitive BM
			Contingency contracting
			Modelling
			Time out
			Token economy
		Talking therapy	Counselling
			Psychotherapy
		Group therapy	Psychodrama
		Environmental therapy	Therapeutic community
02 Weeping with little or no provocation	As above	As above	As above
03 Pre-occupation with self	Reduce	Behaviour modification	Cognitive BM
			Contingency contracting
			Extinction
			Modelling
			Paradoxical intention
			Prompting
			Time out
			Token economy
		Cognitive	Social skills
		Talking therapy	Counselling
		Group therapy	Group counselling
			Group modification
			PPC
			Psychodrama
			Role-play
		Environmental therapy	Therapeutic community

Behaviour	Aim	Method	Techniques
04 Self-pity	Eliminate	Physical Behaviour modification	Chemotherapy Assertiveness training Aversive conditioning Cognitive BM Contingency contracting Differential reinforcement Extinction Modelling Paradoxical intention Prompting Time out Token economy
		Cognitive Talking therapy	Social skills Counselling Psychotherapy
		Group therapy	Group modification Psychodrama Role-play
		Environmental therapy	Therapeutic community
05 Lack of attention to others	Establish appropriate interest	Physical Behaviour modification	Chemotherapy Cognitive BM Contingency contracting Differential reinforcement Modelling Prompting Time out Token economy
		Cognitive	Social skills
		Group therapy	Group modification PPC Role-play
		Environmental therapy	Therapeutic community
06 Helplessness	Establish coping	Service delivery Physical Behaviour modification	Seek specialist advice Chemotherapy Assertiveness training Cognitive BM Desensitisation Differential reinforcement Flooding Prompting Token economy
		Cognitive Talking therapy Group therapy	Social skills Counselling Group modification PPC Psychodrama

Behaviour	Aim	Method	Techniques
07 Persistent lethargy and apathy	Establish motivation	Physical	Chemotherapy
			Exercise
		Behaviour modificaton	Cognitive BM
			Contingency contracting
			Differential reinforcement
			Prompting
			Token economy
		Group therapy	Role-play
		Environmental therapy	Therapeutic community
08 Gross underactivity	Increase activity	Physical	Chemotherapy
			Exercise
		Behaviour modification	Cognitive BM
			Contingency contracting
			Differential reinforcement
			Modelling
			Operant conditioning
			Prompting
			Time out
			Token economy
		Cognitive	Social skills
		Group therapy	Group modification
			PPC
			Role-play
		Environmental therapy	Therapeutic community
09 Self-deprecation	Establish self-worth	Physical	Chemotherapy
		Behaviour modification	Cognitive BM
			Differential reinforcement
			Extinction
			Modelling
			Token economy
		Cognitive	Social skills
		Talking therapy	Counselling
			Psychotherapy
		Group therapy	Group modification
			Psychodrama
		Environmental therapy	Therapeutic community
10 Guilt feelings	Reduce to appropriate level	Physical	Chemotherapy
		Behaviour modification	Cognitive BM
		Cognitive	Feedback
		Talking therapy	Counselling
			Psychotherapy
		Group therapy	Psychodrama

Behaviour	Aim	Method	Techniques
06.10 Anxiety			
01 Tense, unable to relax	Reduce tension	Physical	Biofeedback
			Chemotherapy
			Exercise
		Behaviour modification	Cognitive BM
			Contingency contracting
			Operant conditioning
			Relaxation
			Token economy
		Talking therapy	Psychotherapy
02 Overactive	Reduce	Physical	Biofeedback
			Chemotherapy
(see also 01.**01**)			Exercise
		Behaviour modification	Contingency contracting
			Operant conditioning
			Paradoxical intention
			Relaxation
			Token economy
			Time out
		Cognitive	Social skills
		Talking therapy	Counselling
			Psychotherapy
		Group therapy	Group modification
			PPC
			Psychodrama
		Environmental therapy	Therapeutic community
03 Apprehensive	Reduce	Physical	Chemotherapy
			Biofeedback
		Behaviour modification	Cognitive BM
			Contingency contracting
			Extinction
			Operant conditioning
			Relaxation
			Token economy
		Talking therapy	Psychotherapy
		Group therapy	Group modification
			Psychodrama
		Environmental therapy	Therapeutic community
04 Indecisive	Reduce	Physical	Chemotherapy
		Behaviour modification	Assertiveness training
			Cognitive BM
			Contingency contracting
			Differential reinforcement

Behaviour	Aim	Method	Techniques
			Modelling
			Prompting
			Relaxation
			Token economy
		Cognitive	Social skills
		Talking therapy	Counselling
		Group therapy	Group modification
			PPC
05 Needs constant reassurance	Reduce	Physical	Chemotherapy
		Behaviour modification	Assertiveness training
			Cognitive BM
			Contingency contracting
			Differential reinforcement
			Extinction
			Operant conditioning
			Relaxation
			Self-management
			Time out
			Token economy
		Cognitive	Feedback
		Talking therapy	Counselling
			Psychotherapy
		Group therapy	Group counselling
			Group modification
			Psychodrama
		Environmental therapy	Therapeutic community
06 Irritable, jumpy	Reduce	Physical	Biofeedback
			Chemotherapy
			Exercise
		Behaviour modification	Contingency contracting
			Operant conditioning
			Relaxation
07 Tics and tremors	Eliminate	Physical	Biofeedback
			Chemotherapy
			Exercise
		Behaviour modification	Negative practice
			Paradoxical intention
			Relaxation
08 Feelings of impending disaster	Eliminate	Physical	Chemotherapy
		Behaviour modification	Cognitive BM
			Covert conditioning
			Differential reinforcement
			Relaxation
		Talking therapy	Counselling
			Psychotherapy

Behaviour	Aim	Method	Techniques
		Group therapy Environmental therapy	Psychodrama Therapeutic community
09 Sleep disturbance	See 01.**14**	See 01.**14**	
10 Palpitations or pallor	Eliminate	Physical Behaviour	Biofeedback Chemotherapy Cognitive BM Relaxation
11 Excessive perspiration	Reduce	Physical Behaviour modification	Biofeedback Chemotherapy Relaxation
12 Nausea	Eliminate	Physical Behaviour modification	Chemotherapy Covert conditioning Operant conditioning Relaxation

06.11 Generalised neurotic disorders

Behaviour	Aim	Method	Techniques
01 Rigid conformist	Reduce	Behaviour modification Group therapy	Aversive conditioning Cognitive BM Contingency contracting Modelling Operant conditioning Time out Token economy Group modification PPC Role-play
02 Inflexible	Reduce	Behaviour modification Cognitive Group therapy	Contingency contracting Modelling Operant conditioning Time out Token economy Social skills Group modification PPC Role-play
03 Fastidious	Reduce	Behaviour modification	Cognitive BM Contingency contracting Differential reinforcement Modelling Operant conditioning

Behaviour	Aim	Method	Techniques
		Cognitive Group therapy	Time out Token economy Social skills Group modification PPC Role-play
04 Intolerant of change	Increase tolerance	Behaviour modification	Cognitive BM Contingency contracting Differential reinforcement Modelling Time out Token economy
		Group therapy	Group modification PPC Role-play
05 Does same things over and over again	Eliminate	Behaviour modification	Aversive conditioning Cognitive BM Contingency contracting Differential reinforcement Extinction Operant conditioning Paradoxical intention Relaxation Time out Token economy
		Talking therapy Group therapy	Psychotherapy Psychodrama
06 Self- justifying	Normalise	Behaviour modification	Aversive conditioning Cognitive BM Contingency contracting Differential reinforcement Extinction Modelling Time out Token economy
		Cognitive	Feedback Social skills
		Talking therapy Group therapy	Counselling Group modification PPC Role-play
07 Complains of persistent un- pleasant thoughts and actions	Eliminate	Physical Behaviour modification	Chemotherapy Aversive conditioning Contingency contracting Covert conditioning

Behaviour	Aim	Method	Techniques
			Extinction
			Time out
			Token economy
		Cognitive	Social skills
		Talking therapy	Counselling
			Psychotherapy
		Group therapy	Group counselling
		Environmental therapy	Therapeutic community
08 Fear of animal	Eliminate	Physical	Biofeedback
			Chemotherapy
		Behaviour modification	Cognitive BM
			Covert conditioning
			Desensitisation
			Flooding
			Operant conditioning
			Relaxation
			Token economy
		Talking therapy	Psychotherapy
		Group therapy	Psychodrama
		Environmental therapy	Therapeutic community
09 Fear of situation	As above	As above + Cognitive	Social skills
10 Fear of person	As above	As above	
11 Fear of place	As above	As above	
12 Fear of object	As above	As above	
13 Exaggerated concern with own physical/ mental health	Reduce	Behaviour modification	Aversive conditioning
			Cognitive BM
			Contingency contracting
			Covert conditioning
			Differential reinforcement
			Extinction
			Modelling
			Time out
			Token economy
		Talking therapy	Counselling
		Group therapy	Group counselling
			Group modification
			PPC
			Role-play

Behaviour	Aim	Method	Techniques
14 Uses extreme measures to safeguard health	Reduce	Behaviour modification	Aversive conditioning Cognitive BM Differential reinforcement Modelling Time out Token economy
		Talking therapy	Counselling
		Group therapy	Group counselling Group modification PPC
		Environmental therapy	Therapeutic community

06.12 Self-concept

Behaviour	Aim	Method	Techniques
01 Does not agree with how others see him	Establish appropriate self-perception	Behaviour modification Cognitive Talking therapy Group therapy	Cognitive BM Contingency contracting Feedback Counselling Group counselling Group modification PPC Role-play
		Environmental therapy	Therapeutic community
02 Unrealistic/ inflated view of self	Normalise	Behaviour modification	Cognitive BM Contingency contracting Modelling Time out Token economy
		Cognitive	Feedback Social skills
		Group therapy	Group modification PPC
		Environmental therapy	Therapeutic community
03 Fluid self-concept	Consolidate self-concept	Behaviour modification	Cognitive BM Contingency contracting Covert conditioning Modelling Time out Token economy
		Cognitive Talking therapy Group therapy	Feedback Counselling Group counselling Group modification

Behaviour	Aim	Method	Techniques
			PPC
			Role-play
		Environmental therapy	Therapeutic community
04 Confused	Normalise	Behaviour modification	Assertiveness training
			Cognitive BM
			Contingency contracting
			Covert conditioning
			Differential reinforcement
			Modelling
			Prompting
			Token economy
		Cognitive	Feedback
		Talking therapy	Counselling
		Group therapy	Group counselling
			Group modification
			PPC
			Role-play
		Environmental therapy	Therapeutic community
05 Self-reproaching	Reduce	Behaviour modification	Assertiveness training
			Aversive conditioning
			Cognitive BM
			Contingency contracting
			Differential reinforcement
			Extinction
			Modelling
			Paradoxical intention
			Prompting
			Time out
			Token economy
		Cognitive	Feedback
			Social skills
		Talking therapy	Counselling
		Group therapy	Group counselling
			Group modification
			PPC
			Role-play
		Environmental therapy	Therapeutic community
06 Negative	Establish self-worth	Behaviour modification	Assertiveness training
			Aversive conditioning
			Cognitive BM
			Contingency contracting
			Covert conditioning

Behaviour	Aim	Method	Techniques
			Differential reinforcement
			Modelling
			Operant conditioning
			Paradoxical intention
			Prompting
			Token economy
		Cognitive	Feedback
		Talking therapy	Counselling
		Group therapy	Group modification
			PPC
			Role-play
		Environmental therapy	Therapeutic community
07 Deviant/ delinquent	Eliminate	Behaviour modification	Assertiveness training
			Aversive conditioning
			Cognitive BM
			Contingency contracting
			Differential reinforcement
			Modelling
			Operant conditioning
			Prompting
			Self-management
			Time out
			Token economy
		Cognitive	Feedback
			Social skills
		Talking therapy	Counselling
		Group therapy	Group counselling
			Group modification
			PPC
			Role-play
		Environmental therapy	Therapeutic community
08 Distorted body image	Establish appropriate image	Behaviour modification	Cognitive BM
			Contingency contracting
			Covert conditioning
			Differential reinforcement
			Extinction
			Modelling
			Paradoxical intention
			Token economy
		Cognitive	Feedback
			Social skills
		Talking therapy	Counselling
		Group therapy	Group counselling
			Group modification
			Role-play

Behaviour	Aim	Method	Techniques
09 Alienated from norms	Normalise	Behaviour modification	Assertiveness training Aversive conditioning Cognitive BM Contingency contracting Differential reinforcement Modelling Operant conditioning Paradoxical intention Positive/negative reinforcement Time out Token economy
		Cognitive	Feedback Social skills
		Talking therapy	Counselling
		Group therapy	Group counselling Group modification PPC Role-play
		Environmental therapy	Therapeutic community
10 Lacks purpose	Establish motivation	Behaviour modification	Assertiveness training Cognitive BM Contingency contracting Differential reinforcement Modelling Operant conditioning Prompting Time out Token economy
		Cognitive	Feedback Social skills
		Talking therapy	Counselling
		Group therapy	Group counselling Group modification PPC Role-play
		Environmental therapy	Therapeutic community
11 Uncertain of gender and sex role	Normalise	Behaviour modification	Assertiveness training Aversive conditioning Cognitive BM Contingency contracting Covert conditioning Differential reinforcement Extinction Modelling

Behaviour	Aim	Method	Techniques
			Operant conditioning
			Prompting
			Time out
			Token economy
		Cognitive	Feedback
			Social skills
		Talking therapy	Counselling
		Group therapy	Group counselling
			Group modification
			PPC
			Role-play
		Environmental therapy	Therapeutic community
12 Distorted self disclosure: quantity or quality	Normalise	Behaviour modification	Assertiveness training
			Aversive conditioning
			Cognitive BM
			Contingency contracting
			Covert conditioning
			Differential reinforcement
			Extinction
			Modelling
			Operant conditioning
			Paradoxical intention
			Prompting
			Time out
			Token economy
		Cognitive	Feedback
			Social skills
		Talking therapy	Counselling
		Group therapy	Group counselling
			Group modification
			PPC
			Psychodrama
			Role-play
		Environmental therapy	Therapeutic community

06.13 Moral development

Behaviour	Aim	Method	Techniques
01 Cannot differentiate right and wrong	Facilitate moral development	Behaviour modification	Assertiveness training
			Aversive conditioning
			Cognitive BM
			Contingency contracting
			Differential reinforcement
			Modelling
			Operant conditioning
			Prompting

Behaviour	Aim	Method	Techniques
		Cognitive Group therapy	Time out
			Token economy
			Social skills
			Group counselling
			Group modification
			PPC
			Role-play
		Environmental therapy	Therapeutic community
02 Only distinguishes acts on fear of external punishment	Establish appropriate concern	As above	
03 Minimal concern for impact of behaviour on others	Increase concern	Behaviour modification	Cognitive BM
			Contingency contracting
			Differential reinforcement
			Modelling
			Operant conditioning
			Paradoxical intention
			Prompting
			Time out
			Token economy
		Cognitive	Feedback
			Social skills
		Group therapy	Group modification
			PPC
			Role-play
		Environmental therapy	Therapeutic community
04 Identifies with and emulates deviant standards	Normalise	Behaviour modification	Aversive conditioning
			Cognitive BM
			Contingency contracting
			Modelling
			Operant conditioning
			Prompting
			Time out
			Token economy
		Cognitive	Feedback
			Social skills
		Talking therapy	Counselling
		Group therapy	Group counselling
			Group modification
			PPC
			Role-play
		Environmental therapy	Therapeutic community

Index

Index compiled by Meg Davies